D1929578

Self Management in Organizations

**Martin De Waele** received his Ph. D. from the University of California, Berkeley. He had prior training in Economics, Management Science and Psychology. He is a member of various professional associations such as the American Psychological Association, the Association for Humanistic Psychology, The Association for Transpersonal Psychology, and the American Anthropological Association. Dr. De Waele contributed articles in books and in journals such as *Omega: The International Journal of Management Science*. He is a professor at the University of Quebec at Montreal and a consultant in management and international development. This included assignments in Japan and as an advisor for the United Nations in several African countries.

**Jean Morval** obtained his doctorate in Industrial Psychology after a Master's degree in Social Psychology at the University of Louvain, Belgium. He is a professor at the University of Montreal's Department of Psychology and directed its Social Psychology program for several years. He published books and articles on topics at the crossroads of social, organizational and environmental psychology. He has initiated French-North American academic exchange programs, and was involved in consulting and teaching here and abroad. Dr. Morval is a member of the Executive Committee of the International Association of Applied Psychology and was previously on the editorial board of *The Journal of Environmental Psychology*. He is presently chairman of the Industrial and Organizational Psychology Program at the University of Montreal.

**Robert Sheitoyan** holds a Ph. D. in Business Administration from Syracuse University, New York, and an M. B. A. from Loyola University of Chicago. He also took specialized training in gestalt therapy at Princeton, Rhode Island, and Syracuse. Dr. Sheitoyan is presently a professor at the University of Quebec at Montreal, in Organizational Behavior and in Real Estate Management. He was director of the Executive M. B. A. Program at the same school and is now in charge of its Real Estate Management Program. Previously he taught at Concordia University, Montreal. Dr. Sheitoyan is a "Fellow" of the Certified General Accountant's Association of Canada. He published books and articles on Group Behavior and Organization Development. His research interests are focused on Team Building, Negotiation Skills and Entrepreneurship in the Real Estate area.

Martin De Waele
Jean Morval
Robert Sheitoyan

# SELF MANAGEMENT IN ORGANIZATIONS

## The Dynamics of Interaction

Hogrefe & Huber Publishers
Seattle · Toronto · Bern · Göttingen

**Library of Congress Cataloging-in-Publication Data**

De Waele, Martin.
Self management in organizations : the dynamics of interaction / by Martin De Waele, Jean Morval, Robert Sheitoyan
p. cm.
Includes bibliographical references and index.
ISBN 0-88937-079-6 $26.95
1. Corporate culture. 2. Organizational behavior. 3. Self-management (Psychology) I. Morval, Jean. II. Sheitoyan, Robert. III. Title
HD58.7.W23 1993 650.1–dc20 91-44946 CIP

**Canadian Cataloguing in Publication Data**

De Waele, Martin, 1948–
Self management in organizations : the dynamics of interaction

Includes bibliographical references and index.
ISBN 0-88937-079-6
1. Organizational behavior. 2. Success in business. 3. Self-realization.
4. Management – Psychological aspects. I. Morval, Jean, 1938– .
II. Sheitoyan, Robert, 1938– . III. Title

BF637.S8D4 1993 650.1 C92-093250-9

Copyright © 1993 by Hogrefe & Huber Publishers

P. O. Box 2487, Kirkland, WA 98083-2487
12–14 Bruce Park Ave., Toronto, Ontario M4P 2S3

No part of this book may be reproduced, stored in a retrieval system or by any means, electronic, mechanical, photocopying, microfilming, recording or otherwise, without the written permission from the publisher.

Printed in USA

ISBN 0-88937-079-6
Hogrefe & Huber Publishers, Seattle · Toronto

ISBN 3-456-82034-8
Hans Huber Publishers, Bern · Göttingen

# TABLE OF CONTENTS

Preface vii

Introduction 1

Self Management 5
- Self Management as a Practical Philosophy 5
- Self Management as Process 19

Generic Processes of Self Management 51
- Self Management of the Appropriation Process 51
- Self Management of the Relation Process 86
- Self Management of the Decision Process 115
- Self Management of the Action Process 144

From Self Management to Directing Others 171
- Developing a Personal Style: Going Beyond Models and Accepted Management Patterns 172
- Difficulties Inherent in Certain Environments 175
- Differentiating Skill in Self Management from Skill in Directing and Supporting Others 178
- Giving Direction and the Issue of Power 182
- A New Look at the Appraisal of Performance in Organizations 192

Conclusions 199

Questions for Developing Insights on Self Management 205

Afterword 213

References Used in the Text 215

Further Readings 217

Index 220

"Whether or not a single objective picture of reality exists is unimportant. What is important is that a changing and more complex picture of reality almost always exists, and gaining control of our organization life depends on our constantly asking the questions that will allow us to discover it. Situations and people change, and what's complex and relevant today won't be tomorrow. We must see to it that our reality pictures keep pace."

Samuel A. Culbert

# PREFACE

How individuals manage themselves has always been an intriguing subject in both professional and academic circles. Many people have dealt with the problems of self management by finding refuge in the complex conceptual environment provided by the culture of the times, the culture of a particular country or ethnic group, or the culture of the organization they work for. Yet, from students to senior executives, more and more individuals find themselves pushed to the limit, as a result of behavior and actions that they have trouble relating to personally. Increasingly, they find their organizational environments unresponsive to what they value most in their lives – sometimes as actually threatening to keep them from being in touch with these values. When people cannot express their innermost values, psychotherapy and counseling become only pseudo-solutions – the increased awareness of fear and anger may only temporarily halt the potential spillover to anxiety and violence. At best they stimulate valuable insights, though these insights may prove difficult to put into practice once one is back on the job.

More and more, the management of oneself becomes a task for which only the individual can take primary responsibility, despite the resources available in one's organizational and cultural environments. This book is about individual self management, but also about the management of interpersonal relations in an organizational setting, and the function of leadership and direction. It is addressed to those who find they are growing as people in their organizational environments, who wish to improve their understanding of the processes by which they themselves as well as others in the organization grow and change, and who have an interest in helping others develop as people. It is also addressed to those individuals, managers and operative personnel alike, who at one point or other have believed in the professed values and policies of their organization, but have come to realize that the reality often does not match the ideal – and who then try to survive as best they can. Finally, it is written for those who want to find an equilibrium between what they value most in life and the turmoil of change and pressure that continuously rocks organizational life, calling into question the very perception of their mission and perhaps their own basic values.

Our initial interest in this project came from a simple observation made by all three of us after years of university teaching coupled with innumerable, and generally high pressure, consulting assignments in many diverse organizations – theory and practice often express different realities. Theory is usually hopeful, dynamic, and presented as capable of producing transformations. Practice, on the other hand, turns out to be less glowing, more stagnant, and at times even appears hopeless.

Therefore, the two questions we asked ourselves were:

1] How can we develop a theoretical framework while staying very close to the facts and feelings of our everyday experience?

2] How can we communicate this theoretical approach to practitioners so they can link it up directly with their own organizational experience?

These two questions, plus the fact that the issues raised by self management are so intimately tied to the way people experience them, have led us to opt for a process of joint inquiry. All through this process, our own experiences in organizations have been conceptualized and questioned. Rather than relying on a body of literature, we have composed the structure of the text following many repetitions of this joint inquiry process. We have chosen to retain only certain fundamental elements that seemed sufficiently amenable to generalization and could form a basis for agreement among all three authors. This joint inquiry has turned out to be an inspiring interpersonal process, in which ideas could be expressed, verified against our own experience, confronted, and modified as we went along. The result is meant to be a tool for personal reflection and interpersonal discussion, encouraging individual responsibility and self direction as a path to greater creativity. It is also meant to be a starting point for those who are actively engaged in organizational practice but have had little time to systemize their thoughts – to translate what they know into conceptual terms.

The discussion in this book is based on the definition of four fundamental processes that are in constant interaction:

- appropriation
- relation
- decision
- action.

Many schools of organization and management consider the two salient elements of management to be decision and action. These are, no doubt, important. The self-management approach, as presented here, takes them into consideration but gives them the same weight as the other processes – relation and appropriation. We hope the book will inspire its readers to assume more responsibility, to develop their capacity for self management, and to become better able to adapt to technological and cultural change. And, of course, we hope the book will stimulate useful ideas for any person who decides that the improvement of self-management skills is a good idea, whatever organization he is in and whatever function he performs.

We wish to thank many colleagues in various universities in the United States, Europe, and Canada for their comments and constructive criticism during the various phases of this book. We also thank many people in organizations who have consulted us as we were in the process of developing our concepts. As well, the remarks and comments from our students have been a constant source of intellectual stimulation.

Finally, the entire team at Hogrefe and Huber Publishers have been patient and supportive throughout this endeavor. We would like to thank particularly Dr. Christine Hogrefe, Dr. Tom Tabasz, Maureen Zimmerman, and Jim Tabasz.

*Note:* As the English language does not have a singular pronoun for the third person that does not imply gender, we have tried to alternate the use of the pronouns "he" and "she," as well as male and female examples, throughout this book.

January 1993

Martin De Waele
Jean Morval
Robert Sheitoyan

"In its widest possible sense, however, a man's self is the sum total of all that he can call his, not only his body and his psychic powers, but his clothes and his house, his wife and children, his ancestors and friends, his reputation and works, his lands and horses, and yacht and bank-account."

William James

# INTRODUCTION

The book is divided into three sections. Chapter One deals with self management as a practical approach to life and as a process. In it, we discuss the challenges inherent in this approach. We then examine elements of the process, and some conditions likely to hinder it. We conclude the first chapter with a list of propositions that will help individuals better manage their careers and personal lives, taking into account their work in organizational settings.

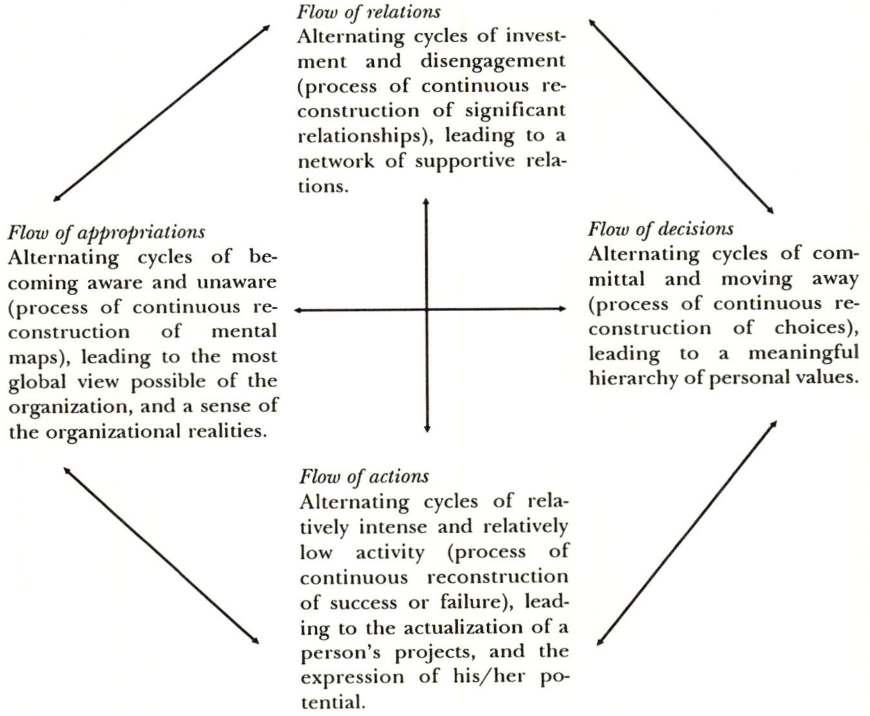


*Chart 1.* Self management as the most harmonious possible distribution of one's energy among four fundamental flows.

The second chapter deals with four generic self-management processes, which constitute the building blocks of the book's conceptual structure: appropriation, relation, decision, and action. We refer the reader to Chart 1 to see how these four building blocks interact. Each generic process will be defined, then considered in its specific relation to self management. Symptoms of obstruction will be identified for each of the four processes, and illustrations will be given of certain organizational conditions that may either reinforce or facilitate the process. Finally, we will discuss conditions which may facilitate managing the process in organizations.

The third chapter deals with the problems and opportunities involved in directing and supporting others, from a self-management perspective. After a discussion of the benefits of a personalized management style, and the difficulties present in some work places, the skills involved in directing others are examined in the light of a self-management approach to leadership. Finally, this chapter sheds new light on the issue of personal power and the use of power in a group context, followed by a reassessment of performance appraisals in organizations.

"Scientists would be wrong to ignore the fact that theoretical construction is not the only approach to the phenomena of life; another way, that of understanding from within (interpretation) is open to us ... Of myself, of my own acts of perception, thought, volition, feeling and doing, I have direct knowledge that represents the 'parallel' cerebral processes in symbols. This inner awareness of myself is the basis for the understanding of my fellow men whom I meet and acknowledge as beings of my own kind, with whom I communicate sometimes so intimately as to share joy and sorrow with them."

Herman Weyl

**Key Points**

- Valued attitudes and behaviors
- Why it is so difficult to self manage
- Seeing life as an explicit process
- The four generic processes of self management
- A healthy process and its obstructions
- Optimal self management

# SELF MANAGEMENT

# 1

## Self Management as a Practical Philosophy

### *Definition*

Unlike philosophy as a system of knowledge, a practical philosophy may be considered an individual way of "befriending wisdom," after the original meaning of the word "philosophy" (from the Greek "philos," meaning "loving," and "sophia," meaning "wisdom"). One's practical philosophy, then, can be seen as one's progressive construction of a certain idiosyncratic wisdom, as it emerges from the understanding and integration of personal experiences. The result is a distillate of values and attitudes that become the general background of the individual's being and acting in the world. They serve both as anchor points and as a mainspring for the expression of a personal style. Conveying elements of one's practical philosophy to another person is usually a straightforward process, even when it is a nonverbal one. In contrast, philosophy as a system of knowledge, conveyed by professional philosophers, often appears verbally complex and sophisticated.

Practical philosophy is not to be confused with lifestyle in a behavioral sense. In fact, certain specialized disciplines have unified the individual's values and lifestyle, establishing broad categories of people based on certain habitual patterns of behavior, then influencing their behavior by appealing to those values. For example, marketing specialists have used this concept to target their market for a product or service. In contrast, the concept of a practical philosophy, as used here, denotes a much more intimate and uniquely individual aspect of personality and behavior.

What happens when self management becomes a practical philosophy? What attitudes and behaviors would be typical for someone who adopts a self-management approach in the context of his practical philosophy? We could probably expect to see most of the following:

1] He takes care of himself first: not in the sense of narcissism or egoism, but rather in the sense of knowing where to set limits – where to draw the line between responding to the demands of the environment and listening to his own needs. Thus, he refuses to neglect himself or to be submerged by environmental demands. He refuses to dissipate his efforts, and he prioritizes his needs.

2] She is interested in working at being a source of physical, emotional, intellectual and spiritual health. She is interested in learning to listen to her own body, emotions, intellect, and psyche, so these different aspects of herself become sources of well-being, both for herself and others.

3] He wants to be aware of the changes in his life and to befriend those changes. Thus, he is interested in assuming a role in the development of his own self.

4] She believes that her learning process depends on her own doing. Even in an unknown context, where it is difficult to respond to learning opportunities, she will accept her share of responsibilities by actively engaging in a minimum of autonomous practice and by realistically evaluating the degree of transferability of previous learnings.

5] He is interested in developing a realistic attitude, in coping with existential issues such as life and death and with sudden changes in general. He is increasingly aware of the emotions that accompany such changes. For example, he recognizes the phases of shock, denial, anger, resignation, and acceptance that may be present after a loss of any kind.

6] She prepares, to some extent, her own exit from the social theaters in which she participates. For example, she refuses to advance to a level in the organizational hierarchy at which she would become incompetent, especially in terms of the demands and pressures of that job on her time, energies, abilities, and skills. She makes sure that her experience and personal vision support the level of responsibility she takes on.

7] His conception of change prioritizes the role of personal attitudes over the importance of changing others or of changing social and organizational structures. For example, he would not pressure another person to change his value system. At the same time, he would not be disappointed in perceived inadequacies in his social environment – he knows there are things he can change and things he cannot.

8] She manages not only her present, but also her past and future. For example, she is willing to accept her prior experiences, even if this is a painful process involving the reemergence of strong feelings. She also manages her future; for example, by preparing herself through professional training, or by acquiring new skills.

9] He tries to equilibrate the energy given to different aspects of life, such as body, emotion, money, love, ethics, environment, and aesthetics. He is sensitive to the multifaceted nature of reality. He applies himself to exploring areas he may have neglected.

10] She sees self management as an active process, enabling her to cope with disappointments, deceptions, betrayals, hopelessness, and burnout.

11] He sees work on personal development as a prerequisite for creating mutually rewarding relationships with others.

12] She is aware that at times her own failure to self-manage may adversely affect others. For example, when one of the partners in a couple mismanages his or her own time or money, this may have repercussions for the other partner.

13] His level of trust in himself and in the potential of others allows him to be directive but supportive at the same time, rather than adopting a coercive or punitive approach.

14] If she is an administrator, she will prefer facilitating self management in those she supervises over encouraging submissiveness in them. For example, she can be genuinely supportive of young people learning directing skills, rather than needing to be competitive with them. She refuses to be drawn into the kind of defensive attitude that may serve to protect herself in the status quo of her own career.

15] He does not leave it up to the organization to ensure his own self development.

16] When interacting with supervisors or group members, she is sensitive in expressing her autonomy while being responsive to the group. In a professional relationship, she can accept authority without abandoning her self-respect.

17] He can keep a sufficient distance from externally defined criteria of success or failure; he values the process of defining his own criteria.

18] His practical philosophy veers away from ideologies and other currents of thought that do not emphasize the development of the person as a priority.

The above list, although not exhaustive, paves the way to a definition of self management. Managing oneself, then, means working toward the optimal integration of one's emotional, spiritual, intellectual, and physical life, at every stage of one's life. It also means recognizing opportunities for using appropriation, relation, decision, and action as resources, to respond to one's needs and develop one's potential.

Besides the above characteristics associated with the self-management approach, it is perhaps equally important to emphasize what self management is not:

1] Self management is not greed, nor does it justify greed. To manage oneself so well that everybody else suffers is a contradiction in terms. Similarly, when greed overwhelms a person he is not managing himself.

2] Self management is different from a social definition of success. Self management transcends culture; it is not a concept that can be easily measured against cultural expectations.

3] Identifying and using opportunities for appropriation, relation, decision, and action is not to be confused with opportunism, which is at the opposite end of the spectrum. Opportunism is behavior enacted at the expense of other people's weaknesses, foibles, or bad luck, and knows no ethical bounds. In contrast, self management often results in sharpening focus on one's most cherished values, and, in so doing, forces one to confront the ethical bounds of one's behavior.

## *Underlying Assumptions*

Having defined self management as a practical philosophy, let's examine some underlying assumptions of the ideas developed in this book. Since our interest focuses on organizations, the assumptions listed below apply chiefly to that context:

1] The more a person develops his self-management abilities, the greater his potential to understand his own value system. Conversely, the greater the understanding of his values, the more he will be able to develop his personal competence and benefit from self-management opportunities.

2] The more a person develops her self-management abilities, the better prepared she will become in managing and directing others.

3] The more a person develops his self-management abilities, the more he will become sensitive to his own internal conflicts and, hopefully, the better he will become at discerning and handling competition and conflict with and between others.

4] The more a person develops her self-management abilities, the more she can be expected to develop and differentiate her own sense of personal power. We can expect her to be less dependent on her organization and less susceptible to manipulation.

5] The more a person develops his self-management abilities, the more he will be prepared to contribute in significant ways to the organizational process. Furthermore, the development of the person is facilitative for the development of groups and productive group processes.

## *The Challenge of Self Management*

### Why is Self Management Difficult?

There are at least three major sources of difficulty involved in self management within an organization. First, some people may find it difficult to express behaviorally certain values inherent in the self-management approach. Second is the realization that one is not alone; others, too, want to manage themselves. A third source of difficulty is that the organizational culture continues to harbor traditional rules of social interaction and conventional views about professional roles and competence.

The first source of difficulty for a self-management approach in organizations resides in the fact that people frequently find it difficult to translate certain implicit values into concrete behaviors. To illustrate, let's examine four values inherent to self management, noting how the behavior related to each can be critical in an organizational environment. They are: a sense of confidence and faith in life, a belief in people's potential and ability, open-mindedness and curiosity, and a sense of autonomy.

1] *A sense of confidence, and faith in life*
A sense of confidence in life is of the basic values of the self-management approach. But it is not difficult to imagine how this sense can be undermined by deceptions, disappointments, feelings of having been taken advantage of, illness, accidents, wars, crimes, the manipulations of politicians, pollution, and so forth. Negative environments (as an example, "depressed" organizations, cf. Kets de Vries et. al., *Unstable at the Top*) always take their toll. In such a setting a person almost always stands to lose. For example, it may become very difficult to display initiative or even to express one's most basic vitality. When the feelings associated with such situations cannot be vented and the mind cleared of negative influences, these influences are left to fester. It is then likely that they will slowly detract from one's own self-esteem and, in the end, undermine one's confidence in life itself. The same effect can be created by taboos, which are linked to fear rather than to a fostering of self-expression. When, despite negative influences, a person wants to manage himself, he may find it necessary to fall back on one of the most valuable resources of his childhood – a blind and unquestioning confidence and faith in life, as well as a degree of naiveté. The ability to nurture these qualities and direct one's life with their support is surely a most valuable attribute for self management.

2] *A belief in people's potential and ability*
This value lies at the basis of a personalized participation in organizational processes. Nevertheless, many large organizations are compelled to enforce standard work regulations, and their management policies do not encourage the emergence of this value. The com-

plexity of rules and regulations is often in proportion to a lack of comprehension, at the top level, of the complex realities present in the organization. True understanding of complexity, and a belief in people's abilities, usually permits someone to express what needs to be done in fairly simple terms rather than passing on the confusion. We can also illustrate the difficulty of maintaining this value in certain government agencies. Typically these agencies have a mission of control – to see to it that government regulations are executed correctly. But, in carrying out such mandates, they tend to become internally self-controlling. How then can they encourage the development of the employee's potential? In some cases, a person who makes a truly original contribution may, in fact, be penalized for it.

On an interpersonal level, disappointing work place experiences may contribute to difficulty in maintaining one's belief in people's potential and ability. Such experiences may often be due to our own projections. Not infrequently one person will think that a colleague has similar interests and abilities in a certain area as oneself, but will later discover that this is quite inaccurate. For example, it is possible to be quite open with someone and think that, judging from observed behavior, the other is being open as well. Afterward, one may be hurt upon realizing that the situation was misread.

From time to time most people need confirmations of their perceptions. When no confirmations are forthcoming, it may become difficult for them to maintain belief in their own potential, as well as in the potential of others. To keep on believing, a self-managing person must keep in touch at all times with his own potential, ability, and personal power, regardless of what is seen in the temporary circumstance.

3] *Open-mindedness and curiosity*

The importance of this third value in self management cannot be overemphasized. However, a newcomer, anxious to explore the organization, and curious to see other divisions or departments, is likely to meet with criticism. Few organizational cultures truly favor the expression of this value. The pretext often used to justify this restrictive attitude is the short-term lack of profitability of such curiosity-satisfying activities. Yet, when we interview people in one department of large organizations it is astonishing to note the number of people who know virtually nothing of other departments, and who ardently wish they knew more. Of course, curiosity also carries the risk of disappointment.

There are also risks with open-mindedness. A person may wish to be open in sharing ideas, but it is possible that colleagues are simply unable to respond. They may even take in the information given and use it to their own advantage further down the road. Many people's experiences in organizations show that open-mindedness and curiosity are to be handled carefully and with a certain circumspection.

4] *A sense of autonomy*

This value refers mainly to the intention of the self-managing person to direct his own priorities as much as possible. He seeks to understand the laws of his own behavior. He learns, for instance, under what conditions he is most productive. The way his work is set up for him in the organization may not harmonize well with these personal conditions. For example, a manager may inappropriately impose his own work-rhythm on his employees without consulting them.

There are other aspects to this valuing of autonomy. Indeed, autonomy implies the capacity to be alone in major decision making and, most of all, the capacity for self-learning on the job. Developing autonomy is often an arduous process. It involves starting with small accomplishments, learning, then building on these experiences to acquire more and more proficiency, and preparing to take on more complex assignments. However, very few organized work systems value this kind of autonomy and its accompanying learning process. Employees are usually integrated into very specific chains of command and control. Often it is critical to quickly prove oneself without the luxury of a process of smaller successes leading to the contextual expertise necessary to satisfy one's own work standards, while still pleasing various supervisors.

No doubt there are other values inherent in the self-management approach that could be treated similarly. For example, the search for integrity, a sense of fairness, and self-discipline. Whatever particular prejudices exist in any organizational culture, the self-managing person can always expect to encounter new challenges that in many cases may conflict with one's personal values. Nonetheless, superiors will expect such challenges to be handled, and the required internal strengths clearly demonstrated.

A second major source of difficulty with respect to self management in organizations arises from the realization that one is not alone. Others, too, can be expected to manage themselves; the person acts within a social system or a business environment. A member of an organization may very well, in efforts toward self management, come into conflict with the group, given the limited nature of resources such as time, space, money, and so on. Conflicts centering around resources such as these may be symptomatic of much deeper disagreements on priorities and values. Sometimes the conflict centers around the short-term or long-term goals of the organization, or is ignited by the question of who is rewarded financially, personally, or with positive reinforcements. Someone with a differing philosophy may view these conflicts as games in which the strongest survive. In contrast, the person who has a self-management philosophy finds that such issues take on a broader aspect; indeed, she cannot refuse others their rights. From such a framework one would resist the view that the conflict is about who gets the biggest piece of cake, more likely maintaining the view that such conflicts are part of an interaction scenario in which power struggles play an important role. Those who practice self management can be expected to understand that power struggles are not efficient problem-solving strategies, because they tend to drain energy away from the real problem. To work out conflicts, including those in which power struggles consume a lot of energy, the self-managing worker will adopt methods such as focusing on a larger or more long-term perspective, widening the frame of reference, easing the synchronization of efforts toward a common goal, and favoring flexibility. These methods allow the group to concentrate on primary goals, and not get sidetracked by secondary considerations.

A third source of difficulty is the prevalence in organizational culture of traditional rules of social interaction and stereotyped views about professional roles and competence. The majority of workers have had little opportunity to learn about self management in any great measure. Family, school, and organizational systems tend to make people excessively dependent on structure and authority. Organizations that constitute an exception to this rule are few and hard to find. The truth is that, consciously or otherwise, many organizations actively discourage autonomy, self-direction, and initiative.

## *The Relevance of Self Management*

In our experience and in many discussions with various groups we have, perhaps naïvely, asked people the question, Is there anything more important than self management? Whenever we have posed this question, those present have been unable to find even one issue that is more important. Of course, relationships are important. So are knowledge, pleasure, money, and so on. But eventually the question always circles back to self management. There are a number of reasons why self management appears to be relevant, not only to a specific group of workers, but to everybody, and why this relevance is rapidly increasing:

1] We realize more and more that a healthy and adaptive organization is the result of personal management abilities of employees at each level, rather than just the result of exceptional talent at the highest level. Genuine power and influence in organizations are rapidly becoming linked more to real problem-solving and communicative abilities than to pre-established status or formal mandate. Further, in many problems the person most directly involved is often in the best position to find a solution. Even if he is not in such a position, his supervisors can rarely afford the luxury of not including him in their decision making. Thus, from the point of view of top management there is every reason to encourage people's self-management abilities, if they do not want to make the fatal mistake of being out of touch with the realities at every level. In turn, whatever one's level or function in the organization, neither outside help nor assistance from supervisors can replace the drive and competence necessary to help a person accomplish his work.
We also realize that in the present economic context, the initiative for training, continuing education, and professional development can be expected to come much more from self-motivated individuals than from global training programs or institutional policy. In

fact, today's enterprises need, more than ever, personnel who are sufficiently autonomous to take initiatives and train themselves.

2] Awareness of limited resources such as time, space, expertise, material resources, constraints on geographic mobility, and an increasing economic and psychological realism require individuals to call upon their own internal resources to create acceptable conditions for themselves and their work environment. Individuals have begun to realize that they can create their own conditions much more efficiently by building creatively on their potential without encroaching on the beliefs, opinions, and attitudes of others.
To illustrate this tendency on a wider scale, even multinational companies are up against a certain saturation in the geographic expansion of their input of raw materials and their markets.

3] When we look at a situation where the members of an organization do *not* practice self management, we find ourselves at the opposite end, so to speak, of the characteristics mentioned earlier. This means that these people do not take care of themselves first; they are not interested in working personally at being a source and a channel of physical, emotional, intellectual, and spiritual health; they do not want to play a decisive role in being aware of and befriending changes; they do not believe their learning process depends very much on their own involvement; they find themselves unable to adopt a realistic attitude toward life and death; and so on. When we go through the whole list of characteristics, each time substituting the opposite of what is there, we realize that in this context people simply become increasingly dependent and vulnerable. Consequently, it is to be expected that they will experience the need to compensate for their lack of self-reliance with various protective strategies, such as an elaborate legal system or set of universal principles. Some may decide to invest their best resources outside their work place and to give their work secondary importance. Others may use a strategy that Argyris has called "distancing," allowing them to keep a certain distance between their actions and their sense of responsibility for them.
Yet all of these strategies fail to make for the teamwork qualities and involvement that are so highly prized for organizational effectiveness. We do not mean to say that a loyal member of an organization should invest everything in it; indeed, one aspect of self man-

agement is understanding that no organization is able to fulfill all the needs of a person, or give complete meaning to his existence. Moreover, in today's world no enterprise can take its economic or moral stability for granted – organizational life spans tend to be shorter, making it even more important for an employee to practice adequate self management to help him adapt to eventual change. When a person does find himself at the opposite end of the characteristics mentioned earlier, and does not manage himself adequately, we can safely predict that much of his vital energy will be used to defend and protect his unnecessarily vulnerable position. While one's energy is being used for defense and protection, creative potential suffers.

4] Many successful managers have by now understood that constraining people to the execution of predetermined strategies alienates them, prevents them from fully living in their jobs and dooms them to mechanical behavior – going through the motions without really believing in them or without really integrating their importance and their consequences. Perhaps the struggle with low productivity levels cited in several recent reports on industrial nations is explained by such limitations placed on employees. When a manager appeals only to a small part of the intellectual and motivational capacity of the people who work with him, and by doing so discourages them from effectively managing themselves, can we expect more than mediocre participation? As the priorities of the times change, it becomes clear that more and more people want to be considered as multifaceted individuals, not merely workers performing tasks eight hours a day in their offices or shops. It also becomes clear that the model of work life that separates the person at work from the "private" person is increasingly seen as unrealistic and artificial. For example, in evaluating the performance of their personnel, managers are confronted with the fact that personal lives and working lives are interrelated and have repercussions on each other. These tendencies illustrate an increasing interest in self management on the part of employees, but they also point to the necessity for managers and planners to come to terms with their own attitudes and behavior regarding self management.

5] Effective management is also important to the working person at the time of retirement. Retired employees who express the greatest satisfaction are often those who prepared themselves progressively for retirement, keeping in mind their overall life (such things as health, social life, and finances) apart from work.

6] Drastic changes brought about by technological revolutions, by recent takeovers and mergers, as well as by changes in planetary and environmental conditions, cause numerous and rapid changes in organizational cultures. The effort required to face changes in mentality, work designs, and organizational values is so great that those who are unable to achieve healthy self management risk finding themselves in a state of burn-out.

7] Finally, for the individual person as well as for the group, self management is about the conservation and channeling of personal and interpersonal energies. It is also about avoiding the waste and dissipation of those energies. Its importance is underscored by the need felt by increasing numbers of people, in many different cultural contexts, to judiciously manage their own potentials, ideals, and talents as well as their fears, apprehensions, and emotional or physical sufferings. The self-management approach, then, gives expression to the desire to come to grips with the ecology of the mind and of consciousness, within the experienced reality of our social theater.

"It is an interesting reflection on the general climate of thought before the twentieth century that no one had suggested that the universe was expanding or contracting. It was generally accepted that either the universe had existed forever in an unchanging state, or that it had been created at a finite time in the past more or less as we observe it today. In part this may have been due to people's tendency to believe in eternal truths, as well as the comfort they found in the thought that even though they may grow old and die, the universe is eternal and unchanging."

Stephen W. Hawking

## Self Management as Process

In this section we will first define the concept of processes and attempt to clarify the meaning of managing a process. After focusing on a definition of the self-management process, we will introduce four generic processes that are considered part of self management. We will then point to some aspects shared by these four processes, in particular with regard to their management. In addition, we will examine the general characteristics of a healthy self-management process, and illustrate some of the conditions that may inhibit it. We will conclude this section with a proposition of what it takes to manage oneself in an optimal manner.

### *On Processes and How to Manage Them*

Examples of processes abound in nature: the earth and the planets evolving within the solar system and the universe as a whole; seasonal changes in weather and in plants; the life cycle of insects; our breathing process; blood circulation; digestion and metabolism; growth, death and regeneration in the ecosystem; and the social process, which can be seen as the changing politics of a people when viewed in a long-term historical perspective. If we had to try and find the essential attributes of such processes in general, the above illustrations would yield at least the following: (1) A continuous movement of some sort (for example, a process may change its tempo, divert its course, or go through transformations and apparent discontinuities, but it is always ongoing). (2) A certain stability in the movement (the movement takes place within a relatively stable structure or environment). (3) Regularities in the movement, in the form of rhythms, phases, or polarities. (4) No one process can be isolated from other processes with which it interacts without compromising its own continuation. (5) Any one process is embedded in, or leads into, another larger process within which it fulfils a meaningful function.

The most conspicuous characteristic of a process is its movement. When we say that we are interested in the process of something, we invariably mean we are interested in the way the thing moves about. Other characteristics such as the way it is shaped, the way it looks, what color it is, and so on, are interesting only insofar as we can see what role they play in the movement. It may be useful to make a comparison with two ways of studying the human body: anatomy is a static description of the structural features of the body (such as lungs, blood vessels), whereas physiology is the study of the body processes, or how a component behaves and interacts with other components (such as respiration, blood circulation).

There is another characteristic of processes worth mentioning. If we found ourselves right in the middle of any process we would probably experience the flow as rather chaotic at times, perhaps even incomprehensible. However, when we are able to view the process from outside, and have a more global perspective aided by distance or over time, then we may notice a definite regularity. What seemed very intense and chaotic would reveal itself as a perfectly logical and purposeful part of a whole. Thus, when a process is understood, and viewed from a distance, and when the regularities have been noted, we gain a certain degree of control over that process – we can see through to what is happening, instead of being swept off our feet by what we experience as random disturbances. Until we find the principles that link different phases together, indeed, that link different processes together, we do not see the process as process – we only see chaotic movement. When we do see the regularities, and when we note what it is that is being "brewed," the meaning of the process becomes clear, and so do its lessons.

The perception we have of a process is inextricably linked with our time perspective. What we perceive as the result or output of a process is merely a snapshot representing what the process looks like at one point in time on certain dimensions. Thus, output measures such as: diplomas after a learning cycle, a company's financial statements, an X-ray of the thorax, or the vote count of an election are designed to mark a point in time and are merely partial perceptions of an ongoing process. In particular, they never provide a clear idea of the dynamic aspects of the processes subjected to such observations. To remain "hooked" on such output measures, or to mistake them for the process itself, often leads to significant errors of judgment as to how a particular process behaves or will behave in the future. This comment about output measures can be extended to plans and statements of intent such as a marriage contract, short-term or long-term corporate objectives, two- and three-year plans. Again, being entrenched in such statements and plans, rather than examining the ever-changing dynamics of a process, is bound to lead anyone who aspires to participate in the process into trouble.

Our perception of a process is equally linked with our notion of spatial dimensions. When we try to isolate one process from the others with which it interacts, we are left with an abstraction, which actually prevents us from getting to know its spatially dynamic characteristics. For example, by looking at the process of bodily immune responses in isolation, we may find out a few things about how it works but we will not be in a position to understand the ramifications of its interactions with other body processes, such as neurotransmissions, or with other environmental processes, such as the role of plants and trees in the regulation of oxygen and air. Similarly, when we transpose theories from one setting into another, as in consulting or in education, we may lose meaningful cultural and environmental connections. By being locked into one particular area in an organizational process – the accounting processes, for example – any person who wants a clear idea of how the organization is performing risks missing out on the dynamic interrelations of the accounting processes with other processes, such as marketing or interpersonal relations. Or when focusing exclusively on the marketing processes, the person risks missing out on their interface with key environmental processes.

Thus, when we are interested in process, we are interested in movement and, more specifically, in dynamic evolution over time as well as dynamic interrelations with other surrounding processes. This leads us into the question of managing a process. First of all, it should be pointed out that most of the processes that have been mentioned so far are natural, self-organizing processes – they are self-regulatory or manage themselves around the maintenance of a state of equilibrium. A second category of processes can be labeled man-made self-organizing processes or systems. These are processes such as transportation systems, sewer systems, and school systems, created by people so they are self-regulatory to a large extent. A third category can be labeled creative processes, when the main characteristics are transformation, moving toward new ways of seeing and towards new equilibria. Finally, a fourth category can be named management processes – the processes that consist of managing processes. We are especially interested in the latter category, since the self-management process belongs to it.

In its widest sense, managing a process can be defined as assisting the flow of movement so as to help bring about, or restore, temporal and spatial harmony within the process and among interrelating processes. Thus, the function of management is especially important at a time of crisis, as when the regular flow of the movement has been disturbed by an unusual or unexpected factor. It would seem, then, that there are two very important instruments in managing a process: knowledge and value. Indeed, management is limited by the knowledge of the person who aspires to manage a process. For example, at this point in time a person could not realistically aspire to manage the process of our planet rotating around the sun. Not only is there no need for such management, since no disturbances have been noted that would threaten the harmony between the two spheres, but even if there were a need, a person would have insufficient knowledge of the forces at work. Other processes, however, are increasingly susceptible to being managed. For example, many body processes have been understood to a degree that allows a certain form of management – knowledge is beginning to build up on the way cigarette smoking may affect body harmony; knowledge has accumulated on how to help the immune system fight bacterial infections, and so on. We are also beginning to use knowledge to examine and manage the relation of body, animal, vegetative, and social processes to physical environmental elements such as polluted waterways, acid rain, unfiltered recirculated air in buildings, and so on. Managing a process implies and presupposes a gaining of knowledge and perspective with regard to that process, including its relations with other processes. Management is also impregnated by values which give the process direction and existential meaning. The focus of management is the harmonious functioning of that process and of its interface with other processes.

## *The Self-Management Process Defined*

We are now in a position to define the process of self management more accurately. As pointed out earlier, the self-management process belongs to the category of processes that consist of managing other processes. In particular, self management involves looking at life as a process in which certain elements are quite stable, predictable, and even self-organizing, and in which other elements are "creative." Managing one's life as a process, then, involves managing both the stable, predictable, and self-organizing elements as well as managing the creative and unforeseen aspects of one's life.

As in managing any other process, managing the self process involves approaching one's life with those two indispensable instruments of management, knowledge and value. Managing the stable, predictable, and self-organizing aspects of one's life involves getting to know those aspects and making sure that the self-organizing personal and interpersonal ecosystem stays harmonious. In addition, managing the creative aspects of one's life involves becoming familiar with, and leading harmoniously through expressive channels – those unforeseen impacts and impulses, from inside oneself or from the outside. From the self-management perspective, nothing can be accomplished by going against the flow of a process, by ignoring it or by trying to stop it. Managing, or helping to bring or restore harmony, even when suffering is experienced, always demands going with the flow of the process.

The management of the self process can of itself be considered a process. When we consider self management as process, we mean that we are interested in the dynamic aspects of self management more than in the background of style and personality. We also mean that we can expect certain regularities and phases in the process of self management. Furthermore, we see the self-management process as being interrelated with and embedded in other processes, such as various levels of social -managerial processes, in relation to which it fulfills a meaningful function. In this book we are mostly concerned with the relation of the self-management process to various work group and organizational processes, but there are many other processes that surround self management – family, education, and political processes, to name just a few. Thus, the self-management process focuses on the individual as he tries to gain knowledge of himself and his environment, and as he tries to bring about or restore harmony to the process of his own evolution, whether physical, emotional, financial, spiritual, and to his interactions with the processes that surround him.

Echoing the simultaneous action of a few processes that constitute human physiology, we have chosen to focus on the interaction of four major processes that we feel are basic to self management. They are: 1) the appropriation process; 2) the relation process; 3) the decision process; and 4) the action process. These four processes can truly be considered generic, in that they transcend the singularity of individual persons. They also transcend the specificity of time (as in history) and space (as in culture).

## *Four Generic Processes of Self Management*

The process of self management can be seen as a constant interaction among the four processes mentioned earlier. We hypothesize the following: 1) These four processes are synchronic - their role is simultaneous rather than in any sequential order - and their interactions are infinitely complex. 2) All four of them are indispensable for a person to manage himself. They can be seen as four different, but necessary, aspects of the self-management process. 3) The four processes operate as if each one were reflected in the other three.

First, the four self-management processes are synchronic and their interactions are complex. Indeed, when a deficiency presents itself in any one of those four processes, other processes will almost certainly become contaminated and self management will be compromised or slowed down. No one process can be said to be more important than another one, nor can any one process claim to be a prerequisite to another one.

Second, all four processes are indispensable. Is it possible to imagine a person in whom only three of these major functions are present? For example, a person may be able to maintain relationships with others, to make choices, and to act; but be unable to appropriate the facts and lessons associated with these three processes. Such a person would quickly risk stagnation, because she would learn nothing from her activities. Her actions, decisions, and social relations would be characterized by uncreative repetitions. This example of lopsided self management shows that the absence of one process can quickly bring a person's development to a halt.

Third, the four processes operate as if each one were reflected, or were at work, in the other three. The process of appropriation is at work in forming relationships, but it is also in plotting possibilities for decision making and in the process of acting. The relation process is present in the work of appropriation and learning, as well as in the various forms of communication that facilitate decision making and concrete action. The decision process is present in appropriation and learning, as in deciding what to learn and what not to learn, but is also present in forming relationships and in determining the means of actions. Similarly, the action process is present in the activities associated with appropriation, with relation building and with decision making.

The process of self management can also be seen as a process of managing oneself that is constantly in interaction with environmental processes, such as physical and social processes. Thus, the process of self management involves continuously combining the widest possible vision and perspective with regard to actual and potential problems, with a focus precise enough to permit practical management. (This constant alternation between widening and focusing the view is similar to the processes of centering and decentering described by Piaget with regard to cognitive development; see Gruber and Voneche.)

The four generic processes of self management (appropriation, relation, decision, and action) can be considered points of reference that allow one to diagnose and direct one's itinerary within an organization – that is, to orient oneself and to act within a given time and a limited space. They can be seen as the moving parts against the background of an individual's unique style and personality.

### *Aspects Common to the Management of the Four Generic Processes*

If the process of self management allows a person to orient himself and to act within an organizational setting so as to bring about, or restore, harmony between different aspects of himself and his environment, the same thing can be said for each one of the four generic processes. Two of the most prevalent aspects requiring such management are: 1) discrepancies between one's own values and those of the organizational culture in which one moves, and 2) the awareness of one's own needs and career aspirations, and one's assessment of the opportunities present in the environment. These same aspects can also be found on the level of each of the four generic processes. To illustrate, let's look at each one in turn.

1] *The appropriation process*

A person cannot accomplish a task judiciously without knowledge of the time available for it or the environment in which it is to be accomplished. Also, the relation between realistic possibilities on his part as well as his present limits must be constantly evaluated. The process of appropriation aims specifically at establishing knowledge about such relevant temporal and spatial parameters. This process also allows a person to gauge his own needs, interests, preferences, limits, and possibilities, as well as any environmental constraints and opportunities, so as to help bring about a certain harmony between them. Usually, a very wide range of possibilities is available in the form of natural resources, objects, tools and equipment, and, not the least, his own imaginative resources, or opportunities offered through the needs and interventions of others. *The appropriation process allows a person to gain a clear sense of reality, both about his own needs and potentials, and about the needs and opportunities present in his environment.*

2] *The relation process*

To manage oneself and carry out one's actions in organizational time and space always implies exchanges, meetings, and confrontations with others. Thus, relations constitute the second generic process of self-management, which is expressed through interactions and communications with other people. Balancing one's own needs, interests, preferences, limits, and possibilities with those of one's colleagues and partners is a challenge. In particular, the reactions of others to those of our actions that affect them may interfere with our self management in a number of ways. They may affect self-esteem, sense of competence, level of intimacy, or creative expression. Thus, the relation process is vital in the process of self management and, even more important, self management is a prerequisite for directing and collaborating with others. *Finding and building a network of supportive people may be one of the gradual outcomes of management of the relation process.*

3] *The decision process*

To orient oneself and to act in an organizational environment involves constant decision making, not only on behalf of the organization but also for oneself. To make decisions, it is necessary to evaluate what is important or of greatest value or priority. Like the other generic self-management processes, the decision process involves a search for balance between what is important for oneself and what is important for others; between cultural and personal priorities; among past, present, and future considerations; and so on. The values that underlie a person's decisions may evolve with age and experience, and may even be expressed very differently under different environmental conditions or depending on the situations. *However, the process itself, which gradually leads a person to a clearer focus on his most important values, can be predicated as a stable and predictable presence in any individual's personal evolution.*

4] *The action process*

Working within an organization further means performing concrete actions that allow one to respond to needs and to obtain optimal results. Often this is only possible when one's rewards from a given action can be balanced with the rewards others receive from it. Many people have experienced the challenge of finding this delicate equilibrium between adequately concretizing their personal projects, and the possibilities and limitations that help or hinder such concretizations in the physical, social, and organizational environment. Every action informs us how well we are in tune or at odds with environmental, cultural, or social expectations. Managing the action process includes exercising an acceptable degree of control over the quality of enacted responses and their appropriateness to personal and environmental demands. *The process may gradually lead to the realization of a person's potential.*

In short, a fundamental common element in the management of the four generic processes is the search for balance, for an equilibrium between what a person desires and what the environment offers in the way of resources, possibilities, or limitations.

In the next section we will explore the characteristics of a healthy self-management process.

*The Characteristics of a Healthy Self-Management Process*

In general, a process can be said to demonstrate health when it can fulfill its function in a fairly smooth and unhindered manner. To illustrate, let's look at the body functions analogy again. The blood circulation process can be considered healthy when the arteries are unclogged, when muscular contractions do not hinder the flow of the bloodstream, when the nervous system transmits the right impulses to the heart muscle, and so on. Similarly, the immune response process can be considered healthy when the appropriate glands respond with appropriate timing to bacterial invasions. Any particular process is healthy insofar as it can fulfill its function unhindered; that is, as its own condition permits an unhindered flow and as the surrounding processes with which it interacts also function without disturbances. Furthermore, the total body process can be considered healthy when all its constituent processes are healthy and functioning synchronically with each other.

When we consider management as a process where the function is to gain knowledge and bring about harmony, then the notion of health can be defined in much the same way. Indeed, the process of managing oneself can be considered healthy when the function of getting to know oneself and bringing about harmony can go on unhindered, when there are no major obstructions either internally or in our relation to surrounding physical and social processes.

Thus, in order for a person to manage herself effectively, major facilitating conditions include getting to know herself rather well and achieving harmony in all four generic processes as well as in the relations between them. In particular, this means that the person can appropriate a multifaceted environment as well as her own inner ecology; that she can effectively manage relations with others; that she can make decisions without major obstructions; and that she can concretize actions in accordance with her potential and limits. Managing oneself effectively also includes a serenity in coping with unforeseen circumstances. In fact, the capacity to resolve crises is perhaps the ultimate test of health for the self-management process. Healthy self management will be facilitated not only by an absence of major obstacles in the four generic processes but, most importantly, by harmonious exchanges among them. In addition, we suggest that the health of these processes is particularly associated with recognition of the following characteristics: 1) the notion of cycles, 2) the coexistence of polarities, 3) free movement between internal and external aspects as well as between the conscious and the subconscious, 4) a synergistic quality, and 5) synchronous occurrence of the four processes. Let's look at each of these characteristics in turn.

1] *The notion of cycles, rhythms, and alternating phases*

Let's return to the image of physical processes to illustrate the notion of cycles and phases. The assimilation of nutrients in the body involves not only the intake of food, but also many other phases, such as breaking down the food, digestion, absorption of nutrients into the bloodstream, evacuation of useless material, new intake of food, and so on. In this bodily process, every phase is equally indispensable. A certain rhythm must be respected during and between cycles, and every part of the cycle is alternately high and low during the whole period.

The above image is useful for understanding what happens in self-management processes. For example, the assimilation of knowledge takes time. A healthy appropriation process consists of intensive periods of observation and learning, followed by periods of rest and integration during which the person puts a critical distance between himself and what he has learned. Other self-management processes also require this variance. For example, in the relation process even our most intimate relationships have their ups and downs. A strengthening of emotional ties may alternate with a period of insecurity and even of questioning the relationship. There is a period for reaching out, building friendship, cultivating intimacy, and moving on to joint projects, or gradually decreasing the intensity. Similarly, it is virtually impossible to maintain a constantly clear and absolute idea of our choices and priorities - an uninhibited decision process will almost certainly consist of acknowledged phases of alternating clarity and doubt. In the case of the action process, this cyclical characteristic manifests itself in periods of intensity and high productivity, alternating with periods of recovery and relaxation. Who has never experienced an intense creative effort, followed by feelings of emptiness after the effort has been accomplished? Contract negotiation, career change, job interviews - all are examples of professional situations that involve the intense mobilization of creative resources. Cycles, rhythms, and alternating phases appear to be inherent and pervasive in many processes, and they command our attention with respect to self-management.

2] *The co-existence of polarities*

Many models of personal and group development have presented the idea of two opposite poles operating almost simultaneously, as in love and hate, or trust and mistrust (Jack Gibb, *Trust)*. In a healthy self-management process there is a recognition that reality includes both poles: both are active at the same time and there is a free flow between them. There is not only alternation, but also coexistence.

For example, a healthy appropriation process entails integrating certain facts, while simultaneously excluding others not pertinent to self management. A sane relation process implies simultaneous association with certain others, and respect for the inevitable separateness from them. In a relation where we have trust in the other person, it is a good idea to at the same time maintain a sense of vigilance so that we remain anchored in ourselves. When we feel love toward a particular person we do well to keep in mind that contrary feelings, such as indifference or hatred, are also present, if only as a remote possibility. We have a similar situation in the decision process. Though one may not appear unduly ambivalent, any choice is made through the double action of two polar tendencies, attraction and rejection. Any chosen object is neither all bad nor all good, and any decision carries some disadvantages even if it is seen as positive and constructive. The coexistence of polarities also holds true whenever projects are put into effect. Any solution that turns intentions into concrete realizations, (that is, any method of implementation) implies a certain number of undesirable consequences. As another illustration, the process of self management can be seen as an alternation between control and the relinquishing of control, while accepting the simultaneous presence of these apparently opposing poles. We could say that a process is uninhibited only to the extent that it is connected with both the positive and negative aspects of reality, as we interpret them. Contrary to Sartre's well-known definition "Hell is – the others," the co-existence of polarities reminds us that hell and heaven are relative concepts. In many ways the "others" remind us of ourselves.

3] *Free movement between internal and external aspects as well as between the conscious and the subconscious*

An uninhibited and healthy process of self management consists of more than a search for a fit between the dimensions of an individual's personal make-up and the external demands made upon him by the organization or the environment. A healthy process is also characterized by an intense interface between the internal and the external, in which each aspect can move freely and flexibly to meet the other. Furthermore, in a healthy process the subconscious mind will be allowed sufficient expression, and not prove detrimental to the development of oneself and one's relations with others. In this context, it is important to mention the role of humor, that can be understood as a highly appropriate means of linking conscious and subconscious aspects of behavior. Have we not all met a situation, for example in an organizational meeting, where humor effectively resolved a group process that threatened to become tense, difficult, or even explosive? Re-framing the rigid thinking often present in these circumstances into a larger context frequently makes it look utterly ridiculous by providing a healthy sense of perspective. To act with humor presupposes just such a free flow between internal and external, conscious and subconscious data. In fact, it is hard to imagine any discovery or innovation without this free interaction.

The role of the subconscious mind is important in all four generic processes of self management. How often do we integrate information without a precise, conscious reason? Is there any interpersonal relationship devoid of subconscious significance? How many decisions do we make after "sleeping on it"? And how many actions are colored with subconscious significance! The importance of the subconscious extends into reminding us of the limitations of overly rigid conscious control. Integrating the conscious and subconscious permits a person to avoid the traps of such self-imposed limitations. We know that Freud chose a fairly simple and stable spatial-temporal device, the couch, which permitted his patients to associate freely and, in so doing, express subconscious data and observe and integrate them. Many intuitive managers practice the art of integrating subconscious clues. When observing them, we sense that these managers are acutely aware of the temporal and spatial structures and limitations of their organization. In addition, they use these data as a stable setting, a background, against which the actions of their colleagues can be understood in all their aspects, including their subconscious roots. They are able to decode the subtle and largely subconscious phenomena that are invisibly woven into the fibers of organizational life.

4] *A synergistic quality*
Contrary to the idea of self management as a rather selfish attitude, it is apparent that a healthy self-management process is characterized by its capacity to generate new opportunities and insights, sometimes unexpected, not only for oneself but for others as well. For example, in a group where people relate dynamically to each other while staying in tune with their own processes, it is quite common to find that many people have the same intuitions about a certain situation, almost at the same time. Thus, it is apparent that they complement each other in terms of resources, skills, and behaviors. Again, this phenomenon holds true for each of the four generic processes, and it leads us to a new definition of synergy: a group can be qualified as synergistic to the extent that its members become generative, for themselves and others, of opportunities for appropriation, relation, decision, and action.

5] *Synchronization of the four processes*
The process of self management can be expected to be healthy to the extent that a certain synchronization is being achieved between all four generic processes. We mean by this that each one of those processes should be in tune with each of the others. For example, a person who finds herself in a very productive phase will need to assimilate considerable information, and be prepared to learn a lot. This geared-up action process can also be expected to tax her abilities to develop and manage relationships and even to make decisions. There may be alternations of rhythms within each of the generic processes. Thus, the process of managing herself will require an awareness of the need for a degree of harmonization between processes, even if this demands certain adjustments in her plans and intentions. Failure to synchronize these processes might

result in obstructions that compromise the whole self-management effort, and may even lead to surprise disappointments.

## *Conditions Likely to Hinder the Self-Management Process*

We are interested here in the conditions that may hinder the self-management process – that is, those general conditions likely to prevent a person from getting to know himself and from bringing about, or restoring, harmony, both internally and in his relation with surrounding physical and social processes. We have identified three types of these conditions, which we will call "obstructions" to the self-management process. The first type of obstruction is related to contamination by an obstruction present in one of the four generic processes, which then has an impact on the others. The second type is related to a lack of synchronization between all four generic processes.For example, one generic process may be in an intense phase while another one may not be geared toward the same level of intensity. The third type has to do with an inappropriate fit between the process of self management and other surrounding physical and social processes, perhaps leading to a relative isolation of the self-management process, or to alienation. Let's take a closer look at each of those types.

### Obstructions of the First Type

They are those generated by obstacles present in one of the four generic processes. As one process becomes clogged, all the others risk rapid deterioration. For example, imagine that employee Bill has not furthered his education and has not had any retraining for quite a while. He has not developed any new competence or knowledge nor enlarged his vision. He has not taken any initiative to deal with the impact of technological changes affecting his organization. His appropriation process is therefore impoverished. The "contamination" may spread rapidly and affect the relation process, hampering the flow of his work relationships, perhaps by making him attach more importance to the status quo than to the dynamic nature of those relationships and, in general, by making him resist change. His decisions will likely suffer from the inflexibility present in other processes and may, for example, lack a sense of contact with the reality around him. We can imagine that his behavior will tend to become repetitive and devoid of any innovation or flexibility. Obstructions such as those present in employee Bill may seem extreme, but they are found to exist in our daily experience.

The contamination or diffusive phenomenon present in the above example is a major cause of breakdown of the self-management process. The chart below illustrates this diffusive character of obstructions. The sequence of the diffusion in the chart is arbitrary, and is not intended as an absolute. In reality we can envision the obstructions as spreading almost simultaneously to all four generic processes, since the obstructions in the different processes influence each other.

*Appropriation Process*
Bill stops attempting to appropriate new aspects of his personal or organizational environment (in terms of knowledge, competence, information, awareness, etc.)

*Relation Process*
We may observe the development of defensive social behavior, intended to protect set opinions; this behavior becomes characterized by a high level of distrust, which, in turn, makes Bill less likely to initiate or maintain genuine social relationships.

*Action Process*
The inflexibility present in the decision process affects Bill's actions: they become repetitive and anchored in the past, rather than being adaptive to changing situations, over time and space. In turn, this behavior can be expected to further reduce his appropriate abilities and to lead the person into a self-destructive circle.

*Decision Process*
Since Bill's social relations in the organization are deteriorating, he no longer benefits from realistic feedback, advice and support; his decision process risks becoming impoverished, and lacking a sense of contact with environmental realities.

*Chart 2.* The diffuse character of obstructions in Bill's self-management process.

To further illustrate the diffusive phenomenon of obstructions originating in one of the four generic processes, we present four scenarios in the pages that follow. Each scenario illustrates the obstruction originating in a particular process.

- *Scenario 1: Obstruction* originates in the appropriation process.
  Let's imagine that Lisa has no problems related to three of the generic processes. The source of obstruction lies in her appropriation process. That is to say, she shows a number of important defi-

ciencies in her appropriation abilities; she has stopped attempts to assimilate new information, to change her point of view, or to recognize the value of modifying her understanding of the organization. Even if Lisa develops relationships with others, these relations will likely suffer from the same pattern. She will be unreceptive, keeping certain fixed attitudes toward some people and refusing to discover new qualities in others. Her decision process is also at risk because it will not occur to her to familiarize herself with novel points of view and new options, or to question former decisions and thus learn from past errors. In fact, her decision-making ability may become so paralyzed that she becomes a chronic procrastinator, or her decisions become imbued with a lack of adaptive judgment and realism. The same type of inhibition will probably infiltrate the action process. Lisa will tend to repeat her responses, even if this means not doing anything at all. When she does act, her actions will likely not be integrated with her personality. For example, she may not commit herself to her actions and may fail to display a reasonable degree of professional responsibility. She is more likely to justify her actions and rationalize them so they fit closely with her preconceived ideas. In general, she will experience an insufficiency of appropriation in her relations, decisions, and actions. The deficiencies present in this kind of obstruction may well lead the person into robotic, mechanical behavior, based on a nonmodifiable "program," an attitude devoid of curiosity, and the willful exclusion of any creative alternative. Therefore, Lisa is likely to be less innovative and less productive overall.

- *Scenario 2: Obstruction originates in the relation process.*
  Let's suppose that Ron is capable of appropriation, decision, and action but lacks openness in the process of interpersonal relations. That is, the obstruction in this process is related to difficulty establishing and nurturing a satisfactory social rapport with other people in his organization. The lack of exchange on this level may well prevent him from fully understanding other people's work rhythms where they differ from his own or from understanding the apparent contradictions in their behavior, or the different and sometimes conflicting aspects of their personalities. In other words, his appropriation process risks being too narrow to fully understand all the factors involved in the organizational interpersonal processes.

Ron's mental image of the organization may gradually become deformed, mostly due to his own biases, since other people may occupy only a secondary place in this image. Ron's decisions may take into account his own personal choices, but not consider the degree to which these choices affect others or the compatibility of his choices with those of others. His actions, although carried through to completion, will likely be isolated acts, not coordinated with the actions of those around him. The most flagrant characteristic of this particular scenario is a lack of sensitivity on Ron's part, both toward himself and his own social and support needs, and toward those with whom he lives and works. This type of obstruction in the relation process may result in rejection by the other members of the organization. Since it may appear that Ron does not really notice them, they may turn away from him rather than risk feeling rejected themselves. Consequently, the greatest danger to Ron's self-management process is that he closes himself up in a sterile effort at self-protection, thereby fueling a self-destructive cycle.

- *Scenario 3: Obstruction originates in the decision process.*
  Let's imagine that Elaine can handle the processes of appropriation, relation, and action with relative ease, but is comparatively weak in the area of decision making. Elaine has difficulty establishing priorities and making choices in complex situations. In those situations, it is as if her entire value system ceases to function, or as if she cannot give it her full, conscious attention. This kind of obstruction will soon carry over into her actions – acts may be performed with a certain indifference, without any clear sense of direction, and without passion or enthusiasm. Her behavior may even resemble the first signs of depression. As she lacks self-assurance, her relations with others may quickly be affected. She may relate to all colleagues and employees in more or less the same way, without forming any special ties. Similarly, Elaine may be capable of absorbing information, but, without real conviction or genuine interest, neglecting to put it in any order of priority or to give it a structure. Very quickly, the same difficulties with creating order, with attaching importance and value to certain things more than to others, and with establishing priorities and eliminating the unessential will find their way into all four generic processes. Given this situation, Elaine's self management will probably express itself in undecided,

emotion-poor, conviction-poor behavior, ill-adapted to achieving the aims of the organization, or her own personal goals. The consequent difficulty in defining and assessing her contribution to the organization may very well lead Elaine to a genuine identity crisis in her work.

- *Scenario 4: Obstruction originates in the action process.*

In this instance, Leo is not inhibited in appropriating, relating, and deciding, but rather in doing. This situation may be equivalent to a sort of stage fright, or may originate in factors such as guilt or anxiety. At any rate, suppose his average level of activity is quite low – he produces little, and consistently resists concretizing any plans or intentions, or implementing decisions he has previously reached. Whatever the reasons for this obstruction in the action process, it is sure to affect his appropriation process. For example, he may become inept at seizing opportunities to learn new things, to expand his experience, or to re-train himself. Leo may even have difficulty seeing, let alone admitting, that his inaction is his major obstacle to adequately appropriating his environment. Similar problems are likely to occur in his relation process. For example, Leo will make few gestures to encourage contact with newcomers, or to deepen relationships with co-workers. This type of interaction may be emotionally difficult to deal with, for himself as well as for his colleagues. Decision making can also suffer from the general level of inactivity, especially in the early stages of preparing to make a decision. Without the initiative necessary to test an idea, or to get information and competent advice, Leo's decisions risk lacking clarity and accuracy with regard to the issues involved in making them. Again, every other process is affected. It seems likely that Leo will be perceived as someone who is relatively unproductive and who is most at ease in jobs requiring little initiative and few responsibilities. Leo himself may not understand why he is relegated to such "low" functions, despite his extensive education. His self management is characterized by a lack of experimentation with possibilities, thereby reducing his ability to reach a satisfying degree of control over his actions and to learn from them. He risks misunderstanding the causes of his situation and becoming more and more frustrated.

## Obstructions of the Second Type

Obstructions of the second type are related to difficulty in synchronizing the four generic processes. Most of the time they point to an excessive development of, and reliance upon, one or more of these processes, to the neglect or exclusion of others. Obstructions of this type remind a person of the desirability of a balanced development of all processes. They also provide a useful indication of where his efforts should be brought to bear.

To illustrate the concept of synchronization in a more or less concrete situation, suppose a person is skillful in applying his energies in the decision and action processes. As a result, he is perceived in his organization as an effective decision maker and as someone who has no difficulty in making himself felt through decisive actions. Despite his abilities in these two processes, he may not have developed a sufficient degree of sensitivity to his co-workers to make them feel worthy of themselves and to instill in them a genuine desire to cooperate with him. On the contrary, his active behavior breeds a climate of competitiveness with his colleagues – they feel that whatever they may accomplish, they will never quite reach his level of performance. Sooner or later, he finds himself facing a complete lack of cooperation from the majority of his fellow workers. In addition, he has trouble interpreting their behavior, due to the fact that he has also neglected the process of appropriations, both with respect to himself as a person and with respect to others' needs and aspirations. He has failed to gauge the impact of his actions and grandiose performance on his colleagues, in terms of the feelings those actions generate in them. By not understanding what has happened between him and his colleagues, he may become hesitant in his future actions or harbor feelings of resentment and frustration. However, neither those feelings nor the hesitations in the action process will likely overcome the obstruction that inevitably forms in his self-management process. In fact, he will effectively prevent himself from bringing about, or restoring, harmony in the process of his own evolution as long as he fails to recognize the lack of synchronization in generic processes.

Synchronization of the four processes means that they back each other up, rather than taking away from each other, going against each other, or not being sufficiently "equal." Other examples would be a person who attaches an exclusive importance to appropriation, without regard for the consequences for others; or a person who acts and appropriates situations quickly, but without due process for relations and decisions. The difference between obstructions of the first type and lack of synchronization resides mostly in the fact that the latter is symptomatic of unbalanced development among the four processes, while in the former the emphasis is more on the inhibition of one particular process, which then leads to repercussions in all other processes.

## Obstructions of the Third Type

Obstructions of the third type find their origin in an inappropriate fit between the process of self management and other surrounding physical and social processes. For example, the process of self management may not be attuned to basic physical rhythms, phases, and polarities, such as those inherent in wakefulness and sleep, work and rest, nourishment and digestion. Most of the time these obstructions have to do with the fact that the person has insufficient awareness of, or pays insufficient attention to, her own body signs, which would ordinarily warn her of her own needs. Another example of this type of obstruction is an inappropriate fit between environmental and organizational opportunities, and the potential of a person in a given area. A manager who is particularly talented in social dealings may find herself in an organization offering few possibilities to use this talent. As a result, in addition to feelings of dissatisfaction, she risks serious obstructions in her relation process. A newcomer in a company may have to face a work place so active and turbulent that her appropriation process is overburdened. Consequently, she risks not being able to respond to many new opportunities at appropriate times, or to integrate possible new knowledge. Her action process may become quite paralyzed due to her failure to achieve a satisfactory balance between her level of activity and the possibilities for action present in the environment.

Whenever an obstruction is due to an inadequate fit between personal rhythms and potentials on one hand, and environmental possibilities and claims,on the other, the person may develop repetitive or defensive behavior. The role of such repetitive or defensive behavior is almost always a trial of adjustment that, as we will explain in the next section, is practically doomed to be ineffectual. In particular, such behavior may create difficulties for the individual as well as for others. Much authoritarian or antisocial behavior may be understood in this light. More generally speaking, a person who fails to deal effectively with obstructions of the third type is likely to end up opting for very stable or routine "quiet" jobs that require little more than the mechanical application of standard procedures. One of the major consequences of these obstructions is that potential opportunities fail to be recognized as such, or may even be misinterpreted as threats, and so are missed; the person enters a vicious circle that eventually becomes destructive.

In the next section we will elaborate on the role of defensive behavior – what types of defensive behavior can be identified, and why and in what ways it is ineffectual.

### *Defensive Behavior and the Self-Management Process*

Sometimes people engage in behaviors that, although they are responses to an obstruction in the process of self management, are ineffectual in restoring a balanced management process. These behaviors are frequently called "defensive" because the aim of the person adopting them is to avoid facing the obstruction head-on. Instead he ends up concealing the presence of the obstruction, mostly from himself and also from others. When this happens, the person may deny the relevance of the particular process where the obstruction is anchored, perhaps by withdrawing from the process altogether and declaring it "useless." Or, the person may try to restore a semblance of a healthy process, perhaps by rejecting the environment that he sees as contributing to the obstruction, or by controlling the environment to such an extent that the obstruction seems justified. Thus, defensive behavior may be of at least three types:

1] Withdrawal from the process that one experiences as being obstructed. In this case the particular process is halted and is no longer considered a valid instrument of self management.

2] Rejection of the environment, which is seen as contributing to the obstruction. This may take the form of revolt or punishment, depending on whether the person finds himself in a subordinate or powerful position.

3] Controlling the environment to such an extent that the obstruction seems entirely justified.

Defensive behavior may avoid the pain or disappointments of an obstruction. But, like taking aspirin for a headache, the behavior is likely to mask the symptom while avoiding its underlying cause. No attempt is made at a constructive resolution and consequent opening up of the process in question. Such attempts are no more likely when the mind tends to resort to defensive attitudes, and consequently defensive behavior, in a rather automatic way. As defensive behavior does not deal directly with either the source or resolution of the obstruction, it may distort, slow down, and eventually permanently damage the self-management process.

Any one type of defensive behavior may be called into action to deal with obstructions in any one of the four processes: appropriation, relation, decision, and action. Let's take an example from the appropriation process, and see how the three types of defensive behavior can work toward paralyzing the process. Suppose the flow of the appropriation process is obstructed, impairing a person's ability to take in relevant aspects of a new environment or, more generally, his ability to learn, to investigate, to chart organizational and personal territories. Common causes for such an obstruction are information overload and fear. For illustrative purposes, let's go through what may happen under such circumstances.

When exposure to information overload or fear leads to an obstruction in the appropriation flow, the person may, as a result, deny herself the full expression of her natural curiosity and fail to go out and seek relevant information. Both information overload and fear are normal occurrences at times, and can be recognized and dealt with directly. However, perceived pressures from outside (such as peers or a supervisor urging conformity to an image) or from inside (such as guilt, shame, a false sense of pride, or a threat to self-esteem) can lead a person to defend herself against the unpleasant experience generated by the information overload or fear. As a result, instead of facing these factors directly, she may resort to any one or a combination of defensive behaviors. Three examples of this defensive behavior are described below.

1] *Withdrawal from the appropriation process altogether, even to the point of denying its usefulness.*

In this case, the person refuses to take in new information or to give credit to the usefulness of the process, either for himself or for others. Learning is not considered a productive or otherwise worthwhile activity. Fortunately, many successful organizations recognize the value of on-the-job training and of personal growth. However, others create situations in which such activities are denied recognition. When the situation seems to lead to a permanent withdrawal from the appropriation process, the person will not only give up most of his capacity for self management, he will also put in place a mechanism that will prevent him from ever restoring a proper flow in his appropriation process. For example, this particular defensive behavior may incite the individual to establish a rigidly defined world view and set of principles. This particular world view and set of principles may have been adequate for the individual at one time, but will now effectively prevent him from accepting data that would entail even a remote possibility of re-ordering his cognitive map.

In effect, preventing the appropriation flow from functioning smoothly as an instrument of the self-management process amounts to making the person blind to himself and to his environment. He may be denying himself vital information for his personal development. The behaviors that express such an obstruction in the appropriation process may range from wishful thinking to prejudice, with corresponding repercussions in other processes. The implications may also be far-reaching if an entire culture condones an obstruction of the appropriation process, and when dogmatically held views discourage people from transcending their self-imposed cognitive barriers.

Even within an organizational setting, a person's withdrawal from the appropriation process may severely handicap the flow of other processes. For example, strategic decision making may lack realism as a consequence of this kind of defensive behavior, mostly because of failure to investigate and to recognize relevant facts. I. L. Janis and L. Mann, have assembled extensive evidence of how internal conflicts, or the wish to protect oneself from potential fear or other painful affects, may interfere with a person's information processing and may lead to rationalizations and highly biased and irrational decisions.

2] *Rejection of the environment that is believed to contribute to the obstruction.*

In this case, the person blames the environment or another person for her own failure to adequately appropriate her environment. She may be locked into the habit of complaining and seeing herself as a victim; learning is then considered impeded by others or outside circumstances. Managers are in a position where they are particularly susceptible to being blamed for preventing others from learning, for they are symbolically close to the father or mother figure. Indeed, in many cultures fathers and mothers have played a culturally sustained role of keeping the lid on exploration and of trying to limit their offspring to rigidly defined norms of social behavior and learning. Where this pattern has led to an obstruction in the child's appropriation process, the adult individual may protect herself against the pain of recognizing the harm that has been done. She may then choose to reject people in her environment who unconsciously remind her of the authority her parents wielded over her during her childhood.

When this type of defensive behavior operates over a long period of time, the person may acquire a negative attitude toward herself or her environment, which is perceived as preventing her from learning or from acquiring all the information she would like. In extreme cases this attitude may lead to depression or open revolt. A habitual negative attitude leads the person to adopt behaviors that contribute to a non-constructive climate in the organization as a whole. Energy that could otherwise be used constructively is being drained from the organization and from others. The person may also willfully sabotage the organization's objectives and create counterproductive political forces that serve as substitute goals.

3] *Control of the environment to such an extent that the obstruction seems entirely justified.*

Rather than confronting the source of the appropriation difficulties, in this case the person tries to mold the environment to conform to his preconceived ideas, which he considers safe and known. This demand to conform may be a defensive mechanism for the employee in relation to his environment, but it may also be a managerial attitude that degenerates into paternalism and authoritarian behavior. The demand to conform may be applied to people,

> to circumstances, or even to data. Data can be interpreted in such a way that one's preconceived ideas are verified. Thus, one is justified in not taking in new information, which could challenge existing cognitive maps or beliefs. Theories about the environment or about people may be elaborated, rationalizing and legitimizing the obstructions in the appropriation process. The demand for others to conform to one's ideas may be a powerful tool in controlling one's own and others' appropriation processes simultaneously.

To summarize, none of these three types of defensive behavior can make the appropriation process a flowing one, nor can they solve the problem or identify the causes that lead to deterioration of the process. However, they can temporarily remove or obscure the unpleasant feelings generated by obstructions. They may impart the illusion that the process is working, or help reinforce the conviction that a free-flowing appropriation process is entirely unnecessary. However, when obstructions are due to information overload, other ways of coping with the problem are more direct than resorting to defensive behavior. For example, one way of coping consists of distancing oneself from the scene, and giving oneself some time to integrate all the information. If fear is behind obstructions in the appropriation process, one may want to recognize and deal with the fear, and seek counsel from people whose insights one trusts. The above types of defensive behavior can also be shown to operate in the other processes – relations, decisions, and actions. In most cases, defensive behavior will tend to turn into self-fulfilling prophecies, or cycles of misperception from which it becomes increasingly difficult to extricate oneself. In particular, such behavior will hinder the self-management process by preventing free interaction among the four generic processes.

In the next section we propose some conditions facilitating optimal self management.

## *Propositions Concerning Optimal Self Management*

### Some Concluding Comments on Obstructions in the Self-Management Process

After the above discussion of the various conditions that can hinder the flow of the self-management process, we might add the following remarks:

1] It is evident that an obstruction takes on greater proportions if it occurs in more than one of the processes at the same time.

2] Only the general nature and the effect of obstructions have been examined. It is not our aim to consider here the multiple causes of these obstructions in an individual's character, personality, or his experiential history. The obstructions are examined as part of the process perspective of self management.

3] An objection that might be raised involves situations in which an environment offers people no opportunity for appropriation, relation, decision or action. Can we speak of someone's self-management problem when the problem is a lack of opportunity for self management? Indeed, we have already alluded to the possibility of environmental conditions affecting personally experienced obstructions in the four processes. There is a point at which personal and environmental conditions overlap significantly, especially through the interplay of projections and other forms of interaction between a person and his environment. These interactions should, of course, be recognized. However, they do not preclude the possibility of awareness and change within the social context in which they occur, and in harmony with this context.

4] Often, opportunity may only appear to be lacking. The experience of those who have survived and developed themselves in exceptionally harsh situations bears witness to this. In the everyday life of an organization, lack of opportunity is frequently invoked to justify an individual's lack of success. If, in truth, an organization offered absolutely no opportunity, only people with serious obstructions in their self-management process would consent to work in it.

5] Finally, we have to say that many people have had the experience of apparent obstructions actually being helpful. Indeed, the flow of self-management processes is the final criterion of what does and does not constitute an obstruction. Seeming obstructions cease to be obstructions when the flow can go on, sometimes after a change of direction.

## Managing Oneself Optimally – What Does it Take?

Attaining an optimum in self management remains a challenge. Some questions that might be raised are the following:

- How can we work, practically and concretely, toward a dynamic balance of the four processes. How can we recognize imbalance; how can we restore balance?
- How can we best balance the characteristics and dynamics of our own personality with the characteristics and dynamics of the organizational environment, especially when personal values conflict with those prevalent in the organization?
- How can we avoid obstructions that take root in the synchronization (or lack thereof) of the four processes? How can we establish a free interchange among the four processes? How can we recognize faulty synchronization?
- How can we pay close enough attention to our rhythms, phases, and polarities so as not to deny their manifestation, especially going through a particularly difficult phase? How do we accept being in a phase of low or high energy? How do we become aware of the differences between ourselves and others in the sense of respecting other people's rhythms even when our own differ greatly, or when we are in a "high" phase?

These rather difficult questions are bound to stimulate reflection. Indeed, we have all experienced the difficulty of dealing with internal and external tensions, with contradictions in both personal and organizational contexts, and even with the nagging questions raised by the most fundamental paradoxes of life itself. Can we find general principles that help us manage ourselves, and realize the best conditions for seeking to fulfill our optimal potential? On the way toward defining such principles, we offer below, in arbitrary order, the following tentative propositions. These propositions also constitute a synthesizing note that concludes the chapter:

1] To manage a situation with a fair degree of control over the management process, it seems evident that the person must try to comprehend and accept the characteristics of the situation that needs managing. This is a crucial point because, when it is the evolution of oneself that is to be managed, we must realize that we do not come neatly packaged and identical. We come in quite unique versions, and every "unique version" has its particular potentialities and difficulties, or limitations. Therefore, the importance of comprehending and accepting one's own characteristics is certainly one of the most essential principles of healthy self management.

2] A second proposition applicable to the process of managing oneself is closely related to the first – it is the necessity of coping and adjusting in spite of difficulties and limitations. By this we mean that self management involves reconciling the continuous conflicts between the cultural trends, standards of behavior, and role models set forth by one's organization, as well as peer pressure to conform, on the one hand, and the concrete and creative actualization of one's personality on the other. In coping and adjusting, a person is likely to create for himself conditions favoring the harmonious linking of all aspects of the management process, so as to avoid obstructing free interaction among them. This adaptive behavior can be seen as the perpetual challenge of striving toward a quality of dynamic equilibrium and balance.

To briefly illustrate this notion of dynamic equilibrium, imagine an employee who has relentlessly pursued ambitious goals and has maximized performance. If, in addition, she excels at innovation and originality in her work and is consequently somewhat ahead of her time, has she achieved the optimum in self management? Not as long as she has problems handling the criticism or envy of her associates. If her relation process suffers, then all her other efforts will be undermined. Thus, without overall good management, she risks becoming an outsider in the group and having no context into which to integrate her accomplishments and potential.

At the opposite end, consider a bureaucratically inclined person who has the tendency to transpose his corporate behavior to all other aspects of his life. By excessively and exclusively identifying with his professional role, this person may jeopardize other important aspects of his existence, for instance his family, friends, or leisure time. It would not be unusual for his deficiency in managing extra-professional activities to eventually lead back to difficulties in his work. In fact, he may identify with his organization to such an extent that the very integrity of his personality becomes compromised. As a result he may unwittingly destroy the possibility of ever bringing creative potential to bear in his work context. However well he controls his behavior, he can be expected sooner or later to come face to face with the need to loosen up in the empathic and creative areas of his life. If he does not, his associates will soon begin to perceive his controls as empty and quite useless, and they may refuse to go along. Indeed, moving toward one's full potential requires managing one's obvious talents, but it also implies managing one's limitations, difficulties, and handicaps. It involves managing pain as well as joy. In fact, it is the management of limitations, difficulties, and handicaps that frequently contains the possibility for a person to find meaning in his work, and in his life.

3] A third proposition for self management is directly related to the concept of process; in particular the need to take into account the characteristics of a healthy process (as they have been formulated earlier) and the need to feel oneself part of a process rather than feel isolated and alienated from what is going on. At the same time, there is a need to maintain a reasonable distance from the environment, and to stay firmly anchored in oneself. In particular, bringing about or restoring harmony within oneself and in one's interactions with surrounding processes requires one to be sensitive to the environment while staying anchored in one's own experience of the events. For example, in joint work on a creative project, nothing will be gained unless each and every person feels part of the creative process; yet creation is likely to stop from the moment the associates become so absorbed in creation that they lose contact with their own experience and forget to focus on the task they have set for themselves.

4] Finally, managing one's own processes is equivalent to managing change. The patterns we can observe in all processes of change can also be observed in the self-management process. For example, in the process of managing ourselves we can expect to find 1) an ongoing, changing flow of events, experiences, feelings, emotions, aspirations, and so on; 2) regularities and predictable patterns in this flow, as well as sudden and unforeseen happenings; 3) ourselves being pushed or pushing in certain directions, as well as resisting changes or meeting with resistance to change; 4) different degrees and different levels of the way changes affect us (organizational changes may impact to different degrees and on different levels our basic beliefs, assumptions and learned patterns, work style, or work habits); 5) time as an important factor – in a way, managing change is also managing time; 6) to do something, to intervene, is equivalent to changing the particular course of the flow of events (when to intervene and in what way?), and that the question of whether to intervene is ultimately an ethical question; 7) managing the changing process of oneself requires the ability to identify the changes, an understanding of their nature, and an understanding of the many ways in which they interact, including their symbolic meaning.

To summarize, to manage oneself optimally is to develop the capacity to bring about, or restore, harmony so aspirations can be realized and, consequently, the self process can move on to interact with other processes at other levels.

In the next chapter we will present, in more detail, each one of the four generic self-management processes.

## Key Points

- Managing appropriations in organizations
  - Obstructions – and their risks
  - Projection as an instrument
  - Double talk – its implications
- The Relation process and self management
  - Dependency and support
  - Intimacy and roles
  - Symptoms of obstructions
- The Decision process
  - Inherent paradoxes
  - Obstructions
  - Choice and the decision flow
- The Action process
  - Symptoms of obstructions
  - Managing action in organizations

# GENERIC PROCESSES OF SELF MANAGEMENT

# 2

## Self Management of the Appropriation Process

### *The Appropriation Process Defined*

The appropriation process can be defined as the continuous flow of a person's knowledge of time and environment, which, through gradual, successive movement toward learning and becoming aware, contributes to the construction of a mental map of himself and of his ecosystem (in this case the organizational environment). The process alternates between focusing on certain data and pushing other data into the shadows of unawareness, which makes it possible for the person to decipher and make sense of both his own and organizational realities. In particular, the process allows him to find his place and to orient himself in the organizations of which he is a member. This "deciphering" is an ongoing activity because information, values, emotions, culture, and myths are all constantly moving and changing. To remain an active, unalienated member of an organizational system, a person usually finds he must constantly identify gaps in information, changes in value priorities, new attitudes and techniques to be acquired, and so on.

Appropriation, then, is a matter of gaining self-knowledge, of identifying one's needs, desires, talents, limitations, and patterns of behavior. But it is also a matter of absorbing the organizational environment in order to acquire sufficient knowledge and mastery of all its aspects

– to identify culture and subcultures, attitudes, general awareness, and prospective policy changes. As such, the concept of appropriation is wider than the concept of learning in classical learning theories. Appropriation is above all an exercise in clarifying unexplored zones, an exercise in which it is important for the person to identify the most reliable sources of information, and to establish a sense of priorities that allows him to distinguish the essential from the secondary. The ideal of the appropriation process is no less than acquiring a clear and global view of the situation. Indeed, how can we intervene and act effectively without it? Acquiring such a view is not easy. It is perhaps easier to acquire a deformed or confused perspective. For example, when something is bothersome we are tempted to try to forget it. However, rather than being discarded, that data is often stored in a "dormant file" in our memory. Without our being aware of it, the data may then unexpectedly color our view of a situation, and influence our communications or some specific action we take (Sigmund Freud, *Psychopathology of Everyday Life*). In addition, ambiguous messages from our environment may cause us to sustain partial rather than global perspectives on situations. Finally, errors are inevitable and can result in painful experiences that we would rather forget quickly. But effective appropriation includes the ability to accept such experiences and transform them into opportunities for learning.

Appropriation is a matter of learning about both the realities of the organization and one's own responses to the ambient social and physical ecosystem. This learning is carried out on many levels of our consciousness, and deciphering has to be done on all these levels – rational, emotional, physical, subconscious, and others. Appropriating an organization is, in a sense, like taming it, allowing oneself to feel comfortable with it. Even if this is a continuous and highly intuitive process, it offers us a fairly simple criterion for determining whether effective appropriation has taken place. A newcomer has effectively appropriated her organization if she can genuinely say that she is able to be herself in it, if she has no need to hide or pretend, and if she has a strong awareness of both herself and the myths and realities of her work environment, in their stabler and more dynamic aspects alike. Appropriation would thus appear to be absolutely necessary for the healthy management of the other three generic processes.

*Understanding the Appropriation Process*

The following are observations we have made in the course of our own experiences in many organizations:

1] We have already briefly alluded to the multidimensional nature of appropriations. Sometimes we grasp the communications of our environment in intellectual ways; at other times we may have a feeling, for example about the "climate" or atmosphere in an organization. We may grasp realities the hard way, as through unexpected punitive feedback from a supervisor, or through a stab in the back from a hitherto trusted co-worker. Or, not least in importance, we take in certain data unconsciously and realize only much later how it all fits together. Similarly, the mental maps we construct about our organizations are multidimensional, or multilevel. The information that has found its way into our mental map of the organization contains conceptual elements, emotional components, physical manifestations, and subconscious elements, for example in the form of general assumptions underlying our view of the organization (E. H. Schein). Moreover, as different people tend to prefer, or emphasize, different modes of information processing, including different rhythms, it is only natural for their mental maps and their ways of learning to be colored by these intrinsic preferences. That everyone learns in his own way, and in different ways at different times, is nevertheless not always fully recognized in organizations. As we will see in the next section, certain obstructions in the appropriation process can be traced to this oversight. In particular, uniform training programs do not appear to be an adaptive response to realities in the appropriation area.

Another aspect of the appropriation process is closely related to its multidimensional nature. It is generally assumed that the conscious activity of appropriating information and knowledge (learning) requires effort. We certainly do not deny that active learning may require effort and discipline, but many people have found that learning is made much easier if they can respect their own personal rhythms, if they can explore the types of discipline that are most conducive to effective appropriation, and if they can select the type of learning effort best suited to their personality and style.

2] Most of the time our appropriation process busily gathers bits and pieces of information here and there, and with time we succeed in constructing partial mental maps of our organization. Thus, as mentioned earlier, chances are that our mental maps will be biased, and from time to time we will realize with some surprise that we "did not have the whole picture." Our personality and our emotions often lead us to select only data that confirm or disconfirm our preconceived ideas and wishes. Whether we take in exclusively confirming or disconfirming information, the result is the same – our mental maps of organizational realities are incomplete. The same is true for the maps we construct about ourselves, for example, as they are reflected in our self-image.

Yet, ideally, the aim of the appropriation process is to see the whole picture, to acquire the most global view possible of the organization and its members – in other words, to see things sufficiently in perspective. Two questions can be raised in this regard. First, how do we know that our mental maps are sufficiently global? By what criteria can we recognize the global nature of our view? Second, given that our maps are probably incomplete, are there ways we can make sure we are moving in the right direction, toward more global views?

Regarding the first question, are there any criteria through which we can tell when our mental images of ourselves and our organizational environment are sufficiently global? One such criterion has already been mentioned: the extent to which we can feel at ease with ourselves, and the extent to which we can feel at ease in the organization. Similarly, we can consider our appropriations to be sufficiently global, in relation to a certain subject or situation, to the extent that we feel genuinely at ease and confident in communicating with other people about that subject or situation. And, we could add, to the extent that we feel genuinely at ease in making decisions and taking action with respect to the subject or situation. Thus, appropriations can be considered sufficiently global to the extent that a person feels at ease carrying them over into the relation process, communicating about them on an equal basis with others, applying them to the decision process ("touching base" with his values and priorities as well as with those of others), and integrating them into the action process (being comfortable with implementing decisions in an ethically justified fashion).

A second criterion complements the first one – our mental maps are sufficiently global so that we can feel and create harmony when we act on the basis of those maps. There is a fundamental assumption behind this criterion. As long as our communications create significant discord; as long as our decisions create conflicts either within ourselves or in the organization; and as long as our actions arouse extensive opposition, we may conclude that our view of the situation is insufficiently global (we do not "have the whole picture"). Many people have experienced the reality of this assumption in their own environments. Indeed, it is precisely from the discordant situations we witness or create, and from the opposition that forms in response to our actions, that we can potentially learn the most, and enlarge our mental maps to encompass more elements. Many have also experienced the likelihood that actions based on partial perspectives, rather than on the whole picture, result in negative, painful, or otherwise undesirable consequences. There is another aspect to this criterion. Suppose a person has been in an organization for a long time and has had ample opportunity to appropriate the organization. To the extent that such a person still does not create harmony, we can hypothesize that however global his mental maps may be with respect to the organization, they are likely to be insufficiently global with respect to his own personal realities.

These criteria lead into our second question. Given the knowledge that our mental maps are often incomplete, are there ways by which we can ensure that we move toward the most global view possible of ourselves and of our organizational environment? One way to ensure that the appropriation process moves toward the most global view possible follows directly from the criteria just mentioned: to adopt an attitude of active inquiry and receptiveness to feedback, without prejudgment of its "rightness or wrongness," including feedback containing disconfirming information. The attitude of active inquiry includes willingness and ability to seek awareness of the partial, or insufficiently global, nature of one's information, and to continually test one's information and one's assumptions about oneself and about the organizational environment. The opposite of this attitude would be to close one's eyes and make unverified assumptions, then act upon them without verifying as a matter of course. The opposite of the most global view possible about oneself and about one's environment is the construction of a make-believe world.

A second way to ensure movement toward the most global view possible is complementary to the first. It is giving free rein to one's spirit of curiosity and passion to "put the pieces of the puzzle together." This way is complementary to the first because a stance of active inquiry cannot live long without this spirit of curiosity, and vice versa – without active inquiry, the spirit of curiosity may be dulled and short-circuited. The best possible example of this spirit of curiosity can be found in the ways children find to appropriate their environment. In her search to know her world, a child usually follows her process through, and asks questions in the order that her mental map needs them answered. In the world of our childhood, no question is useless or gratuitous; every inquiry follows the thread of previous inquiries and of "natural" curiosity about the next piece of information that takes on importance in our mental and physical systems. When important questions are not answered for any reason, such as uneasiness or ignorance on the part of parental figures, and when this unresponsiveness includes punishment, the child's spirit of curiosity may eventually be blunted. As a result, her "maps" of the world may miss crucial information, or crucial dimensions such as the emotional, physical, or spiritual, for a long time, leading to process difficulties in certain areas of her self management. What is important in this regard is the knowledge that the very same factors that can blunt the child's spirit of curiosity are capable of the same result in the well-meaning adult intent on managing himself. For example, most members in organizations find it important that their questions be answered in a satisfactory manner by colleagues and supervisors, or that their questions be treated as valid instruments of inquiry. We will come back to this point further on, while dealing with the subject of management of the appropriation process.

Another aspect of the appropriation process is the role of intuition in providing the clearest and most global view possible. To a large extent, our mental maps of ourselves and our organizational environment can also be seen as intuitive maps. Indeed, many persons have experienced the ability to orient themselves adequately in their environment while following an "intuitive trail." They experience the ability to orient themselves without being fully aware of the "map," or of the important parameters of such a map. In other words, they realize only afterward what the important parameters of their maps were. Thus, they have found that being in tune with their intuitive processes is a valuable asset in using their mental maps for practical purposes.

3] In recent years there has been a marked interest in the analysis of organizational culture. Like the concept of culture traditionally applied to societies and nations, organizational culture refers to the beliefs, values, and assumptions dominant in a particular organization, as well as to their visible manifestations (for example, in the way offices are laid out, or the ways people communicate with each other). Every organizational system sooner or later develops a culture in this sense – it is a common reality binding the members of the organization together. Organizational culture is a multifaceted reality. Its traits can be seen and touched in many ways (office layouts, for example), or its invisible traits may be elusive and difficult to trace. These traits may include myths and general beliefs concerning the nature of the organization's mission, or how it should be accomplished; what kind of behaviors and attitudes are acceptable, and which are not; and the written or unwritten "rules of the game." Some of these myths and beliefs may be expressed in meetings, memos, internal training programs, or annual reports. Others may find their way into ambiguous messages, rumors, or performance appraisals, and still others are never consciously expressed.

It is becoming increasingly clear that if a person is to find his place in an organization, and retain his own identity without becoming submerged in a quagmire of cultural assumptions and beliefs, the deciphering of culture is crucial and a vital part of the appropriation process. Those who have not concerned themselves with the organizational culture (elements of which may even be conflictual) risk becoming less aware of what is happening in the organization, causing themselves useless difficulties in adaptation. They also risk becoming prisoners of the organization's myths. For culture can be seen as a widely agreed-upon mental map of the organization, held simultaneously by most of its members. It is a map that may include certain beliefs and assumptions and exclude others, and it can change in the course of time. Consequently, deciphering culture realistically involves demystifying the multifaceted currents flowing through the organization. Obtaining a clear and global picture of organizational culture also involves remaining firmly anchored in one's own potential –

remaining sufficiently detached to avoid confusing one's potential with the perceived cultural characteristics of the organization.

To summarize, the appropriation process potentially enables a person to identify environmental opportunities for appropriation. By seizing those opportunities, exploiting them, and acting upon them with discernment, one can then orient oneself and define the parameters of one's contributions. To do so presupposes that one becomes capable of re-evaluating one's appropriations, jettisoning what becomes relatively unimportant, and continually transforming one's mental maps of oneself and of the organization as new information becomes available.

## *Symptoms of Obstructions*

Obstructions in the appropriation process refer to those states of mind, attitudes, and behaviors that play an inhibiting role in the process – those that prevent the smooth and adequate flow of focusing and unfocusing, those that prevent learning and awareness, and those that systematically prevent a person from obtaining the most global view possible of the organization and of specific situations within it. Many obstructions in the appropriation process find their origin in fear, ignorance, or both.

*Fear is a natural response when people are faced with new or unexpected situations for which they have no ready-made model at hand.* The better someone's appropriation process has worked in the past, and the more he has appropriated new information, the less susceptible to fear he is likely to be. Conversely, the less someone knows, the less he has appropriated new information in the past, the more he can be expected to display fear when faced with new data. There are also connections between fear and the other processes. For example, the more supportive relationships a person has developed, the less he is likely to be fearful in the face of new information. Conversely, the less a person has benefited from authentic and genuinely supportive relationships, the more susceptible to fear we can expect him to be. Similarly, the more someone has acted on and integrated the lessons from his actions, including his mistakes, the less he may succumb to fear in new situations, even if they require him to use new and previously unexplored abilities. The more a person has refrained from acting, or the less he has truly integrated any lessons from his actions, the more he may become fearful when an unexpected situation arises, taxing both his abilities to integrate data quickly and his capacity to adapt his old models to new evidence. Fear leads a person to resort to old models; he fails to accept new data and explore their significance and value.

*Fear can also be a cultivated response in people with a history of being chastised or rebuffed for expressing disconfirmation with regard to models held by individuals who abused their power.* The more a person has been exposed to such put-downs, and the less he has subsequently been able to express his own views, to test his own models, the less likely he will be to handle new information in a harmonious fashion, or to view that new information in a sufficiently global and realistic perspective. As the repeated rebuffs may have instilled in him a low sense of self-esteem, together with an eagerness to regain his freedom of expression, his appropriation process may become biased toward finding data that would increase his self-esteem or would allow him to express himself more. Alternatively, his appropriations may consistently force data into confirming his low self-esteem. As a result, he may relate new information excessively to himself, rather than seeing it for what it really is – information about conditions experienced by other persons, or about circumstances that do not depend on him. When something goes wrong on the job, the employee may blame himself excessively rather than realistically evaluate his own role as well as that of others in the situation.

*Ignorance too can be a cause of obstructions in the appropriation process, not only because it tends to breed fear, but also because it fails to provide the person with the necessary basis for making connections.* The more a person has learned about herself and her environment, the more varied and the more global we can expect her mental maps to be. More varied and global mental maps provide a person with the necessary confidence to explore new territory, and augment her capacity to integrate new data within the old models, thereby helping her to see more readily the many possible ramifications and linkages of new data with the information she already possesses. Conversely, the less a person knows, and the less diversified her mental maps are, the greater the likelihood that she will reject new information as worthless, simply because she cannot spontaneously connect it to anything that is already familiar to her, and the more we can expect her to be manipulated and misinformed. The less a person knows about a certain area the more likely she will be to revert to old mental maps, and the more likely she will be to prejudge a situation on the basis of old maps, thereby increasing her mishandling of complex situations. Ignorance breeds ignorance in the sense that it can cause the appropriation process to remain paralyzed at a very low level of information input and output. The appropriation process can move toward more diversified levels only to the extent that new information reaches the rare points of attachment available in the individual's mental maps. In the extreme case where no such points of attachment are available, the person risks being mired in a rigid system of thought where no new learning is possible.

Consistent bias in the appropriation process – the tendency to interpret data systematically one way or the other – can also have repercussions on his action process. Indeed, his biased mental maps may lead him to overly restrain his own actions, or to intervene with inappropriate timing; or he may misjudge the extent to which a newly formed mental map is applicable in his present organizational environment. More specifically, his eagerness to regain his freedom of expression may make him view his possibilities for intervention too idealistically, without taking realistic stock of the obstacles he may find on the way. In short, when rebuffs have denied him confirmation of his own mental maps at a time when he needed it most, his appropriation process risks being caught in a double bind – if he accepts new information and adapts his old mental maps to take it into account, he may miscalculate the possibilities for application of his new map. On the other hand, if he rejects the new information and sticks to his old mental maps, he is likely to forego valuable lessons and fall back on outmoded and ill-adapted behavior (from his own self-management point of view), thereby creating for himself, and possibly also for his associates, a no-win situation.

Symptoms of obstructions in the appropriation process may take many and varied forms. The symptoms invariably point to a mental map that is insufficiently global, or to maps that are insufficiently adaptive in a dynamic sense. The underlying cause of these symptoms may be related to fear, ignorance, or other factors. The following constitutes behaviors and attitudes that we have frequently found to be symptomatic of such obstructions:

- systematic failure to let go of prior data that are no longer pertinent;
- systematic failure, or refusal, to take in new information;
- habitual overburdening of the appropriation process;
- blind spots, or the systematic exclusion of certain types of information;
- consistent inability to discriminate between facts that are pertinent and facts that are not;
- tendency to get so absorbed in the organizational environment as to forget to map it.

First, symptoms of obstruction in the appropriation process may be related to failure to let go of prior data that are no longer pertinent. One person related the following experience: *"Alastair was always nice to me. One day I found out that he was nice to me because he wanted something from me; with his subordinates I saw him behave like a punitive madman. For days and months I could not bring myself to let go of the exclusive image of niceness that I had of him. I felt myself denying the fact that he simply could be artificial with me, until he directed his anger against me at a moment when I least expected it . . ."* Often people refuse to let go of prior data, which have outlived their pertinence, because they have emotional attachments to those data or to whatever it is the data represent for them. By clogging the appropriation process with the debris of past emotional attachments, failure to resolve and clear out such attachments may prevent the person from developing the curiosity and openness necessary to perceive and integrate new information.

This leads us to a second symptom of obstructions in the appropriation process: systematic failure, or refusal, to take in new information. This symptom may express itself as a person's apparent inability to consider information that would risk enriching, disconfirming, or otherwise modifying his mental maps; his world view is closed. He may go even further, and by authoritarian or persuasive means try to convince others to adopt the same rigid mental maps. He may demand that they conform to his own view of the world or to his own conception of how the organization should be. Failure to take in new information may result in mental maps that are hopelessly out of date, or that deform or limit organizational realities. Such maps may be temporarily useful for a person who wishes to avoid dealing with complexity, and who is content working and concentrating on his task in a setting that permits him to be relatively closed off from the environment. However, when this person comes face to face with the necessity of expanding his mental map (for example, under the pressure of unexpected problems arising in the organization), he will be prone to making serious mistakes for which he or others may have to pay the price. An event like this is likely to bring only disappointment and confusion.

A third symptom of obstructions is the habitual overburdening of the appropriation process – the habit of taking in more information than is necessary for the healthy flow of the process. In this case, the other generic processes may be neglected, or may themselves become overloaded with useless information. The person also risks creating an imbalance within his learning process – not only does she make it difficult for herself to discard data of minimal value for her, she also foregoes an optimal learning process by wasting time. Such overburdening may only have value when the person really has no idea of what interests her. In such a case, the exaggerated information intake may provide her with an extensive range of data that she can then filter to determine what data are meaningful to her. Even then, the overburdening strategy may well become counterproductive unless the person knows how to stop it.

A fourth symptom of obstructions in the appropriation process can be labeled "blind spots," or the systematic exclusion of certain types of information. In this case, the person is extremely selective with regard to information intake, leading him to unwittingly limit his mental map. The most important characteristic of this kind of obstruction is that the person is unaware of the limits of, or the limitations he imposes on, his mental maps. There may be many purposes to such systematic exclusions. For example, the maintenance of one's self-image in the face of threatening information; a false perception of the need to protect one's self-esteem; the avoidance of dissonance or emotional distress; the avoidance of recognizing one's limits or one's needs to learn more about certain areas; the wish to maintain an atmosphere of certainty rather than face the possibility of uncertainty. Consider the example of an accountant who only sees his organization in terms of figures on a balance sheet. Such a fractional, limited view is inadequate for interpreting the firm's overall results, the climate prevailing in the work place, or changes in the organizational culture. Not only can this accountant continually find data in his environment that confirm and justify his limited view, he is also likely to systematically ignore data that would broaden his view and oblige him to face the nature of limits he imposes on his mental maps. Consider also the example of a policeman whose training has familiarized him with a code of rules and regulations. If he ends up seeing people only in terms of "good" and "bad" - those who observe the rules and those who do not - his mental map will no doubt make it easier for him to interpret events. But the result may be that he eventually no longer perceives the gradations between "good" and "bad" because they make him uncomfortable.

Similarly, a business woman preoccupied with marketing her products may lose sight of the significance of other dimensions of life. Thus, the appropriation process is obstructed when the person does not succeed in identifying and accepting the limits of her mental maps; when she is unable to know in what circumstances and for what types of activities her map is adequate, and for which ones it is not; when she does not know how to improve her maps and make them more flexible without courting imprecision and lack of clarity.

Blind spots, or the systematic exclusion of certain types of information, can be seen as a permanent danger for people who are members of exclusive professional associations, especially when the protection of interests is confused with rigidity of the mental map. In fact, the protection of one's interests is often better assured by getting to know one's blind spots, as they may contain valuable directions for new learning and adaptive actions.

A fifth symptom of obstruction is consistent inability to discriminate between facts that are pertinent to oneself and facts that are not. This may be simply due to a habit of not testing enough, of blindly accepting data without checking it against what one already knows. Often the person is not aware of the value of testing, or has not learned how to test efficiently.

Finally, obstructions to the appropriation process can be signaled by a tendency to get so absorbed in the organizational environment as to forget to map it. In this case, the person is likely to become submerged in the organizational culture, having no ideas of his own, and feeling tremendous pressure to conform to trends or to the demands of powerful organizational figures. He confuses perception of characteristics of the organizational culture with the need to adopt them as his own, without questioning their usefulness for his purposes or for those of the organization. On a more personal level, he may become so absorbed in someone else's style and personality that he starts imitating that person, without really understanding the mental maps with which this "model" operates. As he is very likely to be blind to certain aspects of the other person's mental maps, his behavior ultimately risks being ill-adapted, not only to his own personality and style, but also in relation to the environment. This type of behavior is common when people try to imitate the work methods of a charismatic pioneer, whether in business or in another profession. The obstruction at work here prevents the person from sufficiently learning on his own - taking in data, testing it with the many dimensions of his own mental maps, and gradually building more comprehensive and global maps of his own.

Before going on to the issue of managing the appropriation process, let's look at two mechanisms which may seriously compromise the appropriation process when they are not managed with care. These are projection and double-talk. Because of their importance, each of these mechanisms is examined in detail in the following pages.

## *Projection Reconsidered as an Instrument for Managing Appropriations*

It should be stated at the outset that we do not refer to the concept of projection in the strict sense as in the specialized literature on projection techniques, such as in Rorschach or the Thematic Apperception Test. We are interested here in the use of projection in its largest sense and from the viewpoint of self management. Thus, we are not concerned with efforts to categorize people's responses to such projection tests, but we consider projection the idiosyncratic signature of the individual, and an indication of the distance between multiple realities and his own perception of them. In particular, we are interested in the role projection can play in a person's appropriation process or, in other words, the role it plays in his efforts to obtain the most global view possible of himself, of others, and of the organizational environment. In the following pages, then, we will first discuss projection as one of the most basic and prevalent mechanisms of the mind. We will go on to briefly discuss the defensive aspects of projection as they relate to the appropriation process and, finally, we will turn to the potentially creative role projection can play in a person's appropriations and in the ongoing elaboration of his mental maps.

## Projection as a Basic Mechanism of the Mind

With regard to the data flow between a person and his environment, projection is undoubtedly one of the most important, but also most imperfectly understood, mechanisms of the human mind. Projection generally refers to the attribution of one's own characteristics, attitudes, feelings, desires, or behavior to another person, an object, or even an occurrence in one's environment. On the most general level, all kinds of characteristics can be projected. In fact, it is our normal tendency to see our own characteristics in others. For example, people tend to believe that others are as interested, as curious, as able to deal with money, as idealistic, as evolved, and so on, as they are themselves, without necessarily being aware of the extent to which interest, curiosity, ability to deal with money, or idealism govern their own lives. People also tend to believe that others are as unimaginative, manipulative, or dishonest as they are themselves, again without necessarily recognizing these traits as facets of their own personalities. Projection is often associated with the attribution to others of characteristics, traits, or behaviors that one considers undesirable for oneself. But, not uncommonly, positive, desirable characteristics are also projected. As a result, the individuals, groups, objects, or occurrences that receive the projection then become either very desirable or very undesirable, as the case may be – they fascinate us or they become a source of irritation.

From the viewpoint of a person's appropriation process, *the importance of projection resides in the fact that the projecting person does not see the other for what he really is.* Instead, he becomes fixated on some partial aspect of the other person's attitude or behavior, and is thus prevented from seeing "the whole picture" in relation to this other person. The same is true when we project our own concerns onto a situation or occurrence, then interpret the situation in a manner colored by those concerns. For example, someone with a broken leg is very likely to suddenly become aware of many people on the street with leg injuries, while someone in a bad mood is liable to see more people on the street as morose than happy, or to see people who look happy and hate them for it. Other examples also illustrate how projection easily causes us to miss the "whole picture":

- A person may suddenly find her employer's salary exaggeratedly high and state a dozen reasons why this is. She may not be taking into account relevant facts, such as workload or responsibility, but merely seeing an opportunity to project her own desires outward to increase her present earnings significantly.
- A person harboring good feelings toward a certain political figure may interpret the reasons behind the latter's sudden disgrace quite differently from one harboring unfavorable feelings toward the same politician.
- Depending on his own feelings about himself (or on his degree of self-esteem, of which he may not be completely aware), a person may be prone to see nothing but good qualities in someone else, and even idealize the other person.
- A person who sees another as very successful in one particular area may unwittingly carry over this perception, and think the other person will do as well in another area.
- People make predictions concerning the future fortunes of a company by clinging to sometimes unrealistic hypotheses that are based on what they wish for.
- Two opposite hypotheses concerning an unknown happening could be equally well defended by means of logical arguments advanced by proponents of either one of the contradicting hypotheses (Immanuel Kant).

The above illustrations show that what is true for projections onto other persons is *also true for projections onto situations. People tend to project their own attributes, traits, beliefs, concerns, desires, behavior, and interests onto an external situation and, in so doing, often fail to grasp the full complexity of the situation. Some of the more important organizational situations that may be misinterpreted in the light of projections are:conflicts, attractions, and a person's job choice or performance on the job.* Fierce interpersonal conflicts can be caused by projections if the person sees the projected content as undesirable, and so can the most compelling attractions when the projected content is seen as desirable. For example, when in our role as group facilitators we want to demonstrate the reality of projections, we sometimes use a simple exercise that helps bring those projections into awareness. The exercise is as follows: We ask each member of the group to find another individual with whom he or she would like to interact. We then ask those who have found a suitable partner to stay with this partner and look him directly in the eyes for two minutes, without talking. Then, we ask the person to write down five characteristics they have perceived in the other person, as well as one question they would like to ask that person. When everything has been written down, we ask them to mark off those characteristics in the list of five that also apply to themselves in significant ways, and to mark off the question if it is one they could also easily ask themselves. Then we ask them how many have made six marks, how many five marks, and so on, to zero marks. Someone with six marks has in fact projected his own traits almost completely onto the other person, while a person with zero marks has probably read the other person's uniqueness. But zero marks are very rare indeed - most of the time people have somewhere between four and six marks. Another exercise can illustrate the nature of projections in an even more dramatic manner, especially when there is a personality conflict between two members of the group (they hate each other, cannot stand each other, etc.). If both of them agree, we ask them to come forward in the group and sit down facing each other, at a comfortable distance for both. We then ask them, in turn, to verbalize three traits they observe in the other and they dislike. We may ask them to write these down, with no talking or feedback. We then ask them, in turn, to find and verbalize three traits they do like, that interest or fascinate them in the other person. This may be done in writing, no talking or feedback. Next, we ask them to give us their respective lists, and we read out loud the lists of what they like and what they dislike about each other. We finally ask each of them the questions: "Are those things you dislike in the other person also characteristics of yourself that you dislike?", and "Are the things you like in the other also qualities you like in yourself?" Most of the time this is the case, and the message comes across. Sometimes it turns out, to everybody's surprise, that they have produced almost identical lists to describe each other.

Another illustration of projections has to do with people's jobs. In a training session with police chiefs, we asked participants the following question: "Why are you in the police force?" Their answers were very revealing of the many possible projective connections between people's own characteristics and the qualities they may attribute to the job. Many of them revealed that, early in their lives, they had encountered injustices that had deeply moved them at the time. We could hypothesize that in many cases we project a part of ourselves onto the kind of work we do. And, more specifically, we could also hypothesize that it is those parts of ourselves that have encountered resistance, or have been prevented from developing, which tend to be projected onto our work. That is why certain types of work "fulfill" us (the unfulfilled part of ourselves can be adequately projected onto the work), while other types of work do not interest us or make us feel bored. As in the other examples of projection offered earlier, we could hypothesize that it is the uncompleted self that is projected in the work we prefer.

*There are three characteristics of projection that take on special importance with respect to its role in a person's appropriation process. First, most of the time the person is unaware that he is projecting* – he is unaware that what he thinks he sees outside belongs also to himself. Indeed, when a person is shown pictures or inkblots during a projection test, and when he is asked to verbalize what he sees in the picture or inkblot, it may or may not be obvious to him that his answers reflect his own inner condition, especially if the pictures are non-figurative. But the daily projections we all make by interpreting the occurrences and facts of our organizational environments may be far less obvious to us, not the least because instead of non-figurative inkblots we face real people and issues we have learned to recognize and label during our many years of acculturation and socialization. Thus, we may be unaware of our own characteristics, which we are projecting. In fact, we may be unaware that we are projecting, and at times singling out one specific characteristic for projection. This lack of awareness often allows us to view the mechanism as a sort of naturally happening confusion between ourselves and our environment, as our own failure to always distinguish adequately between ourselves and our environment, or simply as an insufficient knowledge of ourselves.

*The second characteristic of projection of interest here is the fact that projection is often a director of attention.* Whenever we are "interested" in something this may be a signal that we are projecting. Thus, projections can be seen as the very fabric of self perceptions and of our perceptions of others, which may create interesting relations between people and offer a multicolored spectacle of organizational realities.

*The third characteristic is that whatever is projected almost always carries an emotional importance for us – it rarely leaves us indifferent.*

In short, projection can be seen as a mechanism that lies at the very core of a person's appropriation process. When projections go unrecognized for a long time, the mechanism may virtually block one's ability to learn about one's personal realities – facts, affinities, values, and the very meaning and direction of one's life. In contrast, when they are recognized they may announce a highly integrative experience for the person, as they allow her to come to grips with and actualize a previously unknown part of herself. As a result, she can adjust her self-image and the image she has of others toward a more realistic one.

## Defensive Aspects of Projection

In some cases, projection can be seen as a defense mechanism. In fact, both S. Freud and gestalt psychologist F. Perls considered projection a defense or neurotic mechanism, constituting a major obstacle to psychological growth. From the self-management perspective, it seems more useful to see projection as a natural mechanism of the mind, always present in varying degrees. Whether projection becomes defensive or not is probably also more a matter of degree than of absolutes.

There may be different reasons for a person's apparent readiness to disown particular characteristics, feelings, attitudes, desires, or behaviors, and to prefer to find them mirrored in someone else. Some of those reasons may be unawareness of the presence of those characteristics in himself: having learned to reject those characteristics of himself through pressure from others; disowning these characteristics, which permits him to avoid cognitive dissonance; or even sheer wishful thinking or idealized self-images. To illustrate how pressure from others can lead someone to reject certain characteristics of himself, whether positive or negative, imagine a person who perceives another as being afraid when it is actually he himself who has feelings of fear (although he may now be unaware of them). At the outset, possibly during childhood or at a time when he was unusually vulnerable, another significant person in his environment may have made evaluative or condescending remarks about his fear in a particular circumstance. Or somewhere in his background a voice has said, "Don't be frightened. Big boys don't get scared!" And now, as a "big boy," he feels terrible when experiencing fright, and finds himself horrified at the thought that he is still such a "little boy." He may have felt such terror experiencing that feeling that when it begins he immediately projects it onto another person. Later, he systematically projects it, thus remaining forever unaware of his own fright, or even the possibility of fright. To the extent that he has constructed an image of himself as someone who should not be afraid, rather than what he actually is, he will experience the dissonance between what he thinks he should be, and what he actually feels, as threatening. One way, then, to deal with that threat is to deny and disown his experience by projecting it outside of himself. In this way he focuses on an image of himself rather than his actually experienced self. It is as if he were saying, "I don't want the part of my experience that is not consistent with the way I would like to be." When "fear" is something one often notices in other persons, and if one finds it disturbing, chances are that "fear" is a significant component of one's own psychological make-up. Sometimes a person will go to the point of instilling fear in his environment as a means of seeing it "out there" rather than within himself. Ideal images of oneself ("I wish to be . . . ") or dark images of oneself ("I do not want to be . . . ") have a lot to do with projection. The previous example of fear can be extended to any of a person's characteristics. In general, we can hypothesize that the projection becomes defensive to the extent it prevents someone from learning about himself. Of course. when it does become defensive, we can expect projection to work together with other defensive mechanisms, such as denial of aspects of reality, rationalization, and so on, all concurring to block the possibility of learning and adapting one's mental maps.

## Creative Aspects of Projections: Managing Appropriations

While projection in itself cannot be labeled in terms of good/bad or right/wrong, the mechanism definitely has the potential for creating perceptive distortions, and therefore tends to block the normal adaptive process at work in the evolution of our mental maps. Alternatively, it also carries the potential for creating perceptive realism, depending largely on the degree of awareness toward which a person is prepared to work to dissolve the projections - at the same time coming to terms with the emotions attached to them - and learn from them.

From the viewpoint of managing appropriations, we are interested in the effects of interpersonal projections. We have to consider two scenarios - one in which the self-managing person projects onto someone else, and another one where she herself is the object of projection. *When a person is the object of a positive projection by someone else*, she may well feel as if she is being charged with energy, and this can undoubtedly help her in the execution of her tasks. However, in that case she is also likely to face a dilemma in responding or not responding to the expectations that come with the projection. It may be tempting to respond, especially if it makes her feel important, even if this is not always the most effective response in the long term. It may also make her feel uneasy, or burdened, due to her preoccupation with not disappointing the other person. Thus, it can be temporarily flattering to receive positive projections from someone else. *Alternatively, when a person receives negative projections*, he is likely to feel as if his energy is being drained, largely because of the unfavorable judgments the other person implicitly asks him to bear. To be the target of negative projections may also be felt as depressing by the "receiving" person. The phenomenon of the scapegoat is an example of such negative projections - one person blames another for the ills he himself experiences, or for the failure of an assignment. It is not always easy to deal with a situation where one is being used as a scapegoat. From the self-management perspective, a certain alertness is called for in this regard. It is always important for the person to discern what is real, and what is an exaggerated image of a part of himself that is being used by someone else as an excuse for their own poor performance.

*The second scenario involves the self-managing person projecting onto another.* Probably the most classic example of such projections involve finding an "enemy" outside, which then effectively focuses one's attention on another person instead of focusing it on one's own condition. Frequently, this strategy allows one to avoid facing certain feelings, emotions, attitudes, behaviors, inner contradictions, or confused priorities in one's life. When the projection involves harboring negative feelings toward others, the person risks becoming so caught up in those feelings that she may become a generally negative person. However, whether the projection involves positive or negative feelings, disowning parts of oneself always takes up considerable energy. Interestingly, when a person starts to recognize a projection, and begins to own up to the projected content (whether it is positive or negative), she invariably feels more integrated. Indeed, in terms of realism she stands to learn more about herself and others, or about her environment. The renunciation of one's emotional stake in vesting another person with certain aspects of one's own personality is a powerful aid to mental map-making, and a potent way to achieve a more complete view of oneself and others. Moreover, the energy previously tied up in maintaining the mirror image, and the defense of that tie, becomes available for constructive action. It is our interpretation that self management is precisely about such a constructive process.

Sheldon Kopp has captured the notion of dissolving projection when he advises, "If you are looking for a hero, look again because you are diminishing some part of yourself, and the way back is to re-own that which you have given away." One may well add, "If you are looking for a villain, look again because you are glorifying yourself, and the way back to reality is to re-own that part of yourself that you think is out there to get you." Indeed, when a person renounces seeing external enemies he is almost always confronted with his internal enemies, such as unresolved conflicts and ambiguities. From the self-management perspective these internal conflicts and ambiguities can be painful, but they may ultimately reveal themselves as allies for growth for the kind of constructive development the person is yearning for.

In summary, whether the mechanism of projection becomes an obstacle distorting the appropriation process, or becomes an instrument for managing it, depends to a significant extent on the person's willingness to work at recognizing and re-owning his projections. Furthermore, a desire inspired by his own needs for development in a particular direction is likely to lead him to such recognition. Projection can become an instrument for development when the visceral protection of one's ideologies gives way to the intuitive guidance of one's aspirations. Projection, then, touches the very core of the process of managing appropriations, which is the exercise of judgment and the discernment of multifaceted realities.

### *Double-talk, or Ambiguity in Organizational Messages: A Challenge*

The relative importance of various organizational communication patterns is often far from clear to the newcomer in any organization. Even for someone who has spent many years in the same organizational environment, the messages coming from up, down, or sideways may not be devoid of ambiguity. The ambiguity perceived may well reflect contradictory motives of different departments within the organization, but it may also bear witness to the inner contradictions of a single individual in a leadership position, or it may reflect some leader's willful manipulation of perceptions. It is noteworthy that the ambiguity of messages circulating within an organization may have a more distressing impact on a person who is only vaguely aware of his own inner contradictions.

Message ambiguity is not a phenomenon exclusive to organizations; rather, it appears to be a pervasive characteristic in many interpersonal communications. The message ambiguity may be unintentional (that is, reflecting internal organizational or personal contradictions), or intentionally manipulated for persuasion (such as in advertising messages) or for power. In either case, the decoding of ambiguity may constitute a serious challenge to the self-managing person. Three questions appear in order: (1) How does one recognize message ambiguity – what are its distinctive features? (2) How can we understand what is happening in the phenomenon of double-talk, or message ambiguity – what purposes does it serve?, and (3) How can the self-managing person appropriate reality in the presence of message ambiguity, and avoid being misled by the confusing signals?

## Recognizing Double-talk, or Message Ambiguity – What Are Its Distinctive Features?

Inside organizations, the myriad of messages confronting a person may have to do with many different aspects – the work itself, remuneration, pension plans, perceptions of himself by others, perceptions of his work by others, standards of work quality, norms of behavior, and so on. Probably the single most important set of messages will pertain to the criteria for evaluating a person's work performance. Some of those messages may originate with individual members of the organization and reflect their own self-interest. Others may also transmit culturally accepted standards of behavior, attitude, or group interaction. *One of the potentially most confusing and, unfortunately, most prevalent forms of ambiguity is the contradiction between what is conveyed verbally and what is conveyed non-verbally.*

When there is a divergence between what is being said, privately or officially, and what is actually being done either in actions or in concrete decision making, the self-managing person is evidently well advised to appropriate both messages (verbal and nonverbal), rather than base his actions only on what is being said. To illustrate this point, let's suppose that nurses and doctors in a particular hospital appropriate only what is being said by management personnel. They could then be led to believe that they provide an essential service to the community, they are deeply appreciated for their work, and the most valued characteristic in work performance is related to the quality of services rendered. However, judging by the *actions* of hospital administrators, such as unhealthy rotation schedules, substandard remuneration, and performance evaluations largely influenced by their degree of competitive obedience, the top priority is clearly not quality of service, but rather a type of cost efficiency that does not take into account the physical and psychological constitution of workers. Consequently, the nurse or doctor who takes for granted the professed ideal of quality service risks experiencing excessive stress and burnout. In addition, he may suffer in performance evaluations based on, say, the average number of patients cared for in a one-hour time period.

Sometimes the intentional manipulation of verbal/nonverbal message ambiguity is more obvious. For example, a political party may make verbal promises even though its managers know that the budget will preclude the implementation of promised actions. Similarly, in the field of persuasive advertising, the self-managing person would do well to appropriate not only what is being said but also the facts of the matter, for they may be disconcertingly different. Indeed, the commercial spot may appeal exclusively to fantasy or ideal images, while we are really interested in the quality and practical usefulness of the product itself. In another example, the person applying for a new position may *hear* from the selection committee, "We would like to hire you; we need someone of your caliber for this important job." Subsequently, she may be surprised when the salary offered is low in relation to the responsibilities involved, or still later, on the job, she may find that the earlier expressions of confidence in her were in fact conditional on her functioning in a certain predefined manner, for which no verbal cues had been provided at the outset.

In all the above examples, one message is verbal while the other is nonverbal, less explicit, and contradicts the first one. These cases are in many ways similar to a well-known ambiguous message parents often give their children, a message of the kind "We love you" (verbally) and, simultaneously, "We will punish you if you do not behave the way we want you to behave" (nonverbally). It is what Gregory Bateson has called a "double bind" message. As R. D. Laing explains, "One person conveys to the other that he should do something, and at the same time conveys on another level that he should not, or that he should do something else incompatible with it." If the person at the receiving end cannot move out of the situation or cannot comment on it, he is in an untenable position.

Some binds, or ambiguous messages, are humoristic - mere mind teasers; some bind the mind - riddles, for example - and are intended to make one aware of certain facts of life. But other binds, instead of promoting awareness, make one blind; they can be emotional killers, or they may sow confusion, conflict, and mystification. They may even, in the words of R. D. Laing, undermine or disconfirm a person's sense of identity. Fortunately, even if we do not immediately recognize the divergence between verbal and nonverbal messages, most of us do have feelings that "something is not quite right" when a message is partial and unclear. The subject is important enough to take a closer look at what is really happening in the double-talk, or message ambiguity, often found in organizations.

Chapter II

## Understanding Double-talk, or Message Ambiguity – What Purposes Does it Serve?

Whereas double-talk can often be recognized by certain signs, for example a divergence between verbal and nonverbal messages, the question addressed here is, What is behind double-talk – what purposes does it serve? There are at least two main reasons why anyone would engage in double-talk in organizations. *One of those reasons can be characterized as a profound rift between what the message sender professes as the ideal, and the reality of his actions. The other main reason is to be found in a situation where declared motives or objectives differ significantly from, or are contradictory to, real motives.* In both cases, the double-talk is either the unintentional result of such a rift, or is an intentionally orchestrated attempt at covering up the inability of the manager to narrow the gap between his ideals and the reality of the situation, or his inability to communicate his real motives and objectives clearly.

When a manager's ideals do not coincide with the reality of her actions, she may be tempted to insist verbally on the importance of the ideal and to neglect working on the real situation. For example, she may say to a newcomer, "In this company we do such and such . . . ," whereas she knows perfectly well that there are severe and unresolved problems between managers or between departments. As a result, her messages may unwittingly lead others to believe she is seriously interested in the ideal and to align their own actions accordingly. In fact, she is incapable of commitment to the ideal and even uses it as a smoke screen to hide the facts. For the sender, the ambiguous messages may work toward relieving guilt or shame with respect to the real situation, or may allow her to save face or fit in with a desirable image despite embarrassing realities. However, for the receiver, it usually results only in confusion, anger, resentment, depression, or indifference. In one example of this kind of double-talk, managers and supervisors say they want "excellence," "quality," or "efficiency," while consistently ignoring or discarding the available concrete means to achieve those goals.

When a manager's declared motives or objectives differ significantly from his real ones, an ambiguous message is likely to result. The message breeds ambiguity whether the incongruence is intentional or not. Many times, the reason invoked for such a strategy is that the real motive or objective is too unpopular and unacceptable and must therefore be covered up by another motive or objective that is seen as acceptable. For example, forced budget cuts may be "sold" to employees as a move toward "excellence." Or the political pressures one company brings to bear on a government may lead it to close a competitive service on the professed grounds of cost efficiency. In some organizations, people at the base level may be asked to execute actions that do not match the objectives as stated. More often than not, the end result is faulty implementation of the tasks, or compromised health for the employee. Indeed, the person at the implementation level can hardly manage his tasks well when he can only guess at the hidden objectives behind the actions he is asked to perform. Not infrequently in such a situation, the employee fumbles and is later blamed for not acting effectively. Even if not actually dismissed, he may feel forced to withdraw quietly from involvement in his work. Perhaps it is not surprising that many people say their work has little meaning for them, when the goals are not only set at another level, but also kept hidden from them. They are being fed goals that could be unrealistic, overly simplistic, or too partial.

Whether double-talk finds its origin in the divergence between ideal and real, or between real and professed, motives, it would seem that in both cases reality is sacrificed for a false sense of power. In terms of self management, the message sender's relation process becomes obstructed, and the message receiver's appropriation process is entangled. It is not difficult to imagine where an organization would be headed if double-talk were regularly used as a strategy to get messages across. The end result could be characterized by considerable infighting and by a passive refusal of employees to implicate themselves at all levels.

## Managing Appropriations in a Context of Double-talk

Despite its drawbacks in terms of the relation process and the appropriation process, the phenomenon of double-talk exists. On the personal level, then, the crucial question is – how does one appropriate reality in such a context?

When a child faces double-talk from the adults around him, we can readily accept the fact that she will experience feelings ranging from vague confusion to utter bewilderment. Yet we seem to forget that adults, too, experience similar reactions with respect to ambiguous messages in their organizations. It is true that a child is perhaps not equipped to decode and see through the contradictory messages and their underlying motives. And a child naturally trusts her environment. It may not surprise us to hear that the feelings generated by the message ambiguities may eventually lead to obstructions in the child's appropriation process. These feelings may lead to an absence of manifest reaction to external messages, as in autism (Bruno Bettelheim, *The Empty Fortress*), or to a potential dissociation between mind and body, for example, between verbal expressions, on the one hand, and bodily and emotional experience, on the other hand. When a child is exposed to ambiguous messages, her appropriation process is in a way being violated; her innocent sense of curiosity is being taken advantage of by repeated exposure to contradictory meanings.

Persons in organizations are, no doubt, better equipped than children for decoding the various sources and contradictory meanings inherent in double-talk. Nevertheless this decoding process remains an ongoing challenge. Most of us feel that something is wrong when we are placed in a bind generated by contradictory motives. But even to adults it is not always clear what is happening, who is pulling the strings, and where we are vulnerable to manipulation. We may feel that someone wants us to behave in a certain way without actually saying so, or we may feel bewildered and confused, having to guess the real criteria that our supervisor wants to measure us up against. Or we may simply feel that someone wants to pull one over on us. The self-management approach, then, implies that a person comes to grips with the possibility that double-talk can take him by surprise, confuse and demotivate him, and block his desire to learn or to further appropriate his organization. If he remembers that, in most cases, double-talk or ambiguous messages find their roots in undeclared self-interests and in the hidden desire to achieve or maintain control, rather than in sharing and empathy, this knowledge may help him maintain his self-respect and motivation. Furthermore, double-talk tends to confuse a person more when the messages can tune into the employee's own inner contradictions or his sense of guilt. The self-managing person's ability to decode ambiguities will increase as he becomes more aware of these inner contradictions or guilt patterns. Indeed, to the extent that he demystifies his own motives, it will be easier for him to demystify those hidden motives he faces in his organizational environment.

## *Managing the Appropriation Process in Organizations*

The management of the appropriation process in the context of organizations aims above all at constructing a mental map of organizational life, a map sufficiently clear and global to be usable for orienting oneself, relating, deciding, and acting in the context of one's organization. To a large extent, this process of managing appropriations will contribute to one's ability to be at ease, to live, and to be recognized in the organization. Thus, one's management of the appropriation process can be deemed the basis of one's ability to make a valuable contribution to organizational life.

Managing this process may be rendered difficult by obstructions of a personal nature. However, there are also organizational conditions that may hinder the flow of appropriations. Three conditions can be singled out as having a potentially damaging effect on the appropriation process. Consequently, those conditions demand vigilance on the part of the person who is interested in managing the flow of appropriations. These three conditions are:

1] *A general lack of access to information, whether because of organizational structure, norms, or specific behavior by certain individuals.* Access to information can be blocked, for example by means of specific or assumed rules of secrecy. Access to information can also be manipulated, as in the case where top managers preselect the type of information that will be channeled to the lower levels, or when employees at the operation levels decide to withhold information from higher levels in the hierarchy. Behaviorally, a lack of access to information often translates as a lack of openness, and excessive control. One middle-level manager had this to say, "When information does not circulate freely, it tends to heap up at certain points in the organization; its quality deteriorates at the same time as its usefulness becomes almost zero. When I am solicited for a new task, and the boss tells me up front that he cannot reveal to me the details of why the task was created, who are the other people involved, who will be my real supervisors; I just get turned off and risk becoming indifferent and letting it go. I will be tempted to search for other work that I can relate to as an intelligent person."

2] *Any behavior that stunts curiosity and spirit.* "Many times in my organization managers use the sell approach; they will tell us what is good for us, tell us what the "facts" are concerning the market and the product. But whatever they say comes in ready-made formulas. Instead of encouraging an exchange of views, they feed us a predigested mix of partial truths and models that we are supposed to accept without questioning. If I had to work there my whole life, I can see the time when I would have become either a mental wreck or a resigned slave!"

3] *A general failure to diffuse complete and timely information*, or any case where the employer lies, is not honest, or does not give feedback. One factory worker said, "It made me so furious and helpless at the same time when I heard yesterday that the plant is going to be closed a week from now. There were rumors but they have never told us anything. They have never been frank with us." Similarly, in periods of fast changes it is hard to appropriate the environment, and it is also hard to keep one's own emotional responses in perspective. Many times, significant changes create a mental block – one refuses to go along with them, and one refuses to keep appropriations going. Without proper support from other people, such times may be very hard to deal with and may undercut the motivations underlying the appropriation process.

In contrast, the following organizational factors have been perceived as facilitating the appropriation process:

1] *Easy, comfortable, and honest access to the employer or supervisor.* "A boss you can trust .... If you mention a personal problem to him, he will listen, be supportive, help you appropriate your job better, give shortcuts, contacts, references. In general, he will open doors rather than close them."

2] *A minimization of rigid hierarchical thinking.* This refers to minimizing the necessity to "reason like the boss" in order for the employee to make his voice heard. When it is encouraged by the top, nonconformity makes it possible to build richer and more realistic mental maps, which are a prerequisite for innovative and creative thinking.

3] *A reasonable degree of access to, and timely diffusion of, information.*

4] *A generally unprejudiced and open climate in the organization.*

Managing the appropriation process consists of bringing about or restoring harmony within the process itself, but also between the appropriation and the other generic processes. The most important instrument for managing appropriations is, no doubt, the extent of knowledge a person has developed about his own process. Gaining knowledge of the appropriation process is therefore likely to be the first objective of the self-managing person. In particular he is interested in becoming aware of his own appropriation needs and opportunities, becoming sensitive to others' appropriation patterns, and becoming vigilant with respect to personal obstructions, and to organizational circumstances that either hinder or facilitate the process. Taking a reasonable degree of personal responsibility for gaining such knowledge allows him to see those obstructing and facilitating factors that are central to his own personality, past experiences, and personal style.

Apart from gaining knowledge of one's own appropriation process, we have found certain additional attitudes and abilities useful for managing this process, in particular for dealing with personal obstructions or harmful organizational conditions. These can be identified as the following: (1) a sufficient awareness of one's own uniqueness; (2) the capacity to sort out the meaning of one's own emotions; (3) the ability to accept mental maps in constant flux and in various dimensions; (4) the ability to deal with order as well as ambiguity; (5) the capacity to listen and observe; (6) the will to test regularly; and (7) an attitude of vigilance with respect to the nature of information and the ways in which it is channelled to us.

First, managing the appropriation process implies a *sufficient awareness of one's own uniqueness.* To appropriate the organizational culture, including eventual subcultures, it is tempting to submerge oneself in the culture to the extent of forgetting one's uniqueness. On the other hand, not submerging oneself in the culture may yield an inadequate reading of cultural characteristics, as they are viewed primarily from one's own perspective. This perspective risks being biased to the extent that one is not aware of many of one's own characteristics, needs, aspirations, and so on. Thus, to manage the appropriation process involves learning enough about one's own uniqueness to be able to perceive the organization with minimal distortion. To the extent that a person is not afraid of discovering aspects of himself, he can afford to reach out more in learning about organizational life.

Second, managing the appropriation process involves a *capacity to sort out the significance of one's emotions*. Emotions play a decisive role in managing the appropriation process, particularly in sorting out what is personal, what is organizational or cultural, and how the personal interacts with the organizational. Most of us have known people who, in terms of knowledge, skills, and competence, possessed all the qualities necessary for integrating themselves into the life of an organization, but who nevertheless failed in their attempts to do so. Often such failures are associated with the inability of the person to sort out the significance of his emotions in the mental map he constructs of the organization. Emotions can be a powerful facilitating factor in integrating new lessons, but they may also make us look at the world around us through a kind of prism, coloring everything in light of our emotional state. Thus, an emotional block can act as a powerful inhibiting factor in the appropriation process, preventing us from modifying a particular outmoded vision of the organizational culture, and compromising our acceptance in the organization.

The third ability useful for managing the process can be formulated as *the acceptance of mental maps in constant flux and in various dimensions*. Specifically, the person who has learned how a mental map operates, and how it undergoes changes, can be expected to more easily establish new links between many disparate elements in his environment. He is also likely to become more at ease with deciphering the symbolic meanings continually created in the organizational interaction flow, and in developing a vocabulary that allows him to verbalize those meanings. The more he is aware and accepting of variety and change, the more he can be expected to adapt his mental maps swiftly to new experiences and situations. Just as knowing several languages usually means that one can learn another more quickly, the person who has experienced more than one organizational system is likely to have an easier time deciphering the explicit and implicit verbal and symbolic meanings prevalent in a new organization.

The fourth ability useful for managing the process involves *dealing with order as well as with ambiguity*. This involves a certain restraint in jumping to conclusions too quickly - the ability to let the ambiguity and vagueness of first impressions gradually form themselves into more orderly pieces of information. It also involves disengagement, which allows a previously established order in one's mental map to slide to the background and give way to ambiguity when new information challenges its validity. When a person can accept the simultaneous presence of order and ambiguity, not only is he likely to acquire a more realistic sense of organizational data, but his energies are also likely to be more available for the other generic processes. Indeed, if he has a tendency to cling to order in his mental maps, he may become defensive, much to the detriment of the other processes. If, on the contrary, he tends to leave too much ambiguity in his mental maps, his energy risks being continuously absorbed in the effort to create order, thereby preventing him from giving his full attention to other processes.

Fifth is *the capacity to listen and observe*. This capacity can be said to support all the other attitudes and abilities discussed here. Indeed, it requires a quality of being attentive to people, behavior, official statements, informal exchanges, moods, climate, and even seemingly innocuous things such as signs on doors. It involves learning to listen to what is being said, but also to what is not being said. It involves paying attention to what is being done, but also to what is not being done. To pay attention only to what is being said and done may provide one with only a partial picture.

Sixth is *the will to test regularly* what has been heard and observed, and to modify and adjust our mental maps. This can usually be done in a variety of ways, for example by asking for feedback, by getting second opinions from other sources of information, and by observing the consequences of our actions.

Finally, an attitude useful for managing the appropriation process is one of *vigilance with respect to the nature of information and the ways in which it is channeled to us*. We have found the following questions especially useful for articulating this attitude of vigilance :

- Does the information contain something new for me?
- Does it satisfy my curiosity?
- Does the sequence and nature of appropriation experiences correspond to my capacity to deal with them?

Often the appropriation process is managed adequately when new information is integrated, curiosity is being satisfied, and the appropriation experiences are adequately dosed. For example, when information is imposed on us, chances are it will not correspond to our own curiosity, acquiring it may overwhelm us, and it may not even be new information. In contrast, when we can appropriate and master a new aspect of our professional role, we usually experience this as very pleasurable and satisfying. To the extent that we can adequately manage our own appropriation process, we will be more at ease to accept a co-worker to do the same. The appropriation process usually works well when we allow ourselves, and others, to identify realistically what we want to appropriate and what strategies we want to use for doing so.

Every organization is first and foremost a social system. Everyone is co-present and co-active, whether in cooperation or in competition with others. The next section deals specifically with this reality – the relation process.

"Our purpose should be to facilitate human interaction, to begin to turn ourselves around, and to loosen the unconscious grip of culture so that instead of being controlled by the past, human beings can face the future in quite a new and more adaptive way."

Edward T. Hall

Chapter II

# Self Management of the Relation Process

## *The Relation Process Defined*

A person's relation process can be defined as the continuous flow of his exchanges with other people, within an organization and outside the organization. As in the other processes, we are especially interested here in exchanges as they pertain to one's work environment. But this does not detract from the fact that the ideas and concepts do apply to other contexts as well, such as educational, familial, and so on.

The process at work in relations within organizations is mostly characterized by an ongoing alternation between phases of affective investment and of affective disengagement, occurring at different levels of intensity and celerity. Ideally, when operating in the presence of mutual and complementary affinities, this process will facilitate the development of a network of mutually supportive individuals. To learn about our own processes we may need other people more than we think. Thus, a supportive network has the potential to confirm a person in his becoming, rather than undermine his strengths.

The work involved in concretizing such a support network includes investing the energy necessary for selecting and nurturing particular attachments that emerge from a multiplicity of social contacts. Thus, we can expect a person to learn to deal with closeness and intimacy, as well as with distance and disengagement, and to deal with attachment as well as with letting go. Indeed, a support network has to be seen as a dynamic concept. Sometimes one must let go of former work relationships in order to form new ones, more in tune with one's changing style and potential. This does not prevent one from maintaining deep friendships with former work colleagues even while moving on to other work challenges. In extreme cases we have to face people who betray such intimacy in order to further their own career.

One of the main characteristics of the relation process is variety in interpersonal exchanges – for example, verbal, nonverbal, and symbolic communications. Thus, the self-managing person must learn how communications work, and identify the obstacles to communication inherent in his dealings with others. People who form a supportive network are generally those who have compatible goals and styles within the organization. Nevertheless, possibilities for conflict and misunderstanding are numerous. A process made up of alternation between investment and disengagement implies the ability to deal with the unpleasant feelings engendered by attitudes of indifference and hostility in others. It also calls for a certain attentiveness to a myriad of possible feelings generated in us by the actions and communications of others, and to the many different ways in which our own actions and communications impact on others. Pertinent literature (E.Jaques, *The Changing Culture of a Factory*; Kets de Vries, *The Irrational Executive*) discussing group dynamics and the role of subconscious forces in relationships and groups often emphasizes the connection between a person's relationships and the amount of work he undertakes in order to develop himself. This seemingly paradoxical connection can also be seen as one of the driving forces in the relation process.

To sum up, a person who manages the relation process with her co-workers effectively will likely be able to play her social role with ease, and minimize the negative impact of any conflicts that may arise. Mastering the selective aspect of the process will allow her to create supportive relationships within the organization, thus becoming stronger both as an individual and as a member of that organization.

## *A Matter of Exchange*

We are all related to one another, as a species – but we do not always exchange with each other significantly, or in the same ways. Relations seem to work best when there is an agreement on important values and, on a more practical level, a concordance of interests. For example, in business relations this perception of common interests often forms the basis of an unspoken complicity, despite opposite positions at the bargaining table.

The perception of commonalities, rather than an exhaustive list of similarities and differences, brings people together and leads to productive exchanges, but even a conflictive relation may ultimately prove helpful in a self-management perspective. One employee shared the following experience with us. "*I worked together for several years with this colleague, and communication had always seemed tortuous and uneasy. It was as if we oscillated between brief moments of trust and long periods of mutual distrust and bickering. Suddenly we discovered one common interest, one common concern – that we had shared all along but which we had never recognized in each other – and all the obstacles faded from then on. The intimacy channel had been opened and a point of contact had been established.*"

Egos are generally fragile, and to establish an information flow that does not threaten one another's dignity and self-esteem is a challenge, especially in the multi-varied context of highly mobile work relations. When, despite good intentions, communications become focused on sensitive personal issues, the interests we perceive in each other may quickly become confrontational, moving the relation process toward mistrust. When that is the case, the exchanges lose their playful quality and perceptions shift toward irreconcilable differences. The intimacy channel is closed and contact is lost. Exchanging nonthreatening information about oneself may be a potent way to open up channels of intimacy through which common values and interests can be discovered.

More generally, intimacy can be characterized as the degree to which persons make themselves accessible or available to one another, in terms of their feelings, actions, ideas, needs, perceptions, intuitions, hunches – indeed, in terms of their wholeness. The exchange of information may in itself be valuable for opening channels of intimacy. However, the degree to which people decide to develop intimacy with one another is often based, to a large extent, on mutual agreement as to what kind of psychological or material contracts can be made. Moreover, as different people speak to different aspects of ourselves, relations tend to follow their own particular path of least resistance. Ideally, communication follows the same personalized path. One of us expressed this as follows, "I*t helps to know where I am at, and where the other person is at. I cannot talk of the same issues with a business partner and with a gardener, not because one is worth more than the other, but because the priority list of interests is so different. Business partners focus on different commonalities than neighbors. The things that can be exchanged in a significant way are different between partners in a couple and between parents and children, or between a child and a parent versus children amongst each other. Those relationships speak to different needs.*"

A degree of intimacy is more easily achieved when persons are aware of their own needs, their own personality, their ways of being at ease or not with certain subjects, and of what the particular relation can offer in terms of exchange. One of us expressed the following viewpoint, "*Eventually, the most important criterion for deepening the exchange process is the feeling the exchange is good for you. When you feel good about it, when it energizes you and empowers you, a positive affect is created that provides a strong channel of intimacy, and that may lead to a sense of bonding, and to responsible co-action. This sense of bonding and co-action can become the foundation for an effective, pleasurable, and supportive interpersonal process. Conversely, when the relation drains you, takes away from your autonomy or from feeling good, when it leaves you with a feeling of emptiness, these are probably signals that an ingredient is missing and that a vital part of you cannot express itself. Such a relation may create a negative affect, which closes more doors than it opens. In contrast , where a positive flow can be created, business can take off and the exchange process shapes itself into meaningful interpersonal transactions.*" Positive affect is a vital ingredient for the kind of commitment necessary for responsible co-action in an organizational context. While many would think that positive affect depends on whether people agree or disagree on very specific issues, it actually manifests itself on another level; it is possible for people whose opinions on such issues vary widely to nevertheless experience a positive affect.

Group work may provide a powerful tool for experimenting with the exchange processes between members of an organization, and for opening new channels of communication. As one colleague observed, "*In working with a group, it is important to realize that when the fear level is high, members will retreat into abstractions and deal indirectly with each other. One of the outcomes of this behavior is that almost everyone becomes bored, apathetic, and withdrawn, resulting in low group energy. Members talk cognitively about the problems without indicating their personal beliefs, feelings, desires, and reservations. The more concrete, the more direct, and the more immediate the communications between members of such a group, the greater the members' involvement in the development of the group.*"

Stated or unstated rules about how much information to make accessible to each other may be strong inhibitors of exchange. Work in communication groups offers a rare opportunity to bring to awareness culture-induced norms about appropriate, but not necessarily healthy, ways of relating. Indeed, our rules may guide our verbal behavior, yet ordinarily do not affect our non-verbal behavior. But non-verbal behavior is rarely brought into full awareness. When it is first brought into awareness by a group consultant, people tend to get "uptight" about their non-verbal language, mostly for fear that it will be found inappropriate in some sense. They fear that the social conventions operative in the group will not condone the messages conveyed by body language, or they may fear that group members will disapprove and withdraw support. Yet most people will acknowledge intuitively that actions and non-verbal behavior speak more loudly than words. When they find an incongruency between words and actions, they are more likely to believe the non-verbal response. We intuitively know that the body rarely lies; and often we make more information available to others non-verbally than verbally. For example, if we say to someone that we really want to get close to them, while pushing them away with a gesture, they will probably believe the gesture more than the words. We may be unaware of the contradiction that expressed itself, and we may be puzzled at the person's subsequent withdrawal, but only if we have in some way colluded not to discuss verbal/non-verbal contradictions.

When in a group several persons decide to take the risk of openly discussing nonverbal behaviors, they enlarge the boundaries of accessible data, and they open up a vast reservoir of hidden messages. They also enlarge the possibilities for empirically testing the many inferences we make about each other's behavior.

The role of much group work in organizations is to bring relations closer to a level of realism and away from abstractions. Ultimately, when persons act in response to the feelings generated in the exchange process, we can practically be assured that the relation will follow its own particular gradient, even if the flow does not concretize in the ways one would have expected.

No doubt, relations are a matter for experience – and for reflection. But, in the end, all relations contain a mystery that can only be savored once the chemistry has done its work. For even strife and conflict contain the seeds of mutual understanding, and of lasting friendship.

### *The Organizational Social System as a Potential Support Network*

A number of types of relationships have been discussed in the literature. Relationships among superiors, peers, and junior employees constitute one type of classification; the emotional tone of attachments - positive, neutral, hostile - is another. Furthermore, specific circumstances have prompted analyses of work relations in instances such as management-union conflict, politically maneuvered administrative appointments, or complications arising in family businesses. In the context of the relation process as described in this book, we adopt a very general view of relationships in an organization, applicable to a wide variety of settings. In particular, we want to focus on the distinction between the organization as a social system and the potential support network of a particular individual within that system.

What types of problems are encountered with regard to the concept of support in the context of organizational relations? Regardless of the nature of the work, relationships are more often than not described as unsatisfactory, and are a common subject of discussion both inside and outside the work place. Even if these more or less confidential conversations act as effective emotional outlets, they do not constitute effective management strategy in the long term. However, the frequency with which such discussions take place, and the importance accorded to the whisperings circulating in every work environment, are signs that the management of relations is not an easy matter. The reasons for this are many. For one, economic difficulties will cause the social mood to degenerate in any organization undergoing a crisis. Even under less difficult economic conditions, however, negative comments about management or colleagues are common. How many of the stories circulated reflect the expression of envy, jealousy, and distrust? One receives the impression that the grapevine is far busier with criticism than with praise, or more objective appraisals. Moreover, difficulties of this nature are not surprising considering that the work situation is not one in which people have come together freely because of shared tastes and interests, but rather on the basis of complementary technical competencies. There may be some rare exceptions to this general rule, as in some high-technology enterprises, certain non-profit organizations, and a few pioneering organizations adhering strongly to their own values.

*In general, however, it is fair to state that few people find fully satisfying social exchanges within the limits of organizational life. We hypothesize that many of the difficulties experienced in handling the relation process in organizations can be traced to the inability of people to form an adequate support network, and to a misunderstanding of the concept of support.* It is frequently the case that an employee feels she is not enjoying the moral support she would wish for in her work environment. This might be due to her integration in a group with problems, or one that interferes with her autonomy and only appears to offer true support. It is also possible that her own inertia, dependence on others, or unfamiliarity with herself are the main factors that prevent her from finding compatible people. In fact, many people do not know how to support themselves adequately as complete persons, or how to support others in their potential, whether the other is a supervisor, a junior employee, or a colleague.

There is no single all-purpose definition of "support." When we ask the question, "When do you experience someone as supportive?," we realize how greatly the answers may differ from one person to another. As well, we have seen that the answers also depend on the time period, the level of abstraction or concreteness at which the person functions, the emotional level at which he experiences problems in task execution, and so on. For example, some people say, "I experience someone as supportive when he provides concrete help in tasks." Someone else says, "I experience my boss as supportive when he shows that he trusts me, when he trusts me as a person and when he trusts my competence." Another person may say, "I find myself to be supported when someone is around whose personality, style and competence I can trust;" or "A colleague is supportive to me if, by his way of interacting with me, he can help dissipate rather than fuel my fears and apprehensions." Yet another person may say, "A colleague is supportive to the extent that he does not have excessive expectations of me, whether related to my personality, my way of communicating, or whatever – when he can generally accept me the way I am."

It would seem from all these answers that the concept of support has less to do with specific behaviors than with the attitudes underlying these behaviors. For example, though someone may be angry at us, we may still experience that person as supportive – or we may experience an outwardly friendly person as totally unsupportive. *In a very general sense, then, we suggest that we experience those people as supportive who uphold our personality and style as valid, and whose behavior and communications with us are up front and reflect this attitude.*

Is there a relation between support and dependency? More specifically, is it possible that excessive support breeds dependency? Is it possible that by receiving support from others in the organizational system a person risks becoming overly dependent? Is it also possible that an excessive dependency precludes a person from extending support to others? Furthermore, how do organizational roles and the concept of intimacy relate to all this? The following section deals with questions such as these.

### *Dependency and Support*

In many ways, our relations are in our image. Frequently, the relationships we like to nurture and cultivate are part of a larger pattern of our life, in ways that we are not always fully aware of. Similarly, those that we want to sever are usually part of a larger life pattern that we have outgrown and need to move away from.

When we are unable to disengage ourselves from a life pattern we have outgrown, we tend to create relationships of dependency rather than ones of support. The difference is subtle but nevertheless significant. When we are dependent we are the helpless partner in the relation. Dependency can be present in many spheres of life. For example, we are dependent on doctors for medical services, on lawyers for help with legal matters, on psychologists, on other professionals such as plumbers and electricians. But we can transform those relations into supportive ones, for example by actively taking charge of our health, our legal affairs, our personal equilibrium, the condition of our house, and so on. We do this by managing these areas of our life to the best of our knowledge – by doing our homework.

*Like the concept of support, the concept of dependency is often misunderstood in organizational settings, and so is the relation between support and dependency*. In particular, dependency is often confused with asking for help, while it is often feared that giving support will breed dependency. Let's look briefly at these concepts. Dependency can be described as a state of immaturity in a certain area, in which we may need help but do not fully recognize or accept this need and do not explicitly say so. Rather than helping ourselves, we implicitly project the responsibility onto another person. For example, a small child depends on adults for food and nourishment only in the sense that he feels hungry and does not know how to fetch food for himself. Hence, he cries helplessly until someone gives him food. He effectively needs help. We can talk of dependency to the extent he becomes aware of the fact he is hungry, and that he can get food by performing a specific sequence of operations, but when despite his growing awareness he still adopts the behavior of crying out loud and waiting until someone comes. Thus, when dependency becomes a more or less permanent state, it almost always refers to a person's inability, or refusal, to learn.

*In organizational settings, dependency equally expresses itself not by the fact that someone asks for help with a task or problem, but rather by his inability to say up front that he needs help, or by his inability or refusal to learn.* For example, a person may order someone else around, telling him what to do and when, without mentioning that, in fact, he needs the other person's help in accomplishing a particular task or problem. Dependency may also express itself in the guise of exaggerated expectations toward another person - colleague, supervisor, or junior employee. For example, an employer may have exaggerated expectations of a new employee, without offering anything in return in terms of support. Or an employee may entertain exaggerated expectations of his employer, for example in the areas of improving the organizational climate or rectifying perceived injustices, also without offering anything in terms of moral and physical support. Some people in a managerial position may also encourage their employees to be dependent, for example by doing everything for them and not teaching them what they need to know to perform their work autonomously. Dependency may express itself in different areas - emotions, finances, communication, and so on. As soon as the person says, "I need your help for such and such," or "I would like you to clarify something," or "Teach me how to do this," he is in fact opening the doors for mutual support.

*It would seem that dependency and support are to a large extent mutually exclusive, as are dependency and openness to learning.* Curiously, it is very difficult for anyone to be supportive toward a dependent person. Indeed, if the dependent person is not learning, then being supportive is like trying to fill a bottomless basket, or exposing yourself to an emotional drain. To receive support from someone else implies the ability to learn, and in that sense a dependent person is unable to receive support; he is only able to find persons who are willing to fill a void for him. Thus, wherever the possibility of dependency is present, support has to focus on the learning process rather than on the task or the situation itself. Only then will support be effective in validating the individual's personality and style. Similarly, it would seem that dependency in a certain area precludes a person from being supportive toward others in that area, as he lacks inner resources to fall back on. By contrast, an openness to learn in that area makes it possible for her to receive support from others. As a result, dependency dissolves and the individual builds up resources; she gains the ability to take an autonomous stance and gradually becomes able to generously support others in turn.

Most of us have experienced the difficulties inherent in starting a new job. We do not know anything, we find ourselves relying on other employees for information, or relying on secretaries, our employer, or staff people for guidelines. It would be counter-intuitive for an employer to expect a new employee to be completely autonomous. Support is then extremely precious to the newcomer. One person, who repeatedly experienced this situation in different organizations, shared his perception as follows, "*As I go along, I listen and I observe a lot. I start creating contacts, exchanging with people, creating relationships of various kinds and intensities. In a way, I guess I kind of sell myself in exchange for their support. I mean, I gradually give them information about myself. In the beginning I have everything to learn; I cannot give much that is of value to the organization. But I can give something that may be of value to the people who are already there. For example, when I perceive that it is appropriate for me to do so, I can extend my trust to certain people. After a while, it becomes more of a give and take. I have noticed that many people do not mind giving me their support, as they are also very interested in learning about me, as a person and as a professional. In some places that initial process has been harder than in others. Once I had an immediate supervisor who liked me to be dependent. He gave me only minimal information. I could not become self-supportive on those terms; and I had to quit after a while. Other bosses do not know how to give support. I usually seek many sources of information rather than only the boss. But if someone had been there who needed support from that boss, he would have had a hard time."*

It is a common misconception that support can breed dependency. It rarely does. In fact, the reverse is true. Lack of support at the moment when it is most needed will tend to breed dependency, as it creates a pattern of behavior that permanently seeks support, and of which the person may be unaware.

In the next section we will pay attention more specifically to the way roles and intimacy in organizations can influence the formation of a support network.

### *Intimacy and Roles: Can They Be Reconciled in an Organizational Support Network?*

When we think of a support network, we think of varying degrees of friendship and intimacy. Ideally, a support network consists of a circle of people we value, whose company we seek, who are available to listen to our problems or indecisions when they arise, and who can also share the good moments. Sometimes they can even work together with us. They are people we like for what they are, and who can like us for what we are. Without support from significant others we can rarely actualize our full potential. Traditionally, such support has been offered by close friends and family.

However, the complexity of task requirements and of relations within organizations makes it most desirable for healthy self management to create a supportive circle not only outside the organization but also inside it. The cooperative spirit required by teamwork presupposes that the individual is able to manage herself, and to elicit the level of support she needs from others. To give and to receive support requires a degree of intimacy. Ordinarily, we do not choose our co-workers, nor do we usually have much time to get to know them at our own pace. Some people find it easier than others to create a supportive circle in these conditions. In addition, intimacy is usually associated with authenticity; that is, it is difficult to be really intimate with someone else when our real selves cannot touch. However, the roles we play in organizational interactions are frequently defined in terms of technical task descriptions and abilities. To the extent that we cannot mobilize our complete self in order to do a good job we may associate the role with some form of non-authenticity, especially if we feel we have to live up to an ideal set of expectations that come with a particular role. *Intimacy assumes that we reveal ourselves the way we are and that others do the same with respect to us. Yet many people in organizations find this very difficult, if not impossible, to do.* Some of the main reasons for these difficulties can often be found in the relationship between roles, on the one hand, and expectations, projections, and image, on the other.

## Roles and Expectations

*In general, roles do not make for good contact, whether it is with peers, with supervisors, or junior employees.* When we feel forced to relate to others from our role base rather than from our reality base, we compromise the possibility of intimacy. As a result we find that we cannot build the kind of support network that makes for effective teamwork on the job. We end up feeling alienated from what is going on and, in the end, our self-esteem suffers. Unfortunately, low self-esteem and the need for approval from colleagues and supervisors may reinforce our tendency to resort to role-based relational patterns, to establish and affirm our place in the organization. But the kind of support that can be gained from stereotyped relational scripts is often short-lived, unfulfilling, and ultimately unhelpful. Many people have painfully learned this lesson after basing their organizational relations on pleasing others, or coaxing others to please them.

Yet roles are ubiquitous in organizations. We get pushed into roles from more than one side - from our job description or our mandate, from the perceptions of our colleagues or subordinates, or from the pressure of cultural traditions and stereotypes, such as subordinate-boss or man-woman interaction stereotypes. The role-based interpersonal process is not only representative of many organizations. It also seems to be the rule in many business relations and negotiations, where the roles the partners play may do more to bring fears and hesitations to the bargaining table than to actually encourage reasonable risk-taking and mutual support. (This may not be current practice in the West, but in other cultures a certain form of intimacy is actually encouraged in business relations. In Japan, for example, getting acquainted on the personal level is often a prerequisite to satisfying business dealings, and the transaction is compromised if one of the partners does not lend himself to that aspect of the relation.)

*One of the main reasons why roles do not make for good contact, and can compromise the possibility of intimacy and supportive relations, is that roles are usually accompanied by expectations.* These expectations may take many forms, for example reverence, punctuality, conscientiousness, power, authority, various aspects related to style of performance and communication, and so on. Most people become very uneasy when they feel pressure from someone else to act according to such expectations. Moreover, expectations are often unexpressed and assumed to be self-evident by the person who holds them. They do stand in the way of intimacy. When we feel pressure to act according to others' expectations, it is important to clarify the difference between expectations related to job performance (such as the nature of the job, or a task description) and expectations of how to be as a person (which is a matter of style). Unfortunately, the two are often confounded. When personal and professional expectations are confounded, a fragmented interpersonal process is likely to result, which, in the end, will be ineffective towards teamwork on the task level. Most of us will readily agree about the difference between expectations related to task and those concerning personality and style. Yet in an organizational setting the line becomes thin, as objective requirements mesh with subjective realities of the persons who execute them, especially when others perceive our personal traits as affecting our performance on the job. Decision and action styles easily get interpreted as "good" or "bad," while concrete task results and the possibility for a constructive interpersonal process become secondary.

Honest communication is often the only way to unclutter the intimacy channel and clarify and adjust mutual expectations, but it is not always clear that taking the initiative for doing so will be effective. For example, a person in a supervisory role may be tempted to use the power usually associated with the role to get personal messages across. He may succeed in doing so for a while, but success will seldom last long because the other person is likely to resent this behavior, and will become more distant. When the role-based messages finally touch both the sender's and the receiver's core reality, one or both may get hurt in the process. Similarly, when we feel that our supervisor resists relating on a personal level through fear of losing control, we may end up with the impression that we are talking to a stone wall, and tension is likely to build up in the relationship. Depending on the context, we may try to talk with him and point this out. However, if it becomes apparent that there is not much we can do, we end up having to absorb his fears, which appear to us in the form of his controlling-defensive attitude. When he cannot tap into our own guilt feelings, we then may get around his resistance by sticking to our own feelings, by using humor, or simply by leaving the organization. But if he does manage to tap into our guilt feelings, we may lose initiative and self-esteem. However, hiding behind a role is not exclusively a prerogative of supervisors. A junior employee too can refuse to come out of his role and open a channel of intimacy, similarly masking fears, hostility, or both.

Not only do roles carry expectations that may be used to one's advantage, but those expectations may also be influenced or reinforced by projections. We may project certain qualities onto our supervisors, junior employees, and business associates, and, conversely, receive projections from them.

## Roles and Projection

Two of the most prevalent kinds of projection have to do with knowledge and authority. When occupying a position of some authority, such as supervisor, consultant, or executive, we may receive projections from other organizational staff. Conversely, as a junior employee or client we may project certain characteristics of knowledge and authority onto supervisors and consultants.

Knowledge and authority are two characteristics that invariably tap into our backgrounds when as children we reacted toward our parents and educators. Depending on the particular personal background both actors bring to the relation, the projection may resonate with positive (supportive) or negative (undermining) connotations. In other words, "authority" can be experienced, for example, as supportive or as punishing, and "knowledge" can be experienced as informative or as possessive. For example, one supervisor made the following statement, "*I had recruited an employee that I perceived to be autonomous and serious. Later on, as I watched him work, I perceived that the jobs were inadequately performed, that the employee had lied regarding the execution of the work, and that he did not live up to my original image of him. When I told him he had one more month to work, his performance increased dramatically, jobs were completed in record time, and they were well executed in terms of quality. Previous encouragements had not worked. But in the end I had to fire him.*" In this situation, the employee had a history of relations with punitive and controlling bosses. He had projected the same expectation on this new supportive supervisor and was unable to accept positive encouragement from him. The supervisor, in turn, felt pushed into a negative, punitive role, and felt considerable discomfort with the punitive-controlling stance. He found it impossible to be himself as a whole person in a long-term relationship with this employee.

Projecting certain characteristics onto someone else amounts to disowning these characteristics. This may induce dependency in the other person, who fulfills the expectations carried by the projection. For example, if a worker projects the trait "punishing director" onto his supervisor, she may feel lost and become task-inefficient and disoriented if the expectation is not fulfilled. For the person who receives such a projection the danger is that she will assume the role being cast for her and act it out. In the above case, the employee's expectation of a punishing boss actually led this supervisor to fire him. For both persons, the relation may become tense, and will probably be terminated by one or by both, thereby losing its potential for mutual supportiveness.

The more the roles we play – secretary, supervisor, lawyer, accountant, consultant, manager, etc. – form an easy screen for projection, the more they challenge us to remain anchored in our genuine selves. Many people often find it difficult to relate to a business partner's full self. However, for the self-managing person who values intimacy and mutual support, the challenge is to learn enough about the different aspects of that role to actually see through them, and keep on sensing himself as a complete person. If, instead, he remains locked into the assumed role, he may feel temporarily satisfied, but is likely to feel a void once the others are gone, or when away from the office. To the extent that we maintain our ability to respond as a whole rather than as a partial person, we may avoid reacting to projections in ways that are unproductive from a relational point of view. It may still hurt us to feel that a colleague, supervisor, or junior employee does not relate to our whole person, but at least we ourselves can stay in touch with our wholeness and maintain a sense of perspective. Another difficulty with assumed roles and supportive relationships is the perceived necessity of maintaining a particular image of oneself.

## Roles and Image

When we find ourselves in a job dealing with the public, we are often confronted with the need to maintain a specific image we believe to be concomitant with the service we perform. Some examples are the secretary or receptionist who is always efficient and agreeable, the supervisor who gets the job done without problems no matter what, the bank teller who is pleasant and correct, and so on.

However, the image we perceive to be required by the role may drain our valuable inner resources and compromise our ability to offer a satisfactory level of support to clients and colleagues. Conforming to an image may get us a quick sale and clients may be briefly seduced by a show of friendliness or cleverness. However, long-term business or professional relations will seldom be satisfying to both parties if some measure of reality, of honesty, of awareness of one's needs (and, ideally, of awareness of the other person's needs) does not pierce through the role. For example, we cannot fail to recognize that the most successful sales representative is frequently the one who can play the selling role while simultaneously being sincere and honest with the client. Conversely, as a client we will almost always be most at ease with, and most reassured by, a counterpart who understands our concerns and can allow empathy to enter the business transaction.

## Summing Up

It would seem that in any organizational context a psychological contract between different categories of employees, between colleagues, or between business and professional partners, has a greater probability of being constructive when those involved in the interaction express more of their real selves, despite differences in roles or hierarchical position. Furthermore, it would seem that a greater congruence between the respective expectations of the actors is likely to increase the possibility of intimacy and of mutual support. In fact, even the open expression of anger may create a constructive intimacy channel, as it is a way of revealing true feelings.

Finally, while there may be organizational or contextual differences in the degrees of freedom that employees enjoy in dealing with their role, it would seem that, generally, the role will be more successful in terms of organizational objectives, and the relations more satisfying to all parties, when the person is sufficiently at ease with the role and its image, so that characteristics of intimacy can transpire in the working relationship. Conversely, we can expect roles to hinder our relation process when we get so absorbed in them that we lose our ability to empathize.

### *Symptoms of Obstructions*

By obstructions in the relation process we refer to those behavioral or attitudinal patterns that are likely to consistently hinder the flow of the process – in particular, those patterns that tend to prevent the emergence of a support network for the individual in any organizational context. As a partial list of obstruction symptoms, we have identified the following:

- consistent inability to alternate between affective investment and disengagement, or to stay in touch simultaneously with relative closeness and sufficient distance;
- consistent inability to communicate and intervene in a timely and effective manner;
- inability to distinguish the role one is playing in the organization from one's real self, or an exaggerated identification with the role;
- inability to decode the significance of certain projections;
- a persistent state of emotional or other type of dependency on the support of others, or the undifferentiated nature of one's needs for support.

The first obstruction in the relation process has to do with *a consistent inability to alternate between affective investment and disengagement, or to stay in touch simultaneously with relative closeness and sufficient distance*. Employees who are unable to practice an alternation between social investment and disengagement risk not having any real place in the organizational system. They may find themselves unsatisfied as members of the group as their social relationships remain undifferentiated. Either they devote too little energy to such relationships, leading to complete withdrawal at one extreme, or they waste energy on unresponsive co-workers from whom they are unable to withdraw emotionally – leading to clinging behavior at the other extreme. From the self-management perspective, it seems as necessary to insist on the importance of disengagement as it is to encourage social investment. Many of us have experienced situations in which someone behaved toward us in dependent, even overwhelming ways, monopolizing our energies to such an extent that we were obliged to disengage ourselves before being swallowed up in a one-way relationship. Failing to invest or failing to disengage may prevent an individual from creating the kind of supportive network of relationships that he needs and hopes for.

Similarly, the failure to maintain an adequate balance between closeness and distance may compromise the flow of the relation process. Relations may be prematurely cut off because of one person's inability to keep a certain distance from the other, or to keep in touch with the other person's rhythm and style. Wanting to be too close too soon, or at the wrong time, can hurt a relationship as much as wanting to be too distant for too long or at the wrong moment. When these behaviors or attitudes persist and become systematic, they risk to unnecessarily limit the scope and potential richness of the relation process.

A second category of obstructions in the relation process has to do with *the consistent inability of a person to communicate and intervene in a timely and effective manner*. Any communication transmits something of the communicator to the other person – ideas, attitudes, opinions, feelings, emotions, and moods. Thus, any communication also has the potential to affect the other person in various significant ways. For example: the receiver may become fearful, very much at ease, defensive, angry, interested, light-hearted, or simply bored.

Thus, the problem of what to communicate to whom, at what time, and in what ways, takes on much greater importance than many people assume it does. To many people it still comes as a complete surprise that their communication has stirred up feelings and emotions in the other person. A number of skills may help increase effective communication. Among them are the following:

1] *listening and observational skills*: if they are inadequate the person will not be sensitive to the impact his communications have on others, and be unable to make corrections if necessary;
2] *feedback skills* (knowing how and when to provide feedback): feedback given inappropriately is rarely productive;
3] *avoiding to push others into a defensive mode*: provoking a defensive mode usually renders communication ineffective;
4] *decoding the image people want to project, or recognizing their communication styles*: this is essential for avoiding misunderstandings; for example, being caught up in a power struggle as a result of failing to decode a specific communication as a search for power;
5] *keeping in touch with one's own rhythms and with those of others* is essential for avoiding the wrong statement or behavior at the wrong moment.

Effective communication in a group context will likely benefit from several other skills as well:

1] ensuring that one's communications are affectively connected with one's environment – otherwise they risk creating boredom and disinterest;
2] accurately "taking the pulse" of the group: an inability to sense "where it is at" carries the risk of intervention at the wrong moment or on the wrong topic;
3] selectivity: indiscriminate communication may lead to merely dissipating one's energies;
4] distinguishing between intervention as a group member and intervention with the aim of furthering the group's progress. This distinction is essential if one is to avoid focusing exclusively on either oneself or the group;
5] identifying the individuals who are strong in their social expression and those who are more fragile, or those who assume the role of leader and those who seem to be going through a personal crisis, perhaps related to self-esteem or stress.

When one or more of these aspects of effective communication is consistently lacking – for example, when the person consistently fails to listen and observe; consistently and unwittingly pushes people into a defensive mode; or tries to communicate with everyone in a group and on any subject rather than being selective – they are likely to generate difficulties in the person's relation process, which will also undermine the possibilities for supportive interpersonal relations.

Third, obstruction in the relation process can be related to an inability to distinguish the role one is playing in the organization from one's real self, or an exaggerated identification with the role. As we have noted in a previous section, playing a role has the potential to be a valuable instrument in the accomplishment of tasks. However, it may also hinder a person's relation process if excessive identification with the role prevents her from being sufficiently in touch with her own intuitive and emotional processes.

Earlier on, we discussed a fourth element of obstruction in the relation process – inability to decode the significance of certain projections.

Finally, obstructions have to do with persistent demands for emotional or other support of others, or the undifferentiated nature of these needs. Most people find it very difficult to sustain someone else's needs without limitations on time and effort, especially when there is no learning on the part of the person claiming support. Many people find the giving of support rewarding when it involves learning on the part of the recipient. Similarly, when a person has trouble specifying what kind of support he really needs, most people will find it a strain to maintain a supportive relationship. It would certainly seem that one of the skills required to unblock such a situation of dependency in a certain area is the ability to express, promptly and clearly, one's need for help. One of the attitudes that would seem to facilitate the unblocking is an eagerness and commitment to learn and to apply one's learning. Curiously, certain organizational settings encourage dependency rather than learning, as we will see in the next section.

### *Managing the Relation Process in Organizations*

Managing one's relation process involves getting to know one's own relational styles and affinities, in order to bring about or restore harmonious relations with others and, especially, to move toward the realization of genuinely supportive relationships within the organizational system. Also involved is seeing to it that the relation process supports rather than detracts from the flow of one's appropriations, decisions and actions.

As we pointed out in the previous section, the flow of the relation process can be hindered by persistent obstructions of a more personal nature. However, a person's relation process can also be hindered by certain organizational conditions that tend to systematically interfere with it. Among such hindering conditions, we have singled out four by way of illustration – a systematic encouragement of a degree of dependency, overemphasis on internal competition, an exaggerated separation of work and private life, and excessive changes in personnel or leadership.

1] *A systematic encouragement of a degree of dependency*. To the extent that some organizations tend to overcontrol their employees, explicitly (by means of records and evaluations) or implicitly (by requiring them to pledge allegiance to a company image), they may unwittingly condone and actually encourage certain forms of dependency among these employees. Indeed, one of the characteristics of dependency is the reliance on the supporting person or institution to take care of you, often in return for your expression of loyalty. But such dependency may make these persons very vulnerable. The objectives and general economic conditions of the organization may change rapidly, while the persons have assumed that the organization, like a protective mother, is looking after their financial and emotional well-being. When the organization encourages this illusion in return for the loyalty of its employees, it contributes to their inability to give full expression to their relation process within the organization, and to manifest themselves as autonomous actors in regard to that process. When, through its models of direction, an organization puts excessive limits on the relation process of individuals, the latter often have little choice but to leave the organization if they want to stay in control of their own relational process.

2] *Overemphasis on internal competition*. Internal competition may be fostered among individuals, for example with respect to possibilities for promotion, or among departments. While competition can be healthy in the framework of a game, it sometimes has a destructive effect on relationships within the organization. For example, competitive thinking may create an orientation toward developing interpersonal strategy rather than an atmosphere of trust or interpersonal support. It would seem that the possibility of working as a creative team, while it does not exclude a healthy level of gamelike competition, also depends greatly on the level of intimacy and mutual support the team members are willing to agree to. When the organizational culture encourages competitiveness to the exclusion of mutual support, the individual will necessarily be limited in the manner in which her relation process can unfold. The same is obviously true for interdepartmental competition.

3] *An exaggerated separation of work and private life.* When the organizational culture exacerbates the separation between work and private life, that is, when the culture upholds an image of employees as producers only, chances are that their relation process will be blocked to a large extent inside the organization. They can be expected to go through the motions, without real commitment and without learning about personal responsibility or professional conscientiousness. To the extent that the organization's objectives reflect such a reductionist view of human nature and behavior, it is very likely that the persons involved will, in time, feel exploited. Thus, they may adopt a stance of indifference and, in the end, may be seduced into corruption and complete alienation from their original values. The ensuing lack of real investment in meaningful relations within the organizational structure, and the abandonment of support as a valid expression of them, may eventually result in a bad reputation turning away competent people.

4] *Excessive changes in personnel or leadership.* It usually takes time before a new member of the organization becomes fully integrated in the group. Moreover, when many people change or new leaders come into the group the whole culture of the organization may change. When such changes take place on a regular basis, they may take their toll in terms of adaptation, trust, and fatigue. Tension can be compounded when the organization recruits new members whose style turns out to be incompatible with the style practiced by the old members, or when new supervisors have privileged links with top-level executives. In the event of excessive changes of personnel, the rhythms of alternation between investment and disengagement are, as it were, forced into a higher gear, thereby straining a person's relation process.

In contrast, we have observed that other organizational conditions may be facilitative with respect to the relation process. These are conditions that tend to facilitate people's getting to know each other and themselves better with regard to styles and affinities. These conditions allow personal aspirations to help creating harmonious and effective relations with others in the organization. They tend to make it easier for people to find supportive networks, and they favor relationships that are supportive of a person's autonomy in realizing appropriations, decisions, and actions in the organizational context. We identify these conditions as follows:

- a leadership that is relaxed and does not feel the need to justify itself, or to manipulate power;
- a context in which the uniqueness of every individual is recognized and valued, and the realization of potential is actively encouraged;
- the initiation of opportunities for social encounters, which also mix well with relations on the task level;
- use of recruitment procedures that ensure that there is a level of agreement on values and interests.

1] *A leadership that is relaxed and does not feel the need to justify itself, or to manipulate power.*

When leaders feel the need to justify themselves, they tend to lose the trust of their colleagues and assistants. When they manipulate power, for example in the interest of maintaining their position or privileges, they tend to encourage an atmosphere of secrecy and of withholding information. By doing so, they indirectly risk breeding low self-esteem among people, as well as low, unmotivated task performance. When everybody thinks only of saving his or her own skin, the relation process cannot operate properly. It would seem that a minimal degree of openness and trust is an absolute necessity for successful relations.

2] *A context in which every individual's uniqueness is recognized and valued, and in which the realization of potential is actively encouraged.*

When uniqueness is not recognized, and when excessive pressures exist either from top management or from peer groups to adopt certain implicit values, people are likely to respond with a defensive attitude. The defensive atmosphere in turn encourages them to adopt a dependency stance rather than a supportive one. In contrast, when the uniqueness of individuals is recognized, in regard to both their personality and their competence, they can usually appropriate their own space in the organizational social system. To the extent that they do not have to fight excessively for their own space, their energy becomes available for productive work. Even training and development programs can be adjusted to correspond to the needs of individuals or to groups of people with similar interests. Many people who have had uniform training programs forced upon them have become disillusioned about such programs, and have been unable to extract the kind of lessons from them that management intended. Recognition of one's competencies and one's personal values by others, and especially by those people one works with, is in many cases an inestimable creator of relationships experienced as genuinely supportive.

3] *Initiation of opportunities for social encounters that also mix well with relations on the task level.*

Many people find that the opportunity for social encounters off the job facilitates their relation process within the organization. This seems to be the case provided that the kind of relation processes initiated through such encounters can be congruent with the kind of processes that are encouraged within the work context itself. The creation of such opportunities can be a powerful signal from higher management that relations are genuinely valued in the organization, but they may also be a tool for saving face and masking an underlying contempt for relational values. When the opportunities do reflect a genuine concern for co-workers getting to know each other better, they may contribute to clearing the work atmosphere of the obstructing effect of previous stereotypes or prejudices.

4] *Use of recruitment procedures that ensure that there is a level of agreement on values and interests.*

Problems can be avoided when there is a base level of agreement on values and interests among the members of an organization. Conflicts and disagreements are energy-draining. Allotting attention and energy to conflicts and disagreements may be desirable and constructive when a group's purpose is precisely the resolution of such problems; as, for example, in certain forms of marital therapy, or in special sessions devoted to group conflict resolution. But organizations typically have other purposes and, more often than not, such basic disagreements only divert the group's energy from the primary goal of the organization. When there is a base level of common values and interests, the individual's energies blend and complement each other more readily in goal-oriented activities.

Managing the relation process, then, involves a number of attitudes and mind states which, we believe, should help her to gain sufficient knowledge of the process, and help bring about, or restore, harmonious relationships with others in the organization. These attitudes and mind states can be formulated as follows:

1] to become aware of obstructions that tend to systematically hinder the flow of one's relation process;
2] to become aware of the organizational conditions that may contribute to difficulties in the relation process, and be able to distinguish such conditions from other obstructions that are of a more personal nature;
3] to become aware of one's relational needs and affinities, and to recognize the patterns in one's previous rewarding and disappointing experiences;
4] to become aware of the importance of interpersonal communications, in particular the role of attitudes and feelings;
5] to maintain a balance between investment and disengagement in relational processes;
6] to be selective in identifying people likely to contribute to a supportive relationship, and to devote an appropriate level of energy to these relationships; and finally,
7] to take care of one's own process.

Let's look at each of these in turn.

First of all, effective management will be facilitated when a person *becomes aware of obstructions that tend to systematically hinder the flow of his relation process*. Management of the process demands attentiveness to those obstructions and to the ways in which they may impede upon or reduce the potential alternation between investment and disengagement. In particular it demands taking care to always keep open a channel of possible intimacy with others, and to maintain adequate receptiveness to feedback from them.

Second, management of the relation process involves *becoming aware of the organizational conditions that may contribute to difficulties in the relation process, and distinguishing such conditions from obstructions of a more personal nature.* Often, difficulties experienced in creating supportive relationships are a result of organizational factors, such as the climate or certain factors related to leadership. Adequately identifying the reasons for the difficulties allows a person to resort to more appropriate actions. For example, when the general climate in an organization is defensive and secretive, the person may feel tense and uneasy. If he thinks the problem is his own, he may be confused and unable to reach out, or invest. But if he correctly identifies the tension as the result of a climate of defensiveness around him, he may recollect himself and try to reach out.

Thirdly, effective management of the relation process can be facilitated by *becoming aware of one's relational needs and affinities, and by recognizing the patterns in one's previous rewarding and disappointing experiences.* This point includes the identification of areas in which one tends to be prejudiced, either in the positive or in the negative sense. Awareness of such areas allows one to be more objective and more balanced in one's social interactions. In particular, this awareness will allow the person to move from interactions based on the mutual perception of disappointing features, to those based on the mutual perception of potentially meaningful exchanges. One's relational needs as well as affinities may lead one to rewarding relationships, but they may also lead to error. Error is especially likely if one's needs and affinities are so strong in a certain area that one interacts with only a partial aspect of the other person. To relate as a complete person to another's completeness requires awareness and perspective with regard to one's own needs and affinities.

For even if a high degree of intimacy is obtained with certain persons, they still remain separate persons with their own projects and agendas. Insufficient awareness of the facts concerning needs for intimacy and privacy may lead to accidental transgressions of boundaries, which may seriously damage potentially constructive relationships. To identify the patterns that emerge from past experiences in this regard allows one to manage the delicate balance between closeness and distance.

Fourth, to manage the relation process effectively also involves *becoming aware of the importance of interpersonal communications, in particular the role of attitudes and feelings in communications*. The communications of other persons have an impact on us in terms of their attitude and the feelings they impart. Conversely, our communications have an impact on others, conveying some of our attitudes and stirring certain feelings in them. To become aware of these interactions on an emotional level is necessary in order to learn not only about our own relation process, but also about relations in general. Many "faux pas" could be avoided in relations if people knew more about the impact of their communications, and learned how to integrate these effects into their efforts to bring about harmonious relations with others.

The fifth ability facilitating the relational process can be formulated as *maintaining a balance between investment and disengagement*. To maintain harmony in terms of one's relation process may demand investment in a particular relationship, but it may also mean that disengagement is called for if the individual wishes to invest her energy in other relationships that are more in tune with present needs. At the beginning of a relationship one often feels that a sufficient social investment is necessary, not only in order to confront the realities of the other person but also to gauge the possibility for deepening the bonds that may exist. In an organization, a person can often feel that there exists a certain threshold of social investment that must be reached for her to be accepted as a member of the group, and below which she would risk exclusion. At the other extreme, someone who invests too much may eventually lose herself in the social system, with the ultimate risk of losing her personal identity. A sort of ongoing dynamic balance is constantly required, which determines the way in which a person relates on a day-to-day basis to supervisors, peers, and junior staff. The capacity to identify what types and intensity of investment and disengagement are necessary to maintain this dynamic balance is a valuable asset for the self-managing person. In this respect it is helpful to discern the nuances this balancing would require in terms of the seniority of the people involved; the group's maturity in terms of supportiveness; the quality of the organizational climate; or the particular assumptions inherent in the organizational culture.

Sixth, managing the relation process involves *selectivity in identifying people who are likely to contribute to a supportive relationship, and to devote an appropriate level of energy to these relationships.* Developing significant relationships without becoming a prisoner to them is a continuous process rather than a one-time-only event. However, even in supportive relationships there is the necessity to remain vigilant, and to cultivate the ability to say "no" when the exchange becomes too unilateral, or when we feel that our energies are being dissipated. To the extent that we exercise an adequate degree of selectivity in our relations, we can expect them to be more effective - our energy is less likely to be consumed by the conflicts and misunderstandings that inevitably arise in our work lives. To the extent that we devote an appropriate level of energy to a particular interaction, we are more likely to avoid excessively buying into the expectations the other person may project on us. We may then cultivate a sense of realism regarding such expectations: "*I do not expect ideal behavior from the persons I chose to interact with; and I am aware that I do not always conform to the ideal behavior others may expect from me.*"

Finally, managing the relation process involves the *need to take care of one's own process.* This need refers to a certain care in preventing situations from recurring that do not further one's equilibrium, or that impede the harmonious expression of one's qualities. This implies not letting other people take undue advantage. Sometimes there is only a thin line between genuine mutually supportive relations and those in which one person really uses the other, or each takes advantage of the other, without a bond of genuine affection.

Next we will consider another process generic to self management - the decision process.

> "The more one sees of human fate and the more one examines its secret springs of action, the more one is impressed by the strength of unconscious motives and by the limitations of free choice."
>
> C. G. Jung

## Self Management of the Decision Process

### *The Decision Process Defined*

This process concerns the continuous flow of an individual's choices and the continuous reconstruction of these choices. The decision process is characterized by alternations between phases of commitment and detachment, which gradually change the direction and focus of an individual's behavior. In the end, the decision process helps one visualize the very backbone of one's choices over time and, thus, to confront the hierarchy of one's personal values. Gaining this insight permits one to attain a better grasp of the specific orientation of one's contribution to the organization.

From a practical perspective, the decision process consists of a person's continuously working through the link between concrete options and more abstract priorities, underpinned by personal values.

The management of the decision process allows one not only to seize opportunities for decision-making and to conceive of alternatives, but also to test the very limits of each alternative, and to experience the ambivalence generated by the contradicting values that may be present in them. An informed choice is made when one has tested the limits of one's commitment to a certain option.

By mastering the full array of possible options as well as their contradictions, one ensures that the chosen problem resolution will clear the way for decisions further down the road.

Wherever the contradictions associated with a particular option have not been adequately confronted, we have found it very likely that the person may remain locked into unsatisfactory options. Furthermore, we hypothesize that the ability to rethink previous decisions critically and to test the limit of one's commitment optimizes the extent to which significant lessons can be extracted from those decisions as well as the ability to recognize the most favorable conditions for adequate decision making.

As with any other process discussed (appropriation, relation, action), decisions are usually considered the outcome of a conscious process. However, many unconscious forces may be at work as well. For example, rather than being grounded in our experience, some values may be introjected remnants from exposure to parental or authority figures when our minds were open and without defenses or discrimination. Similarly, early childhood experiences can play a role in shaping unsuspected dimensions in the structuring of one's personality. Thus, they may guide and orient our choices to a far greater extent than we are aware. Finally, unconscious collective forces are transmitted by the culture in which we live or, in the Jungian sense, by symbolic forces that transcend time.

Despite the fact that the analysis of the decision process is limited by these unconscious forces, certain paradoxes that are more accessible to conscious scrutiny are the subject of the next section.

### *Paradoxes Inherent in the Decision Process*

One paradox characteristic of the decision process is the necessity to maintain congruence with one's personal values while at the same time allowing for flexibility in choosing options appropriate to the situation at hand. There is no doubt that the closer a decision comes to the real priorities of an individual at a given time, the more satisfying the decision will be. But the external realities may very well make this goal seem hard to come by. The most rewarding decisions are probably made when we are sufficiently aware of our own values and priorities. However, we also need to be aware of those larger organizational dimensions over which we have little control. Excessively self-centered thinking is also often self-limiting, in that it makes it difficult to recognize that other people's values and priorities may be different from one's own. Making decisions in an organizational context means inserting them into a reciprocal stream of decisions: what we decide affects others, and what others decide affects us. One of the issues that seems to be important in managing our decision flow is the ability to realistically assess the impact other people's decisions have on us, especially if we experience them as limiting or negative. For example, when we must yield to decisions made by a supervisor, this ability to control the extent of the possible effects of these decisions on our own system becomes indispensable, at least if we are interested in maintaining an adequate level of self-esteem and emotional security.

Another paradox inherent in the flow of decision making relates to the frequent necessity to make a choice on the spot and under considerable uncertainty, while at the same time having rigorously prepared for the decision by a thorough and persistent information search. For example, unforeseen incidents always occur, and the fact of having prepared for them often generates the necessary energy to respond appropriately to these unexpected calls. In general, organizational realities often require decisions to be made before all the necessary information has been collected or integrated. The difficulty then lies in determining what amount of information is sufficient for responsible decision making.

Maturation of a person's value system has a great impact on her decision making. In her twenties, an individual's personal decisions tend to be influenced by role models such as family, peer group, senior colleagues. In her forties, the same individual will balance the influence of others with her own needs and values. Later, more and more decisions are made on the basis of personal priorities. At this stage, people have a greater capacity for emotional detachment, and, at the same time, somewhat paradoxically, a greater loyalty to their personal values.

A crucial moment in the decision making process occurs when the person discovers the advantages of another option and the disadvantages of his original choice. Such phases of ambivalence are not only natural but even necessary. Indeed, at the core of all decisions lies the inherent contradiction between opposing tendencies, for instance, pros versus cons, gut feelings versus rational arguments, waiting or acting immediately. One manager gave the following example: "*Everyone who has participated in business meetings knows that many people want to intervene quickly and get out whatever it is they have on their mind. Many times these interventions just fall flat and have little impact except for raising the level of stress for everyone. In most cases their interventions are related to another time, that is they relate to unfinished problematic situations they have been experiencing in the past. How many times have we not had the sensation without saying so out loud that the conversation topic had little to do with the present agenda? My personal decision to intervene in the discussion is never clear-cut. There is always ambiguity as to what is the right thing to say and as to what is the right moment to say it. Of course, I am tempted to react immediately to a comment I do not like, but at the same time I also know that if I want my intervention to be a seed for fruitful discussion I have to wait for the right moment. The contradictory merit of affirming my standpoint right away or of waiting for the right moment never makes for an easy decision."*

How are such contradictions to be handled? How much time and energy must be invested in tolerating the disconcerting presence of contradictions, before finally deciding to transcend the ambivalence inherent in the situation? When should we stop investing our time and energy in such an evaluative process? The same issue applies to organizations, or to persons, who have a history of obstinately sticking to deadlines. This rigidity is logically understandable. However, wherever there is a process at work, there is also ambivalence. Many times it would be to the advantage of the organization, or to the person in question, to take enough time to feel through the ambivalence and endure it for a while, in order to let the decision ripen, for that is how understanding develops. If one cuts the period of ambivalence short too quickly, people will often refer back to the past mechanically, repeating decisions made earlier and possibly in a different situation. Thus, the ensuing decision is of questionable relevance to the circumstances at hand. The low-level satisfaction generated in the process will inevitably lead to further problems in the flow and in the person's motivation to make decisions. In contrast, the ripening that takes place in an optimal decision process often generates just the novel idea that constitutes an adequate or brilliant response to current requirements, and then permits the person to move to the desired level of meaningful and decisive action.

The perspective presented in this book values the optimal functioning of individuals as an organizational priority. Therefore, flexibility in handling the paradoxes is not seen as a threat to hierarchical structures, but rather as a guarantee that people can fulfill their personal goals as well as those of the organization.

## *Symptoms of Obstructions*

Obstructions in the flow of the decision process may, among other possibilities, generate constant postponement of decisions, decisions that do not adequately reflect one's priorities, which consistently have a negative impact on others, which are consistently ill-timed, or which simply do not move the individual any closer to the stated goal.

Behaviors and attitudes that we have frequently found to be symptomatic of obstructions in the decision process are, among others, the following:

- an insufficient sense of discernment;
- an excessive dependency on the organization;
- an inadequate or superficial reading of previous decisions;
- a restriction of openness and a lack of flexibility;
- a history of incongruity in decision making.

First, an insufficient sense of discernment may obstruct the decision process. For example, the decision maker may confuse the organization's mission with the means to attain it. In fact, an excessive concentration on methods may make her lose sight of objectives. Frequently, the tendency to increase the number of people on committees or the multiplication of the number of committees within an organization may indicate a disproportionate mobilization of resources with respect to the problems to be resolved. In addition, when these committees debate specific issues, they easily become blinded by their internally generated logic and may lose a vital connection to the wider problem. Paradoxically, even in organizations such as hospital rehabilitation centers, whose mission is predominantly community-oriented, we have frequently observed a very low level of awareness of, and concern with, the real mission of the organization. In many cases, immediate concerns with salary, grappling with red tape, or fixation on internal problems of an interpersonal or administrative nature, clutter the real issues and prevent adequate tackling of the real problems of patients. They also prevent an adequate system for real problem resolution from taking hold.

Second, excessive dependency on organizational priorities often goes together with a lack of balance among the different aspects of a person's life. For example, a person who takes on ever-increasing responsibilities within the organization may overlook and neglect the rewarding experiences that can be associated with the cultivation of his personal relationships and family life. By doing so the person misses valuable opportunities for enriching his own personal development. Unless this behavior constitutes a conscious choice, it may also place him in a position of vulnerability with respect to his personal satisfaction and self-esteem, reinforcing his overdependency on his professional role. If this is the case, his decision-making process may reflect unresolved inner ambivalence and, in extreme cases, lead to erratic or compulsive choices.

Third, an inadequate and superficial reading of previous decisions tends to cut short the kind of reflection that can help identify important parameters of our decision making habits. Choices tend to present themselves to us regularly. If these choices have not consistently reflected our value dynamics and if we have not recognized and analyzed the discrepancies, then former errors are very likely to be repeated in a virtually mechanical manner. In addition, inadequate readings of successes or failures in one area of decision making may be transferred into other environments, making for confusing signals to colleagues and co-workers. For example, a professionally successful person who has failed to achieve a satisfactory level of harmony in her emotional life will often find herself struggling with residues of negative feelings such as resentment, anger, or jealousy. Despite the best of intentions this negative state may lead her to mobilize her energies into a pattern of self-destructive decision making. As a result, her choices and behavior may be poorly understood by colleagues. She may misinterpret feedback and information received from these colleagues, as they react more to her attitudinal state than to the issues at stake. Consequently, her own decisions down the road may also be based on erroneous and incomplete information. In this case, an inadequate reading of decision issues in one area of life propels the person into a deficient decision process in another area.

Other behaviors and attitudes that may be symptomatic of a deficient decision process are a chronic restriction of openness and a lack of flexibility in sifting through the various choices. Organizational systems tend to evolve rapidly in terms of their structure and technologies, their members' skills and attitudes, and also in terms of work styles. The more a person is entrenched in an unbending mind-set and the more oblivious he is to ways of thinking different from his own, the more difficulties he may experience in adjusting to environmental changes. Not only might he be out of touch with his own personal changes, he is also likely to be out of phase with fast-paced organizational changes. By not having cultivated sensitivity to these transformations, this person may have blurred his choices or even blotted them out within his range of perception. For example, we have all seen people who have stubbornly developed their own company against difficult odds and who find themselves, thirty years later, clinging to the same outmoded operating rules that were successful in the past. In the same vein, by neglecting to upgrade one's skills and abilities and to touch base with the changes in one's own interests, one eventually fails to make the choices that would effectively orient one to new requirements, whether personal or work related. In both cases, the process of decision making has become ossified.

A history of incongruity in decision making denotes a lack of consistency between one's values and one's choices over time. The dissonance that results from such inconsistencies, and the acute sensation of an internal conflict, may very well paralyze an individual and inhibit her from making further decisions. For example, a business person may ardently wish to support local artistic productions. Her motivation may even be reinforced by the sympathy and affection she harbors for certain artists in the municipality. On the one hand, she may wish to sponsor and promote artistic programs with a high aesthetic appeal. On the other hand, she may not have accumulated sufficient capital to realize this project. In other words, this person has not made economic decisions of the kind that would allow her to respond adequately to her own philanthropic values.

The same would be true for a person who wishes to help other people, or even be active in a helping profession, but who has failed to make the educational decisions that would allow him to adequately prepare himself for the job, not only cognitively but also by acquiring the necessary emotional strength. For example, he may even have made decisions with respect to his personal life that have had a negative impact on his emotional stability, and which make it increasingly difficult for him to function in a helping role toward others. Furthermore, changing priorities over time may make it difficult for a person to adjust her decision process accordingly. For example, many women feel a blockage in decision making when the attention they want to give to child-rearing suddenly gives way to the realization that they have neglected their once-promising professional life. In addition, men or women may have followed in the professional footsteps of their parents, only to find their decision process blocked much later when it dawns on them that their real preferences lie in other areas.

Among the many factors that may impede congruence in decision making, we have found the area of financial transactions and the exchange of affection to be of special importance. Where intimacy and mutual affection are high, as they usually are in couples, failure to differentiate between these two dimensions may often lead to inappropriate decisions in both areas. For example, when affection is discussed between two people with unequal financial inputs, one may cajole the other into financial obligations by using the affective bond. Poor financial decisions may be made when affection confuses the issues, and, similarly, poor decisions in the domain of affection between two persons may originate in unequal financial needs. In fact, affective-emotional sensitivities are often used to pressure people into making certain financial decisions. A dictionary salesperson may appeal to one's sense of concern for loved ones, or may exploit one's sense of guilt. A case of hostage-taking illustrates the exploitation by one person of another's feelings, and especially fears, in order to obtain money or other advantages – in the confusion one may forget to double-check priorities before making a decision. Similarly, when at some point a person finds himself on loose ground in terms of the emotional-affective area of his life, he may become unsure of himself in the area of his financial decision making, and vice versa.

When all the above mentioned behaviors or attitudes accumulate and coalesce, they may easily point to a real sense of obstruction in the flow of the person's decisions, for example by interrupting the alternation between commitment and detachment. Such an interruption in the flow of decisions may manifest itself as clinging to a previous choice and failing to move away from it when the time has come to do so. The obstruction can also manifest itself as repeated failure to commit oneself by maintaining a state of non-commitment. But the result is that the backbone of one's choices – one's real values – never become quite clear. For some people this situation may lead to a state of boredom and, eventually, to a point where they feel quite unable to make balanced decisions for themselves. With the incapacity to make even minor decisions, one's behavior pattern may come close to an experience of depression.

*Choice and the Decision Flow*

When we look carefully at the decision process from a self-management perspective, a number of key reference points can be distinguished. If we had to draw a map of a person's decision flow, these reference points would be like beacons that could help determine the degree to which the flow is optimal, and point to the nature of difficulties when they arise. These reference points are:
- gestation and need,
- desire (will),
- direction (orientation),
- openness (information),
- choices (options),
- decision (values), and finally
- action.

When the decision process is fluid, we can expect a person to move fairly smoothly in and out of these reference points.

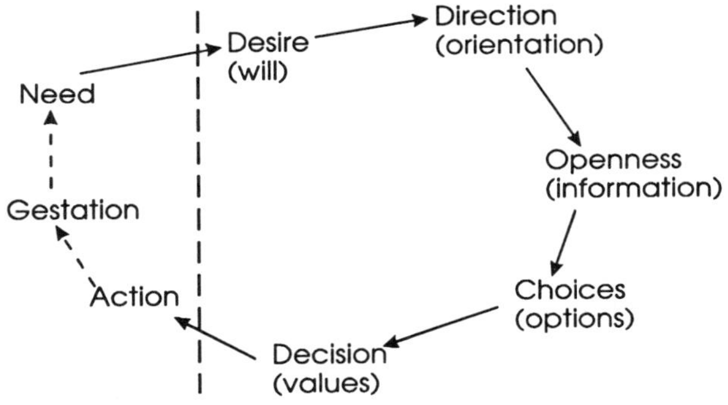


Chart 3. A person's decision flow.

This model assumes that one's decision process evolves from one's needs. We want to define needs in a very large sense here, not only in terms of basic biological or psychological needs, but also in terms of higher-order needs, for example, those related to a person's "life project." Needs vary in time and space, and from one person to another. They are also influenced by the general culture as well as the specific organizational culture. They oscillate continuously between basic physical and diverse higher order needs. Needs generally arise out of a period of gestation, a development period during which one reviews the results or implications of one's actions, finds ways to improve them, and develops new scenarios. Gestation prepares the way for new decision and action cycles. When focused needs are backed by will, they become desires. Desire then refers to the active motivation to work toward personal need fulfillment, and provides a sense of direction. Without the awareness of desire, it is difficult to imagine how one would know in what direction to proceed in carrying out one's decisions and actions. Once identified, direction requires the next stage: openness. Openness refers to the attitude of receptiveness to, and active seeking of, information. It is the bridge between one's sense of direction and the awareness of choices. Choices refer to the identification of the concrete options that would permit one to respond to needs and desires. In turn, choices call for a decision based on values, in order to cut through the multiplicity of options, and to prepare the way for the action flow.

It is important to note that, in an organizational context, a person's decision process can be blocked at any point. For example, the needs may be present but the person unaware of them, and therefore unable to recognize the desire to fulfill them. In turn, one may be aware of the desire to go in a certain direction, but unable to transcend the limitations of cultural programming or other barriers. The same reasons may prevent one from identifying a sense of direction corresponding to one's desires. The appropriation process may be too cluttered or too diversified, and may prevent openness to the information that really matters to the person. As a result, he may not have enough clues to identify the real choices that are available. In an organization, a person may find himself feeling that he has "not much choice" and may consequently need and seek direction from someone else. Very often it is not so much a matter of having choices or not having choices, but rather a matter of finding ways in which to channel one's choices into a direction aligned with one's desires. Once a person has identified choices, he may find it difficult to sift through them and decide on an option.

Finally, one of the key stopovers on the road to a fluid decision process is the gestation period. Many entrepreneurial endeavors turn into failures because the person has not taken sufficient time to think through the project. Also, by putting constant pressure on people to produce and be creative, a manager may unknowingly force people to figuratively abort or "give birth" to a "premature child," in the form of low quality products and services. The product of such inflexible pressure may be like a weak child for the rest of "its life," and may predetermine an unsuccessful conclusion to the business, the research and development project, or simply the intended contribution of the employee.

The following are a few notes with respect to the above-mentioned model of choices and the decision flow. We discuss successively (1) the role of cultural and other programming; (2) the role of defense mechanisms in the decision flow; (3) reactive and proactive movements in the decision flow; (4) the role of experienced freedom; and (5) freedom, choices, and another look at job satisfaction and motivation in organizations.

(1) *The role of cultural and other programming.* Programming refers to the thinking patterns or beliefs that have taken hold in our minds. Most of the time they are remnants of the influences other people have exercised over us, especially at moments when we were most vulnerable to such influences – in childhood or during fragile periods of change. Patterns or beliefs originate in undefined cultural influences, we call them cultural programming. An example would be the beliefs we adopted as the result of exposure to the dominant religion in the country where we were born or raised. Patterns or beliefs can also originate in the influence of a person we experienced as having authority over us. These occur when, for example, a set of norms and prescriptions become part of our system, not because we choose to adhere to them but because we are consistently penalized for daring to resist them.

Programming, or the fixation of thinking patterns or beliefs, may also originate in oversimplified reasoning. For example, due to a single experience that occurred in specific circumstances, we may proceed with theoretical deductions or generalizations, which we have not verified or otherwise analyzed. Consequently, the experience has been prematurely generalized, as in the formation of prejudices.

Wherever programmed beliefs find their origin, the fact is that they may severely limit the flow of a person's decision process – they may block the awareness of needs, they may even clog desire, limit direction, lead to a closed rather than open attitude to available information, restrain choices, lead to decisions based on unclear values and, in the end, cause actions that one may regret. By feeding on fear and on the uncertainty that surrounds us, programming limits the choices we perceive and may considerably hamper the fluidity of the decision process. Thus, whereas choices and decisions are mostly a conscious process, programming usually operates without our being aware of its influence.

From the viewpoint of self management, the most important consequence of any kind of programming is that it consists of patterns and beliefs that, completely outside of our awareness, regulate our behavior in such a way that we follow programmed patterns. Hence, our actions are not the outcome of conscious choices and of a deliberate decision process. Dim awareness of the decision flow often translates consciously as a sense of helplessness or powerlessness, or the experience of having "no choice" - being trapped or imprisoned with no way out. It is not difficult to imagine that despair and depression are only a few more blocks down the road, or that one can completely resign oneself and even transmit the programming to others in the form of imposed rules, expectations, and the like.

In the context of the organizations to which we belong, the same phenomenon of programming occurs with respect to the organizational culture, the assumptions that dominate the organizational value system, and the organization's communication patterns. When asked, many of us will probably confirm that we perceive certain choices in the ways we relate to colleagues, supervisors, and so on. But in daily routines, we often find ourselves caught up precisely in those programmed patterns that produce the sensation that there is "no way out." Consequently, questions may arise. What does it take to see choices where we saw none before? And, when we see our choices, what does it take to go through the process of decision making and plot the next turns in our action flow?

It is plausible that whatever has been programmed can be deprogrammed or reprogrammed. In this respect, mental hygiene can in many ways be remarkably similar to physical hygiene. For example, if one wants to restore the flow of a clogged-up water pipe one must first find out exactly where the obstruction is located. To locate the obstruction, some preliminary work is necessary. The work to be done can be characterized as one of analysis and hypothesis testing in order to create understanding. The same kind of work is useful to restore mental hygiene, as in the case where a decision process is clogged. What can prevent us from doing this work of analysis and understanding? We may have the same kind of reactions as in the physical example. We may stall for time, delay our investigation of the problem, hoping that it will go away; we may try to find a shortcut – a temporary remedy. When these defensive reactions become a habit, we unknowingly program our own defense mechanisms. They then become a programmed habit of refusing to be aware of, and neglecting to investigate, certain disturbances in the flow. Defense mechanisms are a special case of programming. They can play a role in our perceptions of choice and the decision flow and notably in our perceptions of choice.

(2) *The role of defense mechanisms in the decision flow.* The purpose of most defense mechanisms is to keep awareness dim – through denying that one is fearful, justifying the fact that one could not make an appointment because of another priority, projecting onto others certain attitudes that one is afraid of recognizing in oneself, etc. By keeping awareness dim, these defense mechanisms may limit the perception we have of our choices, not only in terms of dealing with others but also in terms of our own priorities, our desires, and the information we have available to us.

When choices are avoided by means of a defense mechanism such as projection, the person may then recognize many choices for other people but may behave as if he himself has none. Alternatively, he may find in a significant other, such as a supervisor, the reflection of his own choice-limiting normative attitude and then blame the other person for his failure to find worthwhile options to consider. As a practical consequence, the more a person avoids dealing with the issue of his own choices, the more direction he will usually need in the organizations and groups of which he is a member. Moreover, defense mechanisms often combine with, and reinforce, the effects of cultural programming. For example, a person may feel fearful and unworthy but deny these feelings. As a predictable result of this denial he will not seek a remedy on his own. Instead, as a compensation for these feelings, and to restore some kind of equilibrium for himself, he may very well boast about his knowledge and power when in the company of other people, or may act as if he were knowledgeable and powerful. Alternatively, a person may feel angry and envious but deny having a problem with these feelings. Instead of seeking to release the emotions and restore harmony within himself, he may very well compensate by appearing overly nice and accommodating to people. In both examples, the defense mechanisms are protective of some status quo, but ultimately unhelpful in solving the problem. Just like physical reflexes of which we are unaware, defense mechanisms mostly operate outside of our awareness and are not an outcome of choice – they act like protective reflexes of the mind. As in the case of learned physical reflexes and habitual behavior patterns, any attempt to change the role of specific defense mechanisms demands becoming aware of the patterns, then experimenting with and getting accustomed to new patterns, and finally, making choices.

(3) *Reactive and proactive movements in the decision flow.* There are times when we clearly feel that we are moving forward in the decision flow – from gestation to need, from need to desire, from desire to direction, from direction to openness, from openness to choices, from choices to decision, and further from decisions on into the action flow. Thus, choices are based on receptiveness to an environment full of information; and, through a continuing chain of events, actions are connected to needs that have been felt and accepted as valuable. Typically, when the movement is clear, things seem to fall into place – we have identified our needs, we have done our homework, and solutions present themselves to us.

But there are also times when we feel that we are moving backward in the decision flow. In that case, we do not experience the possibility of choices and of personal decisions leading into the action flow. Rather, things present themselves to us as if the flow were reversed. Instead of moving forward toward decisions and actions, we can feel ourselves moving backward toward unfulfilled desire, and we end up with an acute feeling of need. In the absence of choices, the decision flow is short-circuited – unfulfilled needs then lead to rash and inappropriate actions, which inevitably leave the person with more unfulfilled needs and more unsolved problems. For example, in such a reactive mode a person may reject choices that others have tried to make for her, leaving herself with the task of working out choices of her own, which is not always easy. In this mode, a person may say to an authority figure: "I don't want to do what you want me to do!" And moments later she may be at a complete loss when the authority figure responds: "Well, what do you want to do?" Reactive movements in the decision flow may be unavoidable during certain periods, for example, after one has experienced a great loss such as rejection by a lover, lay-off from a job, or the end of a significant contract. After such an experience one may have to deal with feelings of frustration, resentment, or anger, and one may get caught up in the belief that there are no more choices to make. As one suppresses imagination and the awareness of one's desires, one may very well fail to find new directions or to be open to one's environment. One is then left with feelings of need, powerlessness and helplessness. When in such circumstances we still manage to express certain choices, they may lack clear direction or the force of intent. In the reactive movement, one becomes a generally passive agent, responding to one's experiences as to capricious life forces.

Both the forward and backward movements can get out of hand. When this happens in forward movement, one risks becoming hyperactive and fretful. When the backward movement gets out of hand, one risks ending up blaming the whole world for one's sorry situation. Cultural and other programming, including defense mechanisms, tend to keep one locked in a reactive mode, while a neglect of the affective aspects of life may keep one entrenched in the proactive mode. Rather than managing proactively or reactively, the self-management approach consists of managing a middle state in which forward and backward movements are handled with moderation and with measure, so as to keep them within bounds that one can still comprehend and enjoy.

How does one move from a reactive or excessively proactive mode to a self-managing mode? The question is an important one, for the mode one is in has an impact, not only on the quality of one's decisions and actions, but also on one's experience of them. Indeed, it is the difference between joy and laughter, and feeling bitter and sorry for oneself. It is not difficult to imagine consequences in the context of organizational relationships, and in the quality of one's contribution in the organization. How does one change from a mode in which one feels bitter and sorry for oneself to one in which one feels like a channel for joy? The question may well be rephrased as follows: how can one restore one's own sense of freedom?

(4) *The role of experienced freedom in the decision flow.* To see choices for oneself, one needs to experience a sense of freedom: freedom to be; freedom to explore; freedom to distinguish among, and to play with, options; and freedom to decide for oneself. One's sense of freedom may undergo pressure from inside or from outside oneself.

*In a decision process with others,* when one party freezes the process by limiting the options she is willing to consider, the other party's process may become frozen as a result. Consequently, one may lose one's own fluidity, even though temporarily, through others' inflexibility. To maintain freedom in a situation where decisions are made together with others, the decision-making must follow its own chemical process, unhampered by predetermined outcomes. It is also necessary to let the information flow freely, and to provide for the possibility of returning to the elements of desire and need. If need and desire can come into the flow unhindered, the group process will likely ripple along its way to an end product, such as a decision, that reflects true choices in harmony with real desires. We have often observed that the mere statement of personal needs by one or a few group members has given a realistic and unhabitual twist to an otherwise fragile group decision process. In a group situation one's freedom can be threatened by one's liability to give in to an overbearing colleague, but only to the extent that one is willing, or is unaware of it happening.

However, even if our colleagues are not overbearing, the tendency to surrender our freedom in a group situation is surprisingly real. Experiments in the field of social psychology and analyses of actual decision-making situations have revealed how easily people are persuaded to act in ways they do not really want to, and how vulnerable they can be to manipulation (Elliott Aronson, *The Social Animal;* Solomon Asch, *Social Psychology;* Stanley Milgram, *The Individual in a Social World;* Daniel D. Wheeler and Irving L. Janis, *A Practical Guide for Making Decisions*). While it is not always clear what factors combine to lead to this situation, it is plausible that our longing to be accepted as a member of a group plays a significant role in our giving up part of our freedom. If so, then the antidote would require a considerable degree of awareness of one's freedom and a solid grounding in oneself.

*In a personal decision situation,* one's freedom can be restricted by defense mechanisms; by cultural programming; and by introjected freedom-suppressors, which then produce guilt, fear, and, in the longer run, anxiety or depression. We have already mentioned the role of cultural programming and of defense mechanisms. As for introjected freedom-suppressors, they signify specific normative or feeling-toned statements, related to values, rules, do's and don'ts; but also to attitudes, feelings, and behavior patterns, which we have adopted from others indiscriminately. They can be compared to food presented to us perhaps with good intentions, but not necessarily acceptable to our own system. F. Perls maintains that introjections are like food swallowed and gulped down without being chewed; ingested outside our awareness, without our evaluation of what was nutritious and what was toxic. Being swallowed whole, outside our awareness, introjections result in behavior that has a driven, compulsive quality to it. Thus, they result in actions that are not an outcome of choice and, again, the person's decision flow is is short-circuited.

Such introjections may be provoked by the authoritarian behavior of significant others, but they can also follow from our desire to imitate others whom we admire. Many introjections have to do with the suppression of feelings – they follow admonitions of the type "don't cry," "don't feel," "don't be close," "don't express affection," "be cautious," "don't let anyone know that you are afraid." But they can also involve statements made by others about one's identity or about the nature of one's intentions, such as "you are ugly," "you are bad," "you'll never be somebody". They may directly induce a feeling of guilt, as in the statements "you should be nice to your parents," "be sure to make your organization proud of you." And they may even reach deeply into the individual's very career choices, as in "don't become a plumber," "choose a job that assures you a lot of money," "you should become a cancer researcher," "you should have a profession like your older brother." Whereas some of these messages may be appropriate in certain situations, when introjected they are torn out of context and become generalized into powerful, subconscious, decision-blocking factors

There is probably no general rule on how to counteract such behavior and decision-blocking elements, except for providing the opportunity to become aware of what was ingested and where, and to analyze what one wants to keep and what one wants to throw out. For example, work on an introjection such as "don't feel" or "don't express feelings" would require determining what one's objection is to the behavior – what would happen if one did feel or if one did show that one is angry, sad, or joyous? When one finds out what the consequences would be, one can then decide to keep the norm as a self-imposed choice or to let go of it. However, it should be pointed out that one of the less well-known forms of introjections is the nonverbal type. Non-verbal introjections are much more insidious and much more difficult to pinpoint and identify than verbal ones. They may involve all kinds of feelings and attitudes unknowingly adopted from our parents' behavior – nonverbal expressions, as well as general attitudes toward life. Frequently, we put them into practice without being aware of their origins. Indeed, they may originate with our parents, but they may also come from significant others with whom we have had, willingly or otherwise, close relationships. They may involve helpful qualities as much as self-destructive attitudes. Even if we succeed in figuring out where these introjections come from, we may find it difficult to eliminate them from our lives. For example, as we enter our forties, we may suddenly discover that we have many fears and anxieties, and be quite puzzled about what brought them on. On closer investigation, we may come to realize that one of our parents was a very fearful or anxious person. When at age forty we live in a close relationship with a person who has many fears, our sensitivity will probably allow us to feel this person's fears, but we will have more discrimination, in that we will likely be able to discern whether these fears are really our own, or whether they are being transmitted to us by the other person. We will also have more choices – will we allow the other's fears to affect us, or will we keep a certain distance from them and remain centered in ourselves? A vulnerable child will more easily introject the other's fear, taking it into his system, unprocessed, especially if he loves the other and needs his love, as in a parent-child relationship. As an adult, he may find that he has to "let go of" those introjections in order to become truly himself. In the example of fear that has just been mentioned, he will have to realize, "They were my parents' feelings, they are not mine."

The major blocking factor of introjections resides in their effect on choices. By recreating the kind of intimacy and vulnerability that made the introjection possible, by grasping the real and fantasized consequences of adopting or not adopting the introjected statement (feeling, attitude, behavior, etc.), one can reconnect with desires and needs, recreate one's own sense of direction, and restore the possibility of choice.

(5) *Freedom, choices, and another look at job satisfaction and motivation in organizations*. There is a definite relation between motivation on the job and job satisfaction, on the one hand, and the self-management processes, on the other hand. Much of the literature on job motivation and satisfaction takes it for granted that the organization's managers or the groups' leaders have to do certain things to motivate employees and group members, or to increase their satisfaction. Even if some of them recognize that motivation and satisfaction are very personal issues, the idea persists that it is a supervisor's responsibility to at least facilitate them. We have no quarrel with the possibility of a supervisor's facilitating or discouraging motivation for his personnel, or of narrowing or widening the distance employees perceive between their own expectations and the extent to which these can be satisfied in the organization. But in the light of the foregoing model of the decision flow, a person will be motivated mainly to the extent that she can express some inner, unsatisfied need to do this kind of work, or some desire to perform in this particular context – a desire to act within the framework of this organization, even if the need is as elementary as to feed her spouse and children. In the context of self management, the responsibility for such an expression will primarily have to be that of the person herself.

Moreover, if one considers the fact that dissatisfaction and demotivation may to a large extent be linked to the lack of experienced freedom and the lack of perceived choices on the part of the employee, and if one considers the fact that, in turn, these gaps prevent her from exercising her responsibility in improving the quality of her work life, then the role of the employee as well as that of the supervisor take on a different color. Indeed, the sense of dissatisfaction, and of demotivation as well, can then be seen as a signal that something is going awry for the person – that some of her natural movement has come to a standstill, and that some vital needs are not being processed adequately. Instead of resorting to easy solutions, which may provide only temporary relief, it then makes sense for her to try to get to the real point of what is blocking the flow of the decision process. From the viewpoint of the employee, it would involve finding out what skills would permit her to go more resolutely in the direction of what she wants and to then nurture this process. From the viewpoint of the supervisor, the question, "How can I motivate my employees?" would perhaps be better put somewhat like this, "What skills and attitudes do I need in order to come through as supportive in a context where an employee is selling herself short in the work environment ?" And, as a complementary question, "How can I help employees to free their own decision process and to make choices that are nurturing to themselves?" Rather than being burdened with the projected obligation to motivate her employees, a professional manager can then commit herself to helping people become aware of and unfold their own choices. The result of such an attitude will likely be that employees move from a deficiency-motivated need to control others and limit themselves, together with an exaggerated need for predictability and security, to a more realistic, opportunity-motivated desire to make a worthwhile and mutually satisfying contribution to the organization.

There is another point worth mentioning. Sometimes we have asked people the question, "What does it take for you to be really satisfied or motivated to work in this organization?" (Note that we intentionally blur the possible theoretical differences here between satisfaction and motivation). Often the answers include some form of the following statement, "I feel satisfied (or motivated) when I can accomplish objectives." But the real issue of satisfaction or motivation often goes much further than these verbal formulations. When pushed to clarify what they really mean, most people affirm that in order to be satisfied or motivated, their life has to be "on track"; and they need to experience that feeling of being on track in their job as well. *From the self-management perspective, then, a sense of fulfillment is more fundamental than either satisfaction or motivation, as it touches and implicates the whole person, rather than a partial aspect, such as: material comfort.* A sense of fulfillment is also more closely related to the choices one exercises in the function of one's life path and, thus, carries a meaning that is wider than the short-term accomplishment of objectives. The sense of failure that some people experience with respect to their life path, the difficulties and complexities they face in choosing careers and in making career decisions and, finally, the precariousness of the directions we often hesitatingly set for ourselves (and the questions they provoke, such as for how long will this be "right choice") all point to the importance of the decision process.

## *Managing the Decision Process in Organizations*

The ideas expressed in the above sections highlight the importance, for decision process management, of a candid confrontation between the values expressed in a particular organizational culture on the one hand, and value-inspired personal priorities, on the other. Where the dominant values in an organization are significantly different from our own, we may then begin to behave as if our decision flow were being dammed up. The discrepancy may not only affect the flow of decisions that we make on behalf of and in the interest of the organization we work for, but also our own personal decision flow.

However, a number of other factors besides the discrepancies in values demand our attention. First of all, management of the decision process requires us to take into account many circumstances, personal as well as environmental and organizational, potentially affecting the flow of our decisions. Second, the impact of these circumstances on our decision flow can be anywhere from constructive and uplifting to damaging and downright depressing. A negative influence does not necessarily mean we will make poor decisions, but it can surely interrupt the flow. As some of the personal circumstances interfering with our decisions have been dealt with in the previous section, we will concentrate here on the impact of incidents related to organizational conditions.

Some of the organizational contexts that people have reported to be damaging to their decision process are the following:

1] Lack of honest contact with one's immediate supervisor. As one person put it: "*It was the first time my colleagues and I had met our new boss. He started by putting down one of my colleagues to the point where, out of anger and humiliation, my colleague left the room. Hours later, he handed in his resignation. I could not help feeling that he had fallen into a trap and that he needlessly hurt himself by brandishing his own resignation as a means to protest what he undoubtedly perceived as unjust treatment. The boss in question couldn't care less.*" Poor contact makes for poor support. By contrast, a minimum of support can go a long way toward bringing about a more focused decision process.

2] An inflexible attitude on the part of work colleagues engaged in the same decision process. One top management employee reported this incident: "*I wanted to create a sense of collaboration with my new assistant and I asked him to participate actively in my decision process. Soon I felt he had very rigid and preconceived ideas on how the project should be run, and we very quickly came to the point where no exchange of ideas or mutual testing of hypotheses was possible. The element of playing with possibilities in order to see which ones would be more useful than others, was completely out of the question. I had the choice between becoming totally depressed and unable to work, or telling him in no uncertain terms that his attitude was plainly unhelpful. Right there, I lost a potentially valuable collaborator, not because of his lack of intelligence but because he just refused to give possibilities a chance. His attitude was not only damaging to the decision task at hand; by his lack of support he nearly wrecked havoc with my own decision process as well!*"

3] Double binds in communication. The following incident offers an example: "*When I took this job my boss told me the decisions in a certain area were mine and that he also expected from me strong proposals for change. In the months following his statement, I made decisions and proposed directions for action, but soon I began to see a pattern in his continuous shoving aside of my initiatives. Instead of listening to what I had to say he practically ignored me and pushed me in directions that he was used to. At first, his frequent rebuffs puzzled me. Then they paralyzed my decision making more and more as I saw that in reality there were not so many decisions for me to make or new initiatives to propose. In the end he had created such a double bind in his communication patterns not only with me but also with his own superiors that he had to step aside and move to another position. His own double bind had become untenable for himself!*" Double binds paralyze the flow of decisions by introducing two or more frames of reference for decision making, both or all of which are contradictory.

In contrast, the following are a sample of organizational factors that various people have reported as having an uplifting and constructive impact on their experienced ability to make choices at appropriate times and places:

1] Supportive power centers. "*We all know that in any organization there are power centers, people wielding power. Nothing is more facilitative for anyone's decision flow than a supportive power center. When the power center is punitive and authoritarian, decisions are duplicate copies of what is expected, that is, they are not decisions at all as there was no ambiguity or choice to begin with. But when the center listens to the needs of people, bases its own decisions on those very needs and, in addition, encourages people to go in the direction of their needs, then the decision process is open and people can learn from their mistakes.*"

2] Clarity as to motivations, interests, available information, and a sense of mutual trust. As one manager put it: "*Nothing's more responsible for our successful decisions over the years than the fact that we have come to know what others really want. Nothing remains hidden. No grudges, no secret deals ...* "

3] Honest communication from the "guts" with work colleagues. One person added: "*Decisions really must come from the heart, not from the head. When my heart is at peace, decisions somehow seem to come more easily. When my heart is in turmoil decisions are difficult. I found that it is very important for me that someone makes me feel he is supportive of me, not against me. That feeling liberates my decision making considerably, even in the work place.*"

The above situations are certainly not an exhaustive list, but they do serve as illustrations of organizational factors involved in the ups and downs of a person's decision process.

Whereas organizational factors surely influence a person's decisions, the reverse is also true – a person's decisions can affect others in significant ways, both personally and as a group. This fact opens up the important areas of ethical behavior, of responsible action and, not the least, of professional competence. Without going into details on these issues, it is useful to raise some questions at this point. How do we come to grips with the many ways our decisions affect others? If we know our decisions affect others in significant ways, how do we deal with this fact? What do we learn from it? What does professional competence mean in our line of work?

While it is true that our immediate environment, in terms of people at the work place or in the family, can influence our decision flow and that we, in turn, can have an impact on others, the thrust of the self-management approach is that we have to take care of ourselves. This caretaking requires more of a long-term vision than a short-term one. In addition, optimal decisions encompass a wider perspective than merely maximizing gains and minimizing losses. The following are a few attitudes and abilities we have found useful for a person to cultivate if he is to manage and take care of the flow of his decision process:

1] the notion of individual freedom;
2] the ability to cut through ambiguities;
3] the ability to access information and to research issues;
4] the capacity to focus;
5] the permission to change focus and direction when the need is there to do so, and
6] the ability to access intuitive/subconscious processes.

First and foremost, managing the decision flow is facilitated when one keeps open the possibility of committing oneself to options or of moving away from them – in other words, when one realizes that one is a free person. To safeguard one's freedom to be committed and to disengage oneself in organizational contexts probably also involves steering clear of circumstances or individuals who would have a negative impact on one's freedom. This entails, in the first place, physical freedom, but also freedom in terms of other, nonphysical choices. With respect to the possible discrepancies between organizational and personal values, freedom can only come from a thorough understanding of both value systems. Testing the organizational value system often requires the questioning of ready-made solutions, at the risk of having others perceive one as making mistakes. Furthermore, developing a greater sensitivity to one's own priorities may demand thrusting deeply into the core of conflicting values and facing up to the possible gap between what is personal and what is organizational.

Individual freedom also relates to the notion of time. Organizations generally foster a kind of myopia with respect to controls over employees' time. How many middle level managers go to great lengths to make decisions that tend to control the time of co-workers without any proven benefit to themselves or to the organization? They think of time as a more or less linear concept, as if all of its subdivisions had the same richness, the same intensity, the same potential in terms of productivity. Most people want to control their own time to a reasonable extent, and there is no reason to believe that their doing so interferes with the optimal functioning of any organization, or that it would interfere with adequate coordination of tasks. In fact, the application of flexible work hours is surely a realistic response to this need.

Second, healthy management of the decision flow is facilitated *by cultivating the ability to cut through the ambiguities when the time is appropriate to do so.* This holds for commitment, as in investing in one option or another, as well as for moving away from options. Not unlike cutting the umbilical cord, this is the ability to cut the link with the gestation period before a decision is made. In other words, it is cutting the link with the unsettling state that is needed while one is gathering information and support. At the same time a sufficient degree of tolerance of ambiguity is called for, the benefits of which may include the ability to read valuable information provided by the subconscious mind. Decisiveness is certainly not called for when one feels vulnerable or excessively tired, or while one is under the influence of someone else's counsel. Indeed, these are all circumstances where one has insufficient contact with one's own resources and where one may not be able to connect with one's subconscious mind. In a wider sense, then, cultivating the ability to cut through ambiguities also involves coming to grips with one's own fears.

Third, managing the decision flow is facilitated by taking care of one's *ability to access information and to undertake whatever research is necessary* in order to arrive at a satisfactory decision. This ability further implies creating for oneself those circumstances of learning which one feels are most appropriate in one's particular context.

Fourth, *cultivating the capacity to focus* facilitates healthy management of the decision flow. This ability includes recognizing different levels of decision making. For example, for the installation of ceramic tiles in a bathroom, one level of decision making involves technical decisions. Another level involves the design of the bathroom, the choice of tiles, their color, the surfaces that need to be covered, and so on. It is important for a contractor not to confuse these different levels of decision making – some decisions may belong more to his client than to himself, while others clearly are his own. It seems important that a person be able to focus on his particular level of decision making and not get unduly involved in the decisions others are entitled to make for themselves. Within the same context, it is not uncommon for organizations to see the number of decisions made within a certain time frame as a measure of performance, without taking into account their relative impact in the long run. It is often more rewarding to make fewer decisions of which have been thoroughly checked than to blindly multiply their number.

The fifth attitude facilitating the decision process is the *permission to change focus and direction* when there is need to do so. Alternation between commitment and moving away also requires that one recognize the possibility of reversing previous decisions. The need to do this often occurs in response to the discovery of new information that leads to a new evaluation of choices and preferences. To reverse a decision may make a lot of sense to someone, even though doing so may temporarily throw his work colleagues or even his friends off balance. In turn, the permission to change focus and direction may necessitate the person's coming to terms with feelings such as guilt, or intimidation by perceived pressures for group conformity.

Finally, the sixth facilitating factor is *to cultivate the ability to access subconscious mind processes through an intuitive approach*. This raises the question of what intuition really is and how it helps a person to access the subconscious mind. Much has been said and written about both subjects; we want to talk only from our own experience. One person communicated his thoughts on the theme in this way: "*How many times do we say: I should have followed my first idea. The first idea is usually intuitive, before I have time to really reflect and ponder. Then I am tempted to bring in rational thought, and to modify my initial response. I believe that the education we have all received encourages us to do so, as we have learned to be analytical. However, when I go through this process I often realize later that I have to come back to my first idea because in the process of analyzing I have left out crucial variables. These are variables that I cannot pinpoint clearly at the time of my decision. My first choice, the intuitive one, often reveals itself to be more harmonious, in the sense that it takes into account my whole person, not just the interiorized obligations, the wishful thinking, etc.*" Intuitively, we can grasp many more things than we are consciously aware of. Intuition is at once an art and an ability – it involves seeing and retrieving relations between things, whether from an external or internal perspective, without necessarily being aware of what causes them. We can assume that our subconscious mind registers everything we have seen, felt, feared, and done at one point or another, even things we may have forgotten. The intuitive approach not only allows us to tap into these subconscious memories, but also to see relations between them.

In a very broad sense intuition refers to the relation between the conscious mind and the subconscious. Intuition also underlies the capacity to fall back on one's own resources when one finds oneself in a situation demanding resolution and when one has no model, no standard way to act. Two of the most important types of decisions that most of us have to make in life are probably: (1) *those in which our material condition is at stake*, as when we make an important investment decision that may imperil all our material resources, or when we emigrate to another country with all our belongings, and (2) *those in which we put our emotional well-being on the line,* such as when we decide to separate from a person with whom we have lived for a long time or when we decide to begin an intimate relationship. Those decisions have to be "right," as they involve all our resources. To make those kinds of decisions we must tap into the subconscious mind and let intuitive processes play a significant role. One simply cannot restrict the decision making process to rational elements since it is *one's whole being that is involved.* One has no choice but to tap into every resource available.

One of the apparent paradoxes with intuition is that it seems to function better in direct proportion to the amount of work that a person has already done consciously. In other words, the more a person has worked on a subject of interest through all the means available - emotionally, through actions, by deductive and inductive thought processes, by abstraction and conceptualization, by relationships - the better he will be equipped to let intuition do its work. The amount of information we all gather is phenomenal and most of it becomes or remains subconscious until the moment where our intuition retrieves it, links it up with other bits of information, and hopefully uses it to guide us toward "the right choice." According to Freud, we can tap into the subconscious mind by means of dreams, lapses of speech, etc. Those phenomena show glimpses of the subconscious mind, as they can bypass the wall of defense mechanisms that we tend to construct in order to protect ourselves. The defense mechanisms we build may very well be the most formidable obstacle against accessing our intuitive processes and, through them, our wholeness. However, there are other ways to access our subconscious mind and bypass the defense mechanisms. One of them is to get to know oneself so well as to be able to do without them, for example through work in group sessions. One group leader had this to say: "*When I am with a group for a prolonged period of time, there is a moment when participants get tired, not only physically, but also psychologically. It is then that real feelings are gradually being expressed. People drop their natural defenses. They kind of give up on all the pretense and all the make-believe that they have learned to use in everyday life to protect themselves against threatening information from inside or from outside. When they let go of the defenses they literally let go of all the intellectual, emotional and social trappings, and they get psychologically naked and real. At such moments, intuition becomes the rule and the subconscious and conscious minds become one. It is also the moment where I, as a group facilitator, can be myself as the projections of expertise make way for humanness and friendship. I suppose that, at moments like that a great number of options may surface with respect to one's life; sometimes even leading to a redirection of one's energies.*"

It appears that, in general, an intuitive approach is facilitated by an attitude of playful distance with respect to experienced reality, an attitude that does not take the events of life too seriously. Defense mechanisms may also be less operative in such a context. It allows one to be less fixed in one's own positions, as one becomes able to view situations differently without losing a sense of basic security and self-confidence. In contrast, being "uptight" or anxious, or feeling threatened by expected gloomy consequences, precludes this healthy "distance" from events. Such an attitude may constitute a serious obstacle to trusting one's intuition, and thus to accessing subconscious processes through an intuitive approach.

"Science and art, cause and effect, plans and operations, means and ends all merge in the instant of the act."

Ralph G. H. Siu

Chapter II

# Self Management of the Action Process

## *The Action Process Defined*

This process consists of the continuous flow of actions. The flow is characterized by phases of intense activity and low activity, alternating in a relatively stable and rhythmic sequence. In the movement of this process, the feedback from trial actions, errors as well as successes, generally provides the clearest guidelines for correcting and adapting our actions in order to implement intentions successfully. The outcome of this dynamic process is the concrete realization of a person's projects.

The action process does not refer solely to the state of being active, nor does it refer merely to the best possible implementation of a previously established plan of action, or to the most perfect application of a set of rules and procedures. Rather, this process refers to the dynamic, and to a large extent self-correcting, implementation of decisions. While the decision process allows for considerable freedom in imagining possible scenarios for action and in effecting delays in the feedback of results, the action process defines the choice and makes the consequences of the choice very explicit to oneself and to others.

Once the action is accomplished, the time lag between the consideration of possibilities and the feedback from results is narrowed considerably. In addition, through this process one seeks an optimal balance, not only with respect to actions on the job but also by incorporating realizations in different aspects of one's life.

With respect to the concrete realization of a person's projects, the action process highlights the importance of internal criteria for successful action, alongside the more external criteria that might be used, for example, in performance evaluations of employees. While it is true that many organizations insist on such external criteria, it may become increasingly difficult for people to manage themselves adequately, as whole persons, should they base their actions solely on these external criteria. For example, a decision not to act after a considerable amount of time has been invested in a particular project may still signify action according to one's internal criteria, even though the organization's cultural context may lead an employer to interpret this process as if nothing had been accomplished. According to a self-management approach, then, merely counting the number of actions without also counting the number of non-actions based on a committed decision process, would constitute a lopsided evaluation of performance. The criteria used to evaluate the flow of the action process will necessarily have more qualitative and exploratory ingredients than those we are accustomed to seeing in many organizations. More will be said on this subject in Chapter Three. Furthermore, the rhythmic character of the action flow points to a need to consider the short term and the long term, as well as time lags, in evaluation of the action process.

When the movement in the action process fails to be alternating and self-corrective, behavior tends to become locked into an automatic mode in which a person's projects lose their dynamic character. Failure to manage the time lags involved in the action process, or failure to differentiate between the short-term and long-term implications of actions, further compounds the difficulties encountered in this mode. For example, when people find that they are stuck in a situation of need with respect to certain resources, we may observe a difficulty with this self-regulating process and with thinking beyond short-term needs for survival. In that case, actions may become automatic, geared toward the immediate satisfaction of urgent needs – there is no time to save energy for later, or, for example, to differentiate between short-term intentions to obtain food and shelter and long-term intentions, for example, to study or to change jobs. In the same vein, a feeling of anxiety is very much a part of the vagaries of the action process. It may signal the difficulties a person experiences in translating and expressing his deepest intentions into actions, whether of a short-term or long-term nature.

In short, the action process can be seen as an alternation between taking the initiative and resting, as a practical exploration of an extended range of possibilities, in order to find actions that adequately express one's personal priorities. The following section addresses some of the more personal and qualitative aspects of this process.

### *Specific Characteristics of the Action Process*

The action process is especially important as a road to concrete validation of decisions, whatever their level of complexity or sophistication.

While decisions happen in the mind, and away from the theater of concrete judgments, actions are tangible expressions that can be observed and evaluated by oneself as well as by others. There is one caveat - actions are tangible, but their meaning, or the way in which they are linked to our own intentions or to our environment, is not always transparent, either to ourselves or to others.

Whatever the circumstances and the sources of a person's actions, they are almost always a vital ingredient of the other processes as well one's appropriations, exchanges with others (relation process), and decisions. The following are a few observations from our own experiences pertaining to the flow of the action process. These observations, given below in an arbitrary order, by no means constitute an exhaustive list of the characteristics of this process.

(1) As actions are the concrete gestures that take place in a specific space and time configuration, this process more than any other raises the question of timing. Besides respect for the natural cycles of relatively intense and relatively low activity,timing above all refers to the desirability of intervening at the right time and at the right place, in such a way that one's intentions are implemented in an optimal manner for everyone concerned. The timing of actions brings into focus the uniqueness of every individual actor. However, it also reminds us that the particular theatre in which our actions take place encompasses many variables over which we may have little personal control, such as: the quality of the organizational environment, the available technology, the particular dynamics of our work team or supervisor-employee relationships, the market conditions under which the organization operates, and so on. Despite all these variables which we experience as uncontrollable, good timing is still very often a highly personal matter, especially because timing summons our personal resources. Consequently, considerable discernment is required in assessing the pertinence of someone else's interferences in one's own timing.

(2) In an organizational context, actions are often connected to the notion of efficiency. To be efficient is then often interpreted as acting swiftly; and the measure of one's efficiency easily becomes simplified as the number of actions a person can carry out in a given time frame. Proverbial phrases such as "time is money" or "not wasting time" are often implicit in the organizational value system, and designate a

linear concept of time. In effect, one is saying: "Do not let time pass by, for we would lose opportunities for action. However, the importance of timing in the flow of a person's action process reveals a problem with this linear concept. The problem can be formulated as follows – the necessity of ensuring that actions will be focalized in the proper time span is often incompatible with the need to translate as many decisions as possible into actions within this same time frame. It appears that the notion of efficiency needs refinement, in that it may be appropriate to temporarily keep some distance (to back off) from actions, and to delay implementation, if doing so warrants a better impact. When efficiency encompasses the need for timing, then the important criterion is not the number of decisions implemented at random, but the quality of decisions implemented at the time and place optimally conducive to the realization of one's intentions.

(3) To act is also to interact with others. Consequently, not only do our actions invite feedback from others who find themselves affected by them, but we also are exposed to our own reality in relation to others. As well, we must bear in mind that others may interpret our actions in many ways, and, in particular, that the feedback we receive does not always reflect a reaction to our true intentions.

In the organizational context, actions tend to generate evaluations in the form of approval or disapproval by others. Often, one's actions also form the basis of more formal evaluations of work. Ideally, those evaluations become part of a more creative process of mutual feedback in which personally satisfying problem-solving processes have a chance to unfold. But this is not always the case. The realization that one is being judged on the basis of one's actions makes it difficult to manage one's social position so there is a satisfactory equilibrium between pleasing powerful others in the organization, and acting according to one's own priorities. If one cannot manage this kind of equilibrium, mutual evaluations can give rise to apparent interpersonal conflicts and, in extreme cases, may compromise one's membership in the organization.

Whenever actions are used as a formal criterion in employee evaluations, one would do well to bear in mind that they are always space and time specific, that a person's actions are interrelated with his past and future aspirations, and with the actions of colleagues and other organizational members. Thus, from a self-management perspective, actions are never isolated events. Consequently, their evaluation calls for care and sensitivity, as well as circumspection with regard to subtle differences and unique circumstances. This also includes one's own evaluations of one's actions. By exaggerating or minimizing their importance and effectiveness one may blow up or diminish one's self-esteem, and cultivate unrealistic expectations with respect to further implementations.

(4) Ideally, a person's actions are closely linked with her intentions and objectives and, on a more practical level with her needs and desires. The flow of actions can be seen as a succession of smaller scale implementations that are all connected to her life project. Despite the fact that a person's real objectives are always very individual, she functions in the context of an organization that can be expected to ask her to act on its behalf or, at least, to act "for the good of the organization." It may be more or less difficult for a person to find a satisfactory equilibrium between acting to implement her organization's objectives and implementing her own at the same time. This raises the question: What does it take to be able to act as a whole person in an organization?

The answer to this question must take into account the fact that much of the work in an organization tends to be programmed. For example, the work of a secretary may consist mainly of typing; the work of an information systems analyst consists of writing computer programs. However, from the perspective of self management, the action process reaches further than the apparently programmed aspects of such work. To be able to work as a whole person presupposes that personal and organizational objectives can overlap to a reasonable extent. Programmed tasks are also one of the many options that are subject to personal needs and preferences.

The link between actions and objectives further raises questions about what constitutes an adequate match between person and task. It seems fairly obvious that nobody can be expected to act with long-term efficiency in a type of work he dislikes, whether he accomplishes that work of his own volition or whether supervisors ask him to do it. If he feels pressured, from inside himself or from outside, to do such work, he will often resort, consciously or unconsciously, to techniques such as passive resistance. Passive resistance refers to a variety of actions taken to avoid doing the work one feels obliged to do. More importantly however, it signals the conflict between those actions the person feels obliged to perform in the organizational context and those which he knows he is able to perform with efficiency and enthusiasm. Instead of applying passive resistance to his work, he may also go through the motions without really believing in his actions. However, even these responses will not prevent him from feeling the unsatisfied longing for his own acts, and to delay them may hurt him emotionally and even physically in the long run.

Organizational settings are often not conducive to the kinds of spontaneous work design that seem to be necessary for balanced self management and optimal performance. Most of the time, one's first requirement is to be able to appropriate the organizational environment adequately, in both its physical and social aspects, and to make a personal imprint on the way one functions.

(5) As actions are the ultimate confrontation with physical and social realities, they are often experienced as entailing risks. Risks refer to the possibility of things happening that one does not really want to happen or that are unpleasant. Most of the time these happenings can not be foreseen or, at any rate, the extent of their impact is difficult to estimate in advance.

The risks one perceives may involve monetary issues, but also one's self-esteem, emotional equilibrium, or relations with significant others. They may apply to the feed-back which one knows will become visible only in the movement stirred by the action; or they may apply to unforeseen dangers, in the sense of situations that thwart the expected implementation of one's intentions. The risks one perceives may also be related to the anticipation of the disappointment that would result if the action appeared to stop short of materializing the objective one had in mind, whether because of one's own miscalculations or due to environmental factors.

Perceived risks are mostly related to one's capacity for foresight and to one's susceptibility to fear. Indeed, some people will perceive risks where others perceive none, simply because the latter may know more, see farther ahead, or have more experience in the area. Similarly, some people are more prone to fear and stagefright than others. In that sense, the often-heard admonition "If you want to be successful you have to take risks" becomes less useful than one that might go like this, "If you act, be sure to learn about the results of your actions."

Perhaps one of the most important perceived risks in acting involves confronting the feelings and emotions that the actions themselves, as well as their results, generate in oneself. Indeed, many times we do not know whether we will like what we see or feel, whether we will be able to cope with those feelings and emotions and, most of all, whether we are sufficiently equipped and sure of ourselves as to be able to learn from them.

From the viewpoint of self management, mastering risks involves, above all, learning from one's actions while not overextending oneself or unduly dissipating one's energies. Consequently, the formal analysis of risks may be a useful exercise for the pragmatic purposes of evaluating one's capacity and developing one's resources, but it will likely be insufficient to alleviate fears about unknown dangers. The more one knows what is pertinent to a particular action and what is not, and what information is needed, the less the concept of risk becomes useful. From the viewpoint of self management, the notion of "taking risks" is neither particularly meaningful nor especially helpful, and certainly it will not automatically lead to success. In contrast, integrating the knowledge pertinent to a particular action allows one to consciously adapt the action to its unique environment in time and space, in an optimal manner.

(6) There is a definite link between the flow of a person's actions and his desire to learn. Not only can actions facilitate a person's learning, but they also seem to be facilitated by this very desire to learn. In the aftermath of an action, even if it did not work out according to our expectations, how many times have we not heard ourselves say that we have "learned something from this." Actions that are repetitive, or that we experience as boring and devoid of challenge, are also those from which we no longer learn.

By testing the limits of our capabilities, we gradually develop a vision of our potential in addition to a sense of security and confidence. In fact, the combined results of learning about the actions themselves and of accumulating certainty-in-process and self-confidence with respect to a particular area, is crucial in the work of building competence and expertise. In the end, failing to act may even reduce one's personal life project to a mere accumulation of hypothetical questions with uncertain answers. Even if one's life project is subconscious, its repeated testing in action will eventually make it visible and clear, and one can contemplate its path. It would seem that many people are capable of acting much more powerfully in the direction of their potentials than they actually do.

(7) In general, when a person's action process functions in an optimal manner, one could expect that most of the following conditions would sooner or later manifest themselves:

- The experience of actions in one's life span provides the basis from which to attain a reasonable amount of insight and confidence to go on, in the sense that a core equilibrium can be recognized from which one's actions can flow forth.
- There will be a certain concordance between the intensity of one's actions and the demands of the situations in which they take place. This characteristic refers not only to good timing but also to the recognition that one's actions may have different qualities depending on one's position in one's own life cycle. When criteria for evaluation of our actions are idiosyncratic (for example, when they are personal), we become more tolerant and capable of change and adaptation.
- Whatever the phase in his life cycle, the individual always has a potential project. He exercises a certain amount of control over his own destiny in that he can identify the projects he is interested in and willing to work for. In contrast, an attitude of mere survival would be characterized by his lacking a project of his own; a tendency to merely react to the demands of others, so as to please them; not knowing what he wants next; and feeling imprisoned by fears.
- The actions he performs are in accord with his priorities. For example, if his priority at a point in time is material (perhaps to save or to invest) he then acts accordingly; if his priority in time is affective-emotional or professional, he acts accordingly.
- He has developed sufficient fluidity in the processes of appropriation and relation and feels sufficiently secure in the flow of his decision process.

(8) Finally, as in the case of the other processes, the flow of the action process implies the presence of apparently opposite poles – intense and low activity. The unhindered flow of the process requires an acceptance of both poles.

## *Symptoms of Obstructions*

When the action process cannot function in an optimal manner, one finds oneself unable to sustain the implementation of one's intentions over a reasonable period of time. Most of the obstructions a person may encounter with respect to this process become visible with one or more of the following symptoms:

1] difficulties related to the harmonious integration of actions in time;
2] a tendency toward spurious activities;
3] difficulties in surmounting internal or external forces which tend to inhibit actions excessively;
4] difficulties related to the adaptation of actions to circumstances, such as failure to adapt the intensity of actions to the demands of the situation at hand, or failure to accept and manage change;
5] exaggerated hesitations on how to act and/or procrastination;
6] one's actions tend to have a negative impact on oneself or on others.

The first of the problem signals relates to difficulties in integrating one's actions in time, in a harmonious fashion. The following are three examples:

(a) *Consistently ill-timed actions.* Such actions take various forms. They can be performed at the wrong moment, as when the person concretizes his intention at an inappropriate time and, as a result, does not obtain the desired response from others; they can be wastefully repetitive, wherein the person insists in performing the actions despite a lack of response from others or despite the lack of personal learning; they can be performed routinely, out of habit, without considering their present usefulness or futility. In essence,this problem signal may reveal a failure to tune in to one's environment. Learning to listen to one's environment as well as to oneself and learning to trust one's own responses to environmental conditions may help to alleviate these deficiencies in the action flow.

(b) *Difficulties in alternating between relatively intense and relatively low activity.* The person may refuse to disengage from a period of high activity and literally overwork herself to the point of breakdown. Alternatively, she may be unable to break away from a period of relatively low activity and become submerged in prolonged lethargy. In both these extreme reactions, the person becomes ultimately unable to follow up on her intentions. In fact, her decision process may itself suffer greatly from the lack of alternation in activity, as may her relations and capacity for appropriation. One may ask what leads someone to behave in this way or what purposes she may be serving by doing so. In essence, she fails to listen to her own inner processes – her needs and intentions, and their changes. Whether her difficulty in recognizing the cyclical nature of her activity originates in her acquiescence to nonempathetic demands from others or whether it is due to her own fears, the remedy probably lies in learning to listen to herself. In listening to herself she begins to trust her own processes and give them their due.

(c) *Difficulties in switching between one type of activity and another.* This difficulty is related to the capacity to be present in the situation at hand, with all of one's resources. The capacity to be present here-and-now, in ever-new situations, requires cultivating a sense of discipline and, simultaneously, an ability to let go of non-pertinent ideas and old situations that may clutter one's mind.

The second problem signal related to the action process is a *tendency toward spurious activities.* This refers to the production of actions that make it seem as if the person is acting efficiently and in accordance with his needs and intentions (he may even believe so himself), whereas in fact he is merely acting out a charade that serves as a smoke screen for himself or for others. In this case, the person does not act because he likes what he does or because he believes in what he does, but for any number of other reasons. It may be to impress others or his employer, for instance to respond to a demand from his employer who, herself, wants to make it appear that work is being accomplished by the organization, or to justify the existence of his job. He may be acting to satisfy a need in indirect ways by using others, by replacing the need for personal power by actions designed to exercise power over others, or to satisfy a personal need while pretending to do something useful for the community. Examples of this might include financing musical productions not because of an interest in music but for his ego satisfaction, tax savings, public relations or visibility; or participating in a research project without having any real interest in the subject, and so on.

In many organizations, there are numerous opportunities for

"smoke-screen" activity, which rarely, if ever, is of real help to either those who make a habit of it or to the organization itself. For example, many people have witnessed the behavior of colleagues who show tremendous zeal in sending out memos, whose purpose is related more to the person's wanting to be accepted or admired in the group than to the usefulness of the information. Many have also experienced a multiplicity of written reports, or meetings where pseudo-problems are invented, none of which address anyone's real needs. The unfortunate result of not addressing real needs is a time-consuming process of pseudo-problem resolutions. The non-realistic nature of these "problems" is often evident in the lack of follow-up and in the subsequent resurfacing of the real needs. Similarly, in the name of democracy or of employee participation people are sometimes invited to get-togethers, but not given power to change anything. After a few disappointments many people begin to participate *pro forma*. In such circumstances, the action process of participants may become blocked and gradually lose its fluidity. Problems are brought to the surface, and in some cases even a consensus can be reached, but no one has sufficient power or responsibility to translate the ideas into action.

The core problem in spurious activities is related to a deficiency of personal power, and to failure to act as a whole person. Instead, partial actions are mistaken for the whole and the person is unable to make the connection to the whole. Consciously or subconsciously, the person fixes his attention on a part of the problem, whereas the action should be understood in relation to the whole. Often, these pseudo-actions will be related to difficulties a person experiences in surmounting internal or external forces that tend to inhibit the very actions that would be meaningful.

Third, the concretization of a person's projects often faces confrontation with action-inhibiting forces that either originate inside herself, such as fear and internalized dogmatic controls, or outside herself, as in the case of external controls; or a combination of external circumstances and internal vulnerability. The action process will likely lose its fluidity to the extent that the person has difficulties in surmounting these action-inhibiting forces. Some of the possible external controls that may excessively inhibit a person's actions, such as procedural or manipulative controls by others in the organization, will be dealt with in the next section.

The subject of fear has been dealt with earlier (see the section on the appropriation process) but it is perhaps useful to repeat some of its features, especially as they are related to the action process. Fear results mostly from the anticipation of unspecified danger to one's life, both physically and psychologically, but mostly the latter. The expression "immobilized by fear" renders well the common association of fear with absence of action. Indeed, when one is in the grip of fear, one's action process will very likely lose its natural movement. Where does fear come from? Our experiences tell us that many circumstances, internal and external, may fuel our fears. The fear that one experiences may have an instinctual quality when one finds oneself in an unfamiliar situation; for example, stage fright experienced prior to giving a performance of some kind. The greater one's involvement in a particular action, the more one can expect to feel fear, not the least because unpredictable feedback may increase in proportion to one's degree of involvement. Furthermore, every new action undertaken can be expected to generate a degree of fear. In fact, the further one reaches out from the action base to which one is accustomed, the more one becomes vulnerable, and the more fear may be present.

The feedback one receives may also be more unpredictable – pleasant or unpleasant – as one reaches out further. Fears can be fueled by perceived external threats to one's physical or emotional well-being or to one's integrity. But they can also be fueled by internal factors, such as guilt feelings, unrecognized hostile feelings or feelings of dissonance related to the acceptance or non-acceptance of one's ideas by the immediate environment. Fears can also be fueled by one's past unpleasant experiences. Some of those experiences may have impressed us strongly enough to have left enduring traumatic scars; wounds may be reopened whenever a situation reminds us of the original trauma. Furthermore, fears can be related to our conditioning to punishment for acting in certain ways. If they are the result of such conditioning, chances are that the fears will have transformed themselves into internalized dogmatic principles. Those principles act like protective devices by means of which one directs oneself, from inside, to act in certain ways in order to avoid those situations that might be similar to the one in which the unpleasant experience occurred. However, the unfortunate side effect of these principles is that they may stifle our actions rather than guide them in novel circumstances that call for flexible thought and adaptive actions.

The difficulty experienced in surmounting fear as well as internalized dogmatic principles, and the latter's potency in stifling the flow of the individual's action process, usually stems from unfamiliarity and misunderstanding. Consequently, the antidote lies in a sensitive approach, and in a gradual process of working through both the acceptance and the understanding of one's fears. It helps to have had prior experiences in facing up to real fears. By going through such a process, a degree of understanding and acceptance may also be gained with respect to the origins and consequences of internalized principles.

The fourth problem area consists of *difficulties related to the adaptation of one's actions to circumstances.* We are referring here to failures to adapt the intensity of actions to the demands of the situation at hand and, on a more general level, the failure to accept and manage change. An example of this would be the case of an executive who dismisses an employee because of recurring absences from work, without having properly analyzed the reasons for the employee's behavior or without having confronted him with the facts. Ideally, the intensity and nature of the action should correspond to what is required in a given situation. Firing an employee for lateness without first discussing the problem with him is an exaggerated response. In this case it is fairly easy to imagine a number of alternative actions that could solve the problem without resorting to such drastic measures. This type of obstruction in the flow of actions is not uncommon in impulsive personalities – those who have difficulty tolerating the low-activity phase of the action process and are willing to act prematurely in order to get rid of the problem. However, impulsiveness may very well end up leaving both parties unsatisfied. At the core of this issue of adapting the intensity of actions to situations is often the good judgment of the actor. To be able to judge a situation quickly and take the most appropriate measures is certainly one of the abilities that a self-managing person would be eager to acquire. At the opposite end of the spectrum, the person may succumb to inertia, especially when the situation demands that a previously successful action be reconsidered or redone. The flow of actions will lose its richness and diversity when the often painful effort of destruction and rebuilding is surrendered in the interest of the status quo. Failure to accept and manage such changes is often at the core of a person's inability to actualize projects. The resulting frustration can only fuel the need to perform spurious activities of the kind described earlier. In addition, one may give up mobilizing one's resources and be prey to a resentful and negative attitude. In contrast, by accepting the changes and learning to mobilize one's resources, one may achieve a useful, positive frame of mind, build faith in oneself and, in the long run, increase one's self-esteem.

A fifth signal of obstruction in the action flow is *exaggerated hesitations on how to act and/or procrastination*. When his mind is scattered or his own intentions are unclear, the person will likely experience serious difficulties in action. Hesitations about how to act and/or procrastination are frequent symptoms of unclear intentions. Often the person will feel that the possibilities for action do not make much difference - he has a hard time discriminating between what really interests him and what does not. Most importantly, the problem is one of focus, and this sends the person back to the decision process - to learn to focus his energies, to identify what he wants, and to identify what fears and obstacles prevent him from acting on what he wants. When the personal process of clarification of intentions comes to a standstill, others can help him focus, for example, by asking straightforward questions. But others can also reinforce his distraction if he simply swallows whole their interests, fears and doubts and ends up being "infected" by them. Consequently, any relationship that purports to help someone focus on his own needs and wants calls for extreme sensitivity and caring, as well as perseverance.

Sixth, the long-term flow of one's action process is at risk *whenever one's actions tend to have a negative impact on oneself or on others*. These actions may be costly not only in terms of relationships and personal credibility, but also in an organization, in terms of long-term productivity and worker morale. For example, a personnel director implements a plan involving major restructuring, the consequences of which include several layoffs. If she does so outside the organization's policy of employee development and training and without personally approaching the employees in question, there is little doubt that her actions will generate a negative impact for many people, and also for the organization as a whole. More generally, an action may be considered negative whenever it reduces the possibilities for appropriation, relation, decision and action for oneself and others. If one realizes the fact that many actions performed in the context of work do exhibit these negative characteristics, then it is not surprising that the psychological and physical toll in terms of stress, sickness, demotivation and burnout, is immeasurable. If the core of this problem is one's unfamiliarity with empathy, then the remedy lies in cultivating the capacity to see through the impact one's actions may have on the psychological and physical experience of others.

Furthermore, perceptions may be distorted due to one's own biases, prejudices or fears, or due to a lack of clear reference points. In general, prejudice or fixed assumptions about situations or people may lead to habitual action patterns in which change is systematically prevented. When one suspects that one's personal perceptions are biased, it may be useful to confront them together with people whose competence and judgment one trusts. Demystifying organizational processes may increase one's sense of personal power and confidence, and clear the way for action initiatives.

In the next section we will address the issue of healthy management of the action flow, and point to factors that may either facilitate or complicate action management.

### *Managing the Action Process in Organizations*

Managing one's actions within the framework of time, for example implementing actions at the most appropriate moment, constitutes without any doubt one of the greatest challenges for an individual in an organizational setting. Her integration in the organization, in particular the quality of her relations with others, will largely depend on her way of managing her own time. However, at least two other aspects retain our attention in regard to the healthy management of the action proces – the ability to utilize the opportunities offered by the organization, and the ability to master one's personal style and let it make an imprint on one's methods of operation.

First, if the process of a person's actions is to remain uninhibited, she should be able to utilize the opportunities offered by the organization. In reality, organizations are always two-faceted – on the one hand, they almost all constitute systems fraught with multiple constraints; on the other hand, they very often present a rich and diversified range of opportunities for action. Neither the constraints nor the opportunities may be very obvious at first sight. Getting acquainted with both is a preliminary exercise that may take the person through a sometimes lengthy process of risk-taking and evaluation of the consequences of her actions. Gradually she can identify the parameters that shape the probabilities for "success" or "failure" in this particular organization. Through failures she may come to understand what channels for action she can use and what their boundaries are. She can then recognize the opportunities and adjust her actions accordingly. This dual nature of organizations, in which constraints mesh continuously with opportunities, puts many a young (or not-so-young) motivated person in a real dilemma – choosing between the uneasy comfort of working in an organizational setting, on the one hand, and the challenge of a rewarding but uneven independent career, on the other.

Second, we have observed that a healthy flow in the action process presupposes that a person works toward mastering his particular style and method of operation. Again, his style and method may be the outcome of a rough learning process, but once he has refined and tested them they will allow him to work out his projects and intentions much more quickly, with much more ease for himself and the people he interacts with, and with much better results. Once an individual has identified and interiorized his style and personal mode of operation, he can then apply it to a whole range of situations. As an added benefit, he is then able to create habits, automatic behavior, or models for those aspects of his work that he has identified as routine. In turn, these models will free him to create new opportunities for actions and to become creative to the fullest extent. Thus, whenever the fluidity of his action process is being challenged, as when he is confronted with a new situation demanding action on his part and he does not know how to act in that particular case, he will have to formulate his own hypotheses as to what actions are warranted, keeping in mind the general characteristics of the process. In general, the action process can be seen as a sequence of phases involving a certain way of looking at situations, seeking significant clues, and choosing the methods most appropriate to one's style and most fitting to the circumstances. Thus, managing this process requires the development of a keen eye, as well as an attitude of determined curiosity.

The action process is no exception: certain environmental circumstances may facilitate or hinder our capacity to act as managers of our own process. We are well aware that organizational contexts can be experienced differently by different people, particularly in regard to the question of whether they tend to inhibit or facilitate the flow of their actions. We have no intention of analyzing the validity of the examples that follow. They are given as illustrations of some contexts that various people, managers as well as other employees, have reported as being unfacilitative or facilitative with regard to their management of the action process in the organizational setting.

Among the contexts that people have reported as being *unfacilitative*, and as having an action-inhibiting influence, are the following:

1] An excessive number of hierarchical levels, leading to a "certain heaviness in transactions". The following is a report that many may have heard: "*For every requisition five forms have to be filled out, five different signatures have to be obtained, and at every level someone wants to exercise some authority over the expenditure. Often people are not even sure whether the item is to be included on their department's budget or on that of another department. First I just got tired of going through all that trouble, then little by little I started getting apathetic. Some of my family members say I am not motivated anymore. I know why. But there is little I can do about procedures put in place at another level.*" The problems caused by the sheer number of hierarchical levels can be compounded by the absence of real power and responsibility at every level. A person who feels powerless is less likely to act in constructive ways than one who feels that his personal power counts, and is valued, in the organization. Furthermore, the opportunities for action cannot be used to their full extent when organizational procedures are a serious drain on employees' energy.

2] Controls used as tools for power rather than feedback. Usually actions are controlled in one way or another in organizations. A degree of control serves as feedback to assure that actions do not stray too far from company objectives and that they produce results within the expected range. Feedback from actions may also be useful to indicate ways in which organizational objectives have to be adjusted in specific cases. Unfortunately, excessive controls may emanate from people who want to push aside others because they consider them enemies, or from those who use controls over others as a means to enhance their own self-esteem. Thus, for the self-managing employee it is helpful to be able to distinguish between forms of control that are useful and constitute an efficient way to obtain feedback, and controls that inhibit action and cover for other reasons.

3] Perceived unfairness or partisanship in the organizational system. The perception of unfairness can assume many forms, and the ways in which it leads to the inhibition of our actions may be subtle. For example, an employee is verbally given considerable responsibility, but subsequently realizes she has not been given the means to assume this responsibility. An employee may be told that initiative is expected from her but, when she does show initiative in dealings with clients discovers that management does not support her and, instead, courts the client as if the employee were not even part of the game. When one gets the feeling that one's own supervisor will stab one in the back at the first sign of trouble, one may logically expect the flow of one's actions to suffer.

Other instances of perceived unfairness may relate to inadequate performance rewards, or the possibility that someone else will take credit for the fruit of one's efforts. Environmental uncertainty, in the case of mergers, acquisitions, takeovers, and lack of support in understanding and coping may express a lack of commitment from the organization toward its employees. For example, if a person sees that for less work of an equivalent nature another person gets paid more than herself, this will probably lead to a certain degree of action inhibition on her part. She may have worked hard on a research project, thinking that she was committed to her organization and that her organization was committed to her. Later on she finds out that the company has now been sold, that her future is uncertain, and that her work will now be used and further developed by others without recognition for herself. An event such as this one may exert a strong pressure to limit her future actions in any other organization as well.

As a contrast, the following are a few illustrations of other organizational contexts that have been seen as facilitative with respect to the action process of its members:

1] *A significant degree of responsibility at all levels and the concomitant level of freedom in organizing the work.* This naturally refers to the practical side of work and work relations, such as the degree of autonomy and initiative offered to employees, but also to the attitudes or philosophy with which managers and employees approach each other and their work. One chief executive of a very successful and rapidly growing company went so far as to say this, *"I don't want to establish a fixed company philosophy for fear of never being able to change it. I prefer to have each employee work on an awareness of his or her own actions, within a structure where a certain flexibility is maintained with regard to the task."* This kind of flexibility is often crucial in adapting actions to even slightly changing personal or environmental circumstances. Consequently, the flexibility will further the flow of actions whereas rigid job descriptions and procedures might hamper it. Whenever the decentralization of power and responsibility imparts a feeling to the employee that he can influence things on his level, the action flow will be facilitated.

2] A context in which the person is not penalized for mistakes, and where feedback is used as a constructive tool for increased communication. This is a rather subtle point. It presupposes that the potential evaluator of actions, usually the person's immediate supervisor, can maintain enough distance from the hierarchical relationship, and allow himself enough closeness with the employee, to be objectively bold and frank, and subjectively sympathetic and forgiving, at the same time. The assumption underlying this point is that merely punishing an employee for a mistake, by, for example, not renewing a contract, ignoring communications, or withdrawing crucial support at times when it is needed, may indeed prevent her from repeating it, but may not lead to any significant learning for her. Her actions can only improve if she becomes capable of learning from her mistakes, and of formulating the necessary conceptual links on her own. She will then emerge from the experience as an enriched and more knowledgeable person, as opposed to one who has learned to respond with fear and who is eager only to please management. The person who manages her action process will build up understanding from her mistakes and be able to adjust subsequent actions in the light of this understanding.

3] A context in which there is an intent to create opportunities for action. This is a situation where actions by members of the organization are not seen as a threat to the organization or the supervisor, but as desirable. The concept referred to here is broader than the mere delegation of tasks. It involves the active encouragement by supervisors of daring initiatives, which not only challenge the collective assumptions of the organization but which lead people to break through their own individual barriers as well. It happens very often in organizations that those who are active at the frontier, such as those who are in contact with the clients, who negotiate the contracts, etc., are the most knowledgeable about what is needed to make the operations more successful. How often do these valuable insights get lost, only to save a supervisor's personal pride? If a supervisor can put aside personal pride, this will often go a long way toward creating genuine opportunities for action. In general, when the supervisor can create a climate of trust between himself and his co-workers, rather than a climate of fear or competition, or a compulsion "to have the last word," the action process will be greatly facilitated.

Finally, with respect to those organizational circumstances that tend to have either a facilitative or a hindering effect on a person's action process, we may formulate an hypothesis of a more general nature. The flow of the action process of an organization's members will be facilitated so long as the organization operates in a developing sector of social life, such as in a domain of rapidly expanding technology; is future oriented; is highly innovative; has a high level of profitability; practices people-oriented management, probably with a high level of decentralized responsibility and commitment; and faces expanding markets or clientele. On the contrary, one may expect the flow of the action process of an organization's members to be hindered when the organization operates in a declining sector of social life, such as in a domain of out-dated technology; lives on the merit of past successes; is not very innovative; has a low level of profitability; emphasizes centralized hierarchy and procedures in its management practice, probably with a low level of personal responsibility and commitment, and faces declining markets or clientele.

In the light of the specific characteristics of the action process, the management of this process is likely to be more adequate when a certain number of precautions are observed by the self-managing person. As in the other processes, this one will operate all the more smoothly when the person stays aware of what is happening, continues to learn, balances apparently opposite tendencies as much as possible, provides for opportunities rather than diminishing them. These precautions constitute basic criteria for a healthy management of the action flow.

More specifically, we will reformulate some tentative hypotheses concerning behaviors, attitudes, or abilities that are worth cultivating in order to ensure that management of the action process furthers the process nature of action rather than inhibit it. In arbitrary order they are the following:

1] seeking a line of work that one genuinely likes;
2] acquiring and developing the awareness of environmental constraints and opportunities;
3] developing the ability to discern when action is or is not appropriate;
4] developing the capacity to mobilize one's resources when there is a need to do so, and
5] developing the ability to tune in to change and to change one's actions when necessary.

The first hypothesis for healthy management of the action flow relates to *seeking a line of work that one genuinely likes*. This refers to the necessity for the individual to make sure that the type of actions required from him in the organizational setting correspond to what she personally finds likeable and satisfying. The question she will need to answer again and again is: "Will this action or this activity further a sense of satisfaction in me?" When an action is satisfying to its performer it is usually done well. On the contrary, when the action is done under obligation or stress, its results may show the strain of this emotional background. Indeed some actions retain an imprint of the affection with which they have been executed, just as we can feel the emotional involvement of the artisan in a work of art. Other actions are neutral to the point of not even being noticed by others. Another question related to the first one is, "Will I learn something new in concretizing this intention?" When she likes what she does, the person will find that actions provide the beacons that allow her to course-correct her most abstract and theoretical viewpoints. Action then has the characteristic of providing clear indications about the missing pieces and, consequently, about the things she needs to learn more about. On the contrary, when someone does not like the activity, there is a high probability that her lack of alertness will prevent her from perceiving the lessons that otherwise might be learned.

The second hypothesis for healthy management of the action flow is to *acquire and develop an awareness of the constraints and opportunities present in one's environment.* This awareness includes the ability to gauge realistically the environmental barriers that he should not waste energy trying to remove. In turn, the development of this awareness goes hand in hand with the acquisition of knowledge about himself and about what he wants. In the process of mastering the continuous interaction between environmental constraints and opportunities, on the one hand, and his own awareness of what he is and wants, on the other, it is not uncommon to see constraints change into opportunities. In fact, many new opportunities are created in this way - by changing the old objectives and dynamics of a situation into a new kind of dynamics, and letting a new vision replace the old objectives. Thus, full awareness of opportunities implies the ability to create them. For example, an old asset may be seen in a new light and can become an instrument for meaningful action. A businessman may buy an old and declining manufacturing outlet, to transform the building into residential lofts if this kind of lodging is in demand. This action would be meaningless if he wanted to continue to use the building as a factory, but by changing its function he creates new opportunities for action that are in accordance with his wants.

A person's strengths are also his weakness, for he will need to build on them and work with them in order to make them bear fruit. If he does not do so he may suffer feelings of guilt and even depression. In contrast, his weaknesses are also his strength. Not only do they erase guilt feelings, but through accepting them he may obtain ways to put these feelings to use and even transform them into assets. In this context of transforming reality from disadvantage to opportunity, it is also useful to cultivate the ability to transform the negative into the positive. This applies not only to the presence of negative feelings in oneself - which have a constraining effect on one's actions, even if one is unaware of it - but also to the presence of persons in one's immediate environment who have difficulties coping with their internally generated negativity. From the point of view of one's action flow, it is much more productive to transform the negative into the positive rather than to combat the negativities with more of the same.

The third hypothesis relates to *the ability to discern when action is or is not appropriate*. This ability is related to answering the question, "Is it appropriate for me, at this point in time and space, to act on (or concretize) this intention, or to implement this decision?" What are the criteria? The action flow will benefit if the person has developed solid criteria for when to act and when not to act. When such criteria are missing, one may find one's actions inhibited for all kinds of misleading reasons, such as guilt or fear. Or one may act impulsively when situations trigger negative affects, such as jealousy, revenge, or anger. The first case may lead one into spurious activity; the second case may very well destroy many of one's future opportunities for constructive action.

The ability to discern when action is or is not appropriate will not develop unless a person feels free to act or not. When she feels obliged on moral or other grounds to act, she will not develop any criteria for herself, and her action process will lack sufficient grounding in her personal intentions. Some useful questions that may help a person to find her own criteria are the following, "Is this action in my best interests?" "Is this action in the best interests of my colleagues?" "Do I have enough information to act now?" "On what level do I want to act (on a detailed level, on a strategic level, on all levels, etc.)?" "Under what conditions do I want to act (alone, together with others, as a 'cog in the wheel,' as coordinator)?" "What are the conditions under which I know my actions to be most rewarding?" "Which kinds of actions do I generally prefer?"

At times, it is wiser to let others act and to refrain from acting ourselves, especially if we do not personally have all the knowledge necessary to act conscientiously. In an organizational context, a person may prefer to act on the level of detailed information or may prefer to delegate that level to others and concentrate on a more strategic level. A manager may prefer to act alone, or may generally prefer the creative influx or the dilution of responsibility that comes from acting in close collaboration with others.

In general, to fine-tune this ability of discernment, the individual will need to come to grips with: (a) the differences and the relation between imagination and action, and (b) the question of whether actions can be inherently good or bad (i .e. the ethical question). Neither of these issues are merely philosophical questions, and the self-managing person will need to understand them if he or she wishes the action process to remain open and fluid at all times.

The fourth hypothesis relates to *the capacity to mobilize one's resources when there is a need to do so*. This is the ability to effectively channel and direct our physical and mental energies into the spatial and temporal structures in which we move ourselves. It includes the ability to assert oneself whenever it is called for, as well as the ability to take care of one's resources. Actions will be more conducive to learning when one can remain in control of them - when one can look after them, observe them run their course, and follow up on them when necessary. Staying in control means permitting oneself to experience all the facets of one's actions with one's whole being, rather than letting them get out of hand and then turning one's back on them, as when the results turn out to be disappointing, or even dangerous.

The ability to mobilize one's resources may come more easily, and the action flow may be smoother, if one has a mental image of the action - when through a capacity for anticipation one already senses beforehand what will happen. Ideally, this mental image will harbor a whole range of alternative actions, one of which will be expressed concretely. In addition, one sees this action as it plays itself out in time - one knows when to put it on hold, and when to execute it.

The fifth hypothesis relates to *the ability to tune in to change and to alter one's actions when necessary*. When the implementation of a decision does not correspond to what one expected, does not yield the expected learning potential, or simply turns out to be a failure, it may be better to remedy the situation immediately rather than to "wait and see." The assumption behind this ability to tune in quickly to change, is that it is better to halt the negative feelings generated by the failure than to allow them to accumulate in oneself or in others. In this way, one can go on to other constructive actions. Acting quickly on unforeseen situations presupposes that the one has also envisioned the possible failure of an action and the concomitant possibility of stopping it even before undertaking it, and that one knows how to deal with such a situation. As mentioned earlier, because negative feelings tend to block our actions, the ability to convert the negative into the positive is a significant tool for unblocking the action flow.

Concrete actions often allow people to clarify and refine their theoretical concepts. They also enlarge the scope of practical knowledge. Actions are an effective way of communication – they transmit messages to other members of the organization. Furthermore, every action is a potential step toward potential self-realization, the making of values, and personal fulfillment.

"We live in a life in which our percepts are perhaps always the perception of parts, and our guesses about wholes are continually being verified or contradicted by the later presentation of other parts. It is perhaps so that wholes can never be presented for that would involve direct communication."

Gregory Bateson

**Key Points**

- How to implement a self-managed orientation
- Giving direction
- The use of power
- Evaluating performance – a different look

# FROM SELF MANAGEMENT TO DIRECTING OTHERS

# 3

A question now needs to be addressed. Does everything we have said about self management apply to the direction of the work of others, or to the classical theme of "leadership"? Additional questions arise in this context. What are the consequences of a self-management philosophy for the feelings and behavior of others? How are others affected by direction inspired by the self-management approach? Once we have adopted a self-management approach and integrated its philosophy, can we transfer some of its principles to the direction of others? What, if any, are the difficulties we may encounter in effecting such a transfer? Does the practice of self management automatically lead to a better understanding of the functioning of others in the organization? These and similar questions assume considerable significance, as popular theories of direction, supervision and leadership do not usually elaborate on the director's, supervisor's, or leader's management of themselves. In the following sections, we will explore tentative answers to some of these questions, while briefly touching on the following topics:

1] development of a personal style;

2] difficulties inherent in some organizational environments;

3] differentiating skill in self management from skill in directing others;

4] the issue of power; and, finally,

5] a new look at the appraisal of performance in organizations.

Chapter III

# Developing a Personal Style: Going Beyond Models and Accepted Management Patterns

Directing the work of others can be facilitated if the director has a model of direction which includes philosophy as well as methodology. However, this model of direction will be effective only when it is in harmony, in many subtle ways, with the director's personality as well as with the style and mind frame of the employees. Thus, working through his own particular style of direction requires the manager to confront and question the usefulness of the myriad old models that he may have collected from one point or another in his lifetime. Many administrators and managers begin their career acting on a basis of role models acquired in their families, during their studies, or from their own supervisors in previous jobs. These preconceptions cause them to manage their employees and even orient their workers' careers without really consulting them about their ambitions, desires, or priorities. Often the style they use is not only out of tune with their employees but has not even kept up with their own maturing personality. Even if it is difficult, it is often necessary for a manager to put aside the way he sees things in order to understand with empathy those reporting to him.

The question to be faced by any manager is how to change an old model of behavior when it is apparent that its consequences are unfavorable or damaging to the employee's self management. Indeed, it is tempting to simply give employees the same treatment one received from one's own former supervisors, ignoring new information or conditions. It is also tempting to ignore the impact of one's particular style on employees, especially if one has not learned to adapt one's models and tends to reproduce the same patterns over and over. But truly successful direction of others' work involves working on oneself as well. When a manager makes the effort to look inside himself, he can recover and re-identify the very assumptions that underlie his style of direction. He can become aware of the models that transpire through his style from sheer force of habit, including an understanding of where they come from and, more importantly, what habitual patterns he has to unlearn and modify in order to be effective. Without an effort to discover how he himself appropriates his world, what he likes in people and in himself, what parameters guide his own choices, and what obstacles inhibit his actions, a manager will have very little power to understand not only what drives others, but also why his direction of others' work succeeds or fails, and what conditions under his control can foster meaningful work relationships with his employees, while leaving everyone's ego intact. Without an ever-widening understanding of what it is that liberates his own potential for appropriation, relationship, choice, decision and meaningful action, the manager will have little to go on to help open up these potentials in his dealings with other people.

We can see that there are very few contradictions between the management of oneself and the direction of others. In fact, self management appears to be the key and the gateway to effectively directing the work of others. In addition to providing additional insight and self-confidence to the manager, a self-management approach will probably provide a less fertile ground for his employees' unproductive projections and expectations concerning leadership qualities. Integrating the self management approach with the direction of others requires the development of a personalized style adapted to the people and the situation that form the theatre of the manager's activities. Changing an established pattern of direction is not always easy. When we have learned our pattern from a favorite role model, it may not occur to us that another style might be more suited to present circumstances in the organization and its environment. However, a previous pattern or a prestigious model need not be completely rejected. What is required is the judicious selection of those elements that are in agreement with one's own personality and environment, so that one's leadership style is enhanced. In short, directing the work of others requires progressively freeing oneself of accepted patterns in order to create an individual way of being and a corresponding style of direction. Ideally, the kind of leadership that a person exercises in her concrete environment is a reflection of the leadership she applies to herself.

The possibility of developing a personalized style of direction and leadership raises the question of training. Do we have training methods that can transmit the possibility of changing and adapting styles to fit circumstances as they arise? How can we empower people to develop their personal style and to change it when necessary? Are there ways to train people to be sensitive to what is needed, and to develop their own style, rather than merely providing exposure to available models? What happens when new technologies become available, adding new dimensions and responsibilities to people in charge of directing others? For example, what happens when the practice of medicine becomes invaded by automated diagnostic systems? What training can adequately prepare medical doctors to use such systems judiciously when they become available? What constitutes an adequate preparation for the use of high technology systems such as radiology and radiation therapy? Is it possible to train doctors in such a way as to provide them with an adequate understanding of the physics, chemistry and biology involved with these techniques, so that they in turn can develop an adequate style for directing their patients? We come to realize more and more that there are few universal answers in these areas. More specifically, we realize increasingly that the problems faced by people who direct others often spring from their own background (which includes personality, and perhaps more importantly, their own life projects), as well as from the particular action theater in which they move and function.

The following list constitutes an attempt to define some of the orientations we believe training should take in order to respond to this need for learning how to develop a personalized style of direction. First of all, it seems imperative that training should equip the person with tools that will allow her to become aware of how she differs from others. Some form of team-building skills or learning situations involving small group dynamics would seem to be useful for these purposes. Work in a receptive group context can be a very powerful means to understanding in what ways one's abilities are most valued by others, how one's interactions affect other people, and how others react. Secondly, it seems important to learn how to manage stress. Change, including changing one's style of direction, almost always involves stress. Thirdly, and most importantly, the training will have to include a methodology for learning how to learn. This is by no means an easy matter, for the trainer will need to have appropriated such a methodology for herself before she can impart it to others. Direction of others requires that the director possesses the ability to continually diagnose and improve her own style of direction. Thus, training will have to include a solid methodology for ongoing self-learning; building on one's experiences; and using all of one's faculties of perception, thinking and feeling; as well as a vision of where one is headed.

In the next section we address some of the difficulties that may arise with respect to the direction of others in certain organizational contexts.

## Difficulties Inherent in Certain Environments

We have already mentioned that certain characteristics of organizational cultures do not facilitate the practice of self management. An examination of the obstacles to healthy self management usually reveals insufficient opportunities for appropriation, relation, decision and action. But what about the leader who wishes to create an environment that is facilitative of a self-management approach in unfavorable surroundings? Even talented leaders with good self management skills are given only restricted opportunities. For example, despite the best intentions, many middle-level supervisors do in fact find themselves crushed between the concerns of their operative personnel and the perceived aloofness of their own supervisors. Is it possible in such conditions to not only manage oneself well but also to provide the kind of direction that opens up, rather than closes off, opportunities for one's employees?

When a director experiences difficulties in opening up opportunities for his employees' self management, this may be due to organizational characteristics (including those of his own superiors), to himself, to the employees, or to any combination of the above. When organizational circumstances are the stumbling block, this may be due to the speed with which environmental factors evolve, leaving little time for the director himself to digest the changes. Similarly, the director may find himself in a totally new environment where his own need for appropriation and assimilation of new information is so great that he does not have enough time to instantly respond to employees' expectations. Usually a person can respond to others' needs and expectations only when he himself has reached a certain equilibrium with respect to his own self-management processes.

Other circumstances that lead to difficulty in opening up opportunities for self management may have to do with the temperament of managers or with major conflicts, such as collective bargaining conflicts or deep-seated personality clashes within the organization. In some cases, the organizational culture may too severely limit the possibilities for expression of different points of view, or may too narrowly define the ways in which the work needs to be accomplished. All these factors may limit the extent to which a director is able to fully develop his own opportunities for appropriation, relation, decision and action. Consequently, he may be unable to marshall all his resources and imprint his own style in dealing with others. When he cannot express his style through his direction, there is little chance that he will have the motivation to lead others to self management.

In other cases a supervisor may face employees who manage themselves inadequately, or may experience a group as energy-draining. How can the leader help her personnel or group re-establish equilibrium? First she must discover where the problem lies – with herself or with the employees or group members. The supervisor's action is likely to be facilitated if she can realistically assess to what extent each employee or group member is capable of self-help. When such an assessment proves impossible or leaves too much ambiguity, the manager then has little guidance in how to deal with those persons.In that case, we find it useful for her to give priority to managing herself well. Sometimes a manager wastes considerable energy on people whose potential is not geared toward the areas the manager wishes to focus on. Or, she takes on too much responsibility for problems to which others have contributed as well. Despite their potential, people may be inadequately prepared to seize opportunities for self management, and there may be a limit to how much they can profit from such opportunities in a short period of time. For example, when a person has felt deprived for a long time in a particular aspect of his life, and if he has developed a nondiscriminating attitude as a result, then he may avail himself indiscriminately of whatever opportunities present themselves. He is likely to jump at the chance for any short-term gratification and, socially in organizations, he will sell his soul in order to create the illusion of belonging.

People can easily take advantage of such a person, but what makes the situation even more difficult for him is the fact that he absorbs what is being offered without really learning anything. Opportunities are merely being burned up and in no way augment his potential for self management. For, indeed, the key to learning lies in discriminating and in making choices - in affirming, "I want this; I do not want that." One business manager had the following story to tell in this respect, "*When I see an employee in such a situation, I tend to ask myself the following question: will this person become a 'survivor' in the system, or will he take charge of himself and break through this non-discriminating attitude? Even if my answer is ambiguous, I will give him a chance - even more than one. Can he do a quality job, within the constraints that he has? Or is he cutting corners at the expense of other employees? I will give him bigger and bigger responsibilities. And I will not hesitate to ask him, 'What have you learned from those small opportunities?' Afterward, when I know I can trust him, there is no limit to the responsibilities I am willing to give him - he is developing himself, and I am developing myself.*" When the opportunities are present, and even if the employee uses them more for his own development than "for the good of the organization," the important factor is very likely to be whether he learns and augments his possibilities for self management. If he does, the manager will not have to worry about immediate returns for the good of the organization. The increased potential will sooner or later be reflected back in his work.

As far as the manager himself is concerned, the key question is this, "Do I, as a manager, feel sufficiently at ease and open so as to help others find opportunities for appropriation, relations, decisions and actions?" To overcome his own difficulties in these areas is the foremost challenge faced by any supervisor, whether they originate in himself or in his surroundings. The assumption of the self-management approach is that the supervision of others will be most rewarding when opportunities for the four basic processes are optimal. In the next section we address some of the differences and similarities between skills in self management and skills in directing others.

# Differentiating Skill in Self Management from Skill in Directing and Supporting Others

In only the rarest cases can a person directing others be all things to all people. More often, we experience one person opening up opportunities for, say, appropriation at certain points in our lives, while another may open up opportunities that belong more to the relational area, and so on. From the viewpoint of the one who initiates such openings it is indeed plausible that she can be more facilitative toward one process than toward another, in function of her own personality, and her own learning process, style and expertise. This being so, we have also noted that many managers do not realize that they can indeed open up or close off opportunities to others. In a more general way, many managers do not realize to what extent their actions and communications with their personnel have impact. If they do not realize their impact, how can they then help others to open up opportunities for themselves? This leads us to a basic question – what skills and attitudes does a person need who desires to lead a group toward self management? The following is a tentative list of such skills and attitudes:

1] A clear intent on the part of the directing person to help the group on the way to self management. One pertinent question for the manager to ask herself is, "Is it my intent to provide opportunities for self management for these particular people? Do I move freely enough in my own management style to be able to commit myself to such an objective?"

2] A corollary of this is the capacity to like and appreciate the persons under one's supervision. Without this kind of unconditional sympathy it is doubtful that one can muster enough feeling for the real needs of one's personnel. "Can I, as a manager, be whole enough that I do not need my personnel to be what they are not, or to pretend to be something that they are not?" "Or do I need them to act in a certain way for my own purposes, such as to admire me?" A related question is this, "Do I like myself enough so that my liking them can indeed be unconditional?"

3] A third important skill is the ability to gauge what impact one's actions and communications have on others. Basic questions in this area are, "What feelings are created in others by my actions and communications?" And, equally important, "What feelings are conducive to others managing themselves well?" It is not always easy to get a clear and unambiguous picture of the answer to these questions. Indeed, feelings may be generated by the person's own situation as much as by a direct response to the manager's actions. It is not clear either whether only positive feelings lead to optimal self management; sometimes negative feelings, such as depression, may help center one's attention on oneself again after a period of excessive dissipation of one's energies.

Perhaps one of the more visible criteria for gauging the impact of one's actions on others is the flow of communication. A person's potential for self management is seldom furthered by a blockage of communication. Consequently, the importance of gauging the impact of one's actions on others' potential to communicate cannot be underestimated. The question for the manager then becomes, "What can I do to further those possibilities for communication and genuine expression on the part of my personnel?" And, in addition, "Am I sufficiently at ease with myself to be able to genuinely listen to such communications without feeling threatened?" "Can I listen intently and at the same time remain on my own ground?" "Can I listen to the things unsaid?" "Am I sufficiently strong inside myself to not feel that I have to do things I do not want to do, even if I feel pressured?"

4] The willingness to confront a person, not with respect to company rules or cultural expectations, but on issues relating to the management of himself. "Am I sufficiently grounded in order to confront the other without hurting him?" "Can I confront her easily without stopping to genuinely like her, and without losing perspective of my intent to help?" "Or does my willingness to confront mask my own desire to get rid of her because her expectations annoy me?" To confront another may imply that one is willing to confront oneself too, or to be confronted in turn. Again, the most important criterion for evaluating the usefulness of confrontation is the way in which it opens up or closes off opportunities for communication. For example, when a manager resorts to memos couched in vague terms, or alludes to issues rather than directly confronting the persons she wants to address, she foregoes opportunities for communication and may close off, rather than help develop, opportunities for self management among her employees. She may feel safer conveying her message in this way, as it does not open a person-to-person communication channel in which she too might be confronted. Finally, we are aware that confrontation may take many different forms, that there is no one good way to handle it, and that it is an ability as complex as communication itself.

5] Besides the awareness of what our own actions do to someone else, we have found it beneficial for the leader to allow himself to be aware of the impact his personnel's self management has on him. Does it make him feel good, enhance his own self-esteem, enhance his own sense of effectiveness? Or does it, on the contrary, threaten him, diminish his sense of control, or make him feel useless or bored? This awareness is likely to bring his own level of self management to the foreground. The prospect of such awareness may be threatening if one uses a position of control to avoid looking at one's own self management. Many of us have encountered managers whose direction tends to fall too heavily on certain employees. Executives who oversupervise in this manner may be compensating for an inability to deal with challenges and opportunities at their own level in the organization. Another question lies in the area of dependence, "Is there a danger that my employees will become too dependent on me if I open up many opportunities for them?" "And when they do become good managers of themselves, can I handle the prospect, as a leader, of becoming interdependent with them?" "Can I handle my inclinations to become overprotective?" These are only a few samples of the intricate relationship patterns and exchanges of feelings that need to be brought into awareness if there is to be an effective transmission, and sharing, of self-management abilities and values.

6] A certain tolerance toward error is called for at the same time as an uncompromising insistence on quality. The self-management approach does not make the leader an advocate of error, of insubordination, or of bad performance. On the contrary, the objective is to achieve a sense of responsibility for one's performance and one's competence, for product quality and the quality of the services one renders. But a person rarely achieves this sense of responsibility if the possibility of error is denied him – he needs to acquire full information as to what the possible origins of error can be and what its consequences may be. Thus, the responsibility of the leader is not so much to punish error but to provide as much information as he can to allow the employee to take his responsibility himself. It is the responsibility of the leader not to require performances from an employee that he knows are unrealistic, but, by the same token, he must inspire the employee toward performances of ever higher standards. To encourage employees and help them to correct errors is one of his most rewarding functions. Through negative reinforcement, punishing errors may lead a person to acquire desired behavior patterns, but it also risks creating toxic by-products, such as feelings of resentment, anger, and low self-esteem. Again, a person who is aware and tolerant of his own mistakes will be better able to deal with the mistakes of others.

7] Finally, and most of all, the activity of directing others should not unduly burden the supervisor. If it does, then something is probably going wrong in the way she manages herself. Ideally, the supervisor knows what the consequences will be, for herself and others, if she does manage herself well or if she fails to do so. She knows that, without heightened attention to her own self, the risks of burnout and of the dissipation of her resources increase dramatically. She knows that as a result of burnout she may fail to be present as a whole person - and when she attempts to respond solely to the multiple and often contradictory demands and expectations of her personnel, her failure may soon reflect itself not only in her leadership but also in the core of her personal stability. Thus, the supervisor knows, intuitively at least, that in order to be a credible leader for others she needs to be, simultaneously, a credible leader for herself. This requirement signifies nothing less than a genuine integration of the leadership dimension into the personality of the person who exercises it. The leader is then in the position to understand the self-management strivings of her personnel with empathy. In turn, those under her supervision can fully understand the leader only if they can both exploit their own potentials and realize the necessity for a leader to manage herself well. Thus, respect for one's own process of self management is a prerequisite for healthy interaction with either leaders or employees.

Management literature has always emphasized the value of setting a good example. Lao Tzu's intimation that the best leader is the one of whom the people can say, "It is we ourselves who have realized this," expresses the feeling of those who have a leader they are sure of identifying with strongly, but with whom they also have the feeling of being responsible for their own results.

> "The best of all rulers is but a shadowy presence to his subjects.
> Next comes the ruler they love and praise;
> Next comes the one they fear;
> Next comes the one with whom they take liberties.
> When there is not enough faith, there is lack of good faith.
> Hesitant, he does not utter words lightly.
> When his task is accomplished and his work done
> The people all say, 'It happened to us naturally.' "

Employees generally respect an executive who takes personal charge of those matters in which he is most skilled, so as to gain maximum satisfaction from his work; that is, a leader who respects himself. Such an executive will likely be even more successful to the extent that his management of himself inspires employees to seek out their own opportunities for appropriation, relation, decision and action.

## Giving Direction and the Issue of Power

In previous pages we have often referred to supervisors and their junior associates, or to managers and their employees. Yet it needs to be emphasized that the giving of direction is interpreted here in its largest possible sense - whether as a government official, a teacher, a parent, an executive, a supervisor, and ultimately, as giving direction to ourselves. Giving direction always involves the use, and possible abuse, of power. We want to look at power in the sense of personal power, then extend our discussion to its modus operandi in groups and organizations.

## *Personal Power*

The issue of personal power has received much attention in the literature of management, politics, and the social sciences in general. Yet, very often our concept of power is tainted by cultural programming or by what we experience as domination by others over significant parts of our lives – for example, life at work, at school, or in the family. Often the concept of power becomes fixed in an either/or framework according to which some individuals have power and others have none. Organizational gossip is full of statements to the effect that X is a powerful figure, that Y is a strong person, or that Z has no power, etc. These are social statements that usually reflect the kind of influence people are perceived as wielding over what happens in the organization. In fact, the either/or definition is often cleverly exploited by some people to dominate others. The power illusion works both ways. Some people maintain the illusion that they have power over and can manipulate others; some live by the illusion that they have no power and do not share in something others have. The power illusion is based on the idea that power is mostly interpersonal, that it is exclusively reserved for some and not for others, and that some individuals are inherently better at using it than others. However, seeing power as a highly personal matter leads us to realize that the concept is better not couched in such simple either/or terms.

Personal power can conveniently be compared to the presence and circulation of energy. The power is "on" when the individual is connected to his energy source and has energy at his disposal to control instruments of life and action. The opposite of power is, then, to be physically or psychologically "off," or to be disconnected from one's energy source. When power is defined as "connection" rather than as "influence over others" the concept gains an added richness that allows us to gain a deeper insight into its consequences. When defined as "connection," personal power is a dynamic and universal human attribute – the ability to tune in to and express what moves oneself. Power is neutral – if the force one is moved by is love, then the expression of one's power is likely to reflect this energy. If one is moved by resentment and anger, then it is to be expected that the expressions of one's power will be imbued with these feelings.

Rather than seeing individuals as powerful or weak, we can recognize the fact that at times one experiences low power; one feels unexpressive, unsure which energy source to tap into, not very confident in oneself. At times the power one experiences surges to record highs. Not infrequently this is reflected in other people feeling attracted to us – we are truly magnetic, we have good contact with people, we experience a sense of confidence and we feel competent. One may ask the question, "What brings about low power or high power?" "What brings about power failures, as when our connection with the energy source is broken, and when we are prone to spurious activities?" No doubt, to master the level of one's power and to bring about a quasi-permanent functional level is a goal worthy of attention. But, as for all human potential, this kind of mastery requires considerable learning, and familiarizing ourselves with our own psychological dynamics. Personal power can be blocked, for example, when obstructions occur anywhere along the "connection"; certain mystified norms or guilt feelings may have led us to diminish our power or to channel it in self-destructive ways. Somewhere along the road we may have learned to see our power as something negative, which made us neglect our connection. As a long-term result, we may fail to control our power sufficiently to be at ease with ourselves. Furthermore, many "power failures" are brought about by the specter of fear and by related problems such as self-doubt.

Our power may be blocked only along certain specific modes of expression but not along others. For example, certain circumstances, or some people's personal expressions, may make us feel "unconnected," while other circumstances (or people) clearly "boost our connection" and even improve our ability to express ourselves energetically. Finally, while it is clear that nobody can take someone else's power away, we may all – at times – be easily influenced, especially if we are not familiar enough with our own power. People can sow doubt in you, even denigrate you and pull your best-intended initiatives to pieces. If you are easily influenced, it may become more difficult to connect with your own energy as a result, but only to the extent that you are insufficiently familiar with your own power. For the person who denigrates another or sows doubt, it is often a sign of a certain dependency, and of failing to be completely centered in himself. Even if the pattern is outside of his awareness and the behavior quite automatic, he is expressing something like this, "I need the other person's power in order to feel on top of myself." However, the more a person has acquainted himself with his own power, the less he will be susceptible to such influence. Conversely, the more a person is aware of the true nature of personal power, and the more he is centered in his own, the less he will be prone to put down someone else for his own satisfaction, and the more easily he will learn to blend his power with that of others in harmonious ways that help achieve the intended results.

To summarize, we have found that personal power is an exciting subject and an extremely important one. It is truly the cornerstone of all self-management processes. Without exaggeration, we could say that power underwrites the ability to function creatively in interpersonal contexts. The ways in which power operates in groups and organizations is the subject of the next section.

### *Power in Groups*

Personal power has been defined earlier as "connection," or the ability to tune into and express what moves one. In a similar vein, the power a person expresses in a group can be seen as his ability to "move" others in the group. Our main hypotheses in this regard are threefold. The first one is that the power a person transmits in a group is directly related to his or her personal power, and it operates chiefly through the processes of attribution and projection. Our second hypothesis is that much of the power wielded by certain persons in groups and organizations is symbolic and mythical rather than palpable or physical. Our third hypothesis maintains that according to the self-management approach, the only truly effective use of power with respect to others is to empower those others. Let's go over each of these statements in more detail.

First of all, power in groups is a matter of attribution and projection. Power is personal, but when group members attribute power to certain individuals it invariably signals projection on their part, whether that projection is prompted by a hierarchical position, by charisma, by certain behaviors of these individuals, or other circumstances. Consequently, the general rules of projection apply to power. For one thing, projecting power onto someone else always involves some degree of unawareness, or even abdication, of our own power in the context of that relationship. In other words, we tend to see the other's personal power more clearly than our own. Invariably we will tend to see power in individuals who are "connected" in areas of our life where we ourselves are not so well connected, such as money management, theoretical thinking, writing, affection, spiritual knowledge, interpersonal communication, or any other possible quality or ability we can think of. In addition, when we see this kind of power in another individual, we may feel vulnerable in that area, and the interpersonal context is wide open to all kinds of secondary feelings, such as love, attraction, and closeness; or resentment, anger, fear, judgment, and even hatred.

As in the case of other projections, the power projection has its origin in the projector but it also "hooks into" the personal power base of the person who receives the projection. For example, an executive may receive projections of power from employees in the area of financial decision making. First of all, by projecting this power onto him they probably give themselves less credit in that area than they deserve, though they clearly recognize his abilities. But at the same time it is very likely that, in turn, he really has developed a special competence in that domain. Similarly, a teacher may receive projections of power from students. Students are likely to give themselves less credit than they deserve, and "look up to" the teacher. But it is also true that the teacher has probably mastered the domain of knowledge that students expect of him. This point leads us to the use and possible abuse of power, which we will discuss later. The important point is that the power wielded by a person in a group is always power attributed to him by other members of the group. In other words, power in groups is personal power that is "recognized" by others in the group. The influence a person can exercise in the group is then a direct consequence of the attributions that others project onto him, whereby they allow themselves to be influenced to a certain degree.

The second hypothesis is that much of the power wielded by certain persons in groups and organizations is symbolic and mythical rather than palpable or physical. In particular, the attributions of power that others in the group make to a certain individual are based much more on her (real or presumed) past accomplishments, future projections about her, and what she wants known of herself than on the "here and now" person. In fact, reducing the relation to the "here and now" will almost always significantly alter the perceived power differentials; it will tend to "equalize" people. One could say that in those circumstances the myth gives way to reality and the symbolic gestures give way to concrete and realistic interactions. However, in ordinary situations the person wielding power is much more likely to use imagistic speech and symbolic gestures, or other nonverbal behavior, to back up her power rather than crude physical force or the enforcement of rewards and punishments. For example, with her background of expertise, a person may withhold crucial factual information from others so that the power attributed to her by another stays on the symbolic level. Indeed, if she conveys this factual information to the other, she thereby annihilates the symbolic power base and empowers the other. For example, this is a reason why education empowers people.

To summarize, power attributed to a person in a group or an organization is based to a far greater extent on the images that people entertain about that person than on real and palpable elements. In turn, those images often find their source much more in what is not said than in what is, and on unshared, rather than communicated, information. Consequently, the challenge faced by the self-managing person directing others is to accept symbolic power while using it to empower others.

The third hypothesis is that according to the self-management approach, the only truly effective use of power with respect to others is to empower those others. Power in a group, or the projection of power by others, has its pitfalls - one can use it, abuse it, or not use it at all. To receive a projection of power from others entails a commitment to do something for them in an area where they are too vulnerable, at least temporarily, to assume their own personal power. To receive such a projection of power is, as it were, an implicit request not to disappoint them. It is a request to use it and to act in a responsible fashion. However, when there is a significant discrepancy between the power projected and one's own capacity to respond adequately, in that case it is probably in the best interests of everybody to refuse the power, to abdicate, or to suggest someone else. This point being made, a question must be raised. When power is projected onto me, what does it mean to abuse that power? And what constitutes judicious use of that power? It seems fairly obvious that expectations will accompany the power attributed to a person. It is also evident that a central goal of the self-management approach is to help people learn to exercise and express their own personal power so that they can be responsible for their own lives.

If, as we have said before, the act of attributing power to someone is indeed a signal of vulnerability on the part of the attributor, then it makes sense to establish as a key rule that the person receiving such a projection not exploit these vulnerabilities for his own ends. While it is likely that he will have to accept these projections from others for a while, his goal must evidently be to return to them in due time what is their own. He would not be able to do this if he intended to feed on those projections for the purpose, say, of feeling good himself. In contrast, he will not be likely to deceive them by accepting the projections for the sole purpose of returning them as soon as possible. Thus, rather than using others' vulnerabilities for establishing control, his challenge is to use them for mutual growth. Many times a leader is faced with individuals who say, "I don't know which way to go or how to behave in these circumstances. I want a leader who can provide clear objectives and clear information." Even in such events, directing others calls for a leader who can call up the "leader" qualities in each group member rather than one who takes advantage of their deficiencies in that regard.

Indeed, the use and abuse of power can be conveniently illustrated by establishing a difference between personal power and group power. Personal power is one's own instrument. As soon as we are in an interpersonal, group, or organizational context; what is truly productive is the power generated in and expressed by interpersonal interactions. To try to restore one's personal power by using others in the group is clearly abusive. In contrast, channeling one's personal power in ways that are compatible with others' power will likely result in mutual enrichment and increased power for everyone. One can go further. We hypothesize that building up excessive power for oneself at the expense of others in an organization will lead to loss of group power in the first stage, and will ultimately be self-destructive to the abusive leader: in the end everybody will lose. Many examples can be found in organizations where the excessive build-up of power by some invariably leads to disequilibrium, and sooner or later brings the organization to its knees. Many cases are less dramatic but nonetheless illustrative of the pattern. How many times have we witnessed people in our organizations who have lost much of their co-workers' credibility and trust after abusing power when in a position that conveniently allowed them to do so? We may be reminded of certain teachers we know who have excessively used up the personal power of their students and created a context in which learning became a nightmare rather than a motivating and pleasurable experience. We may be reminded of parents who, by excessively using up their children's personal power, have destroyed their children's "connection" with themselves, or have caused them to leave the family in disgust. We may also be reminded of supervisors who had no respect for the personal power of employees and created a bitter and unproductive atmosphere in the work place; or of chief executives who led a money-making company to bankruptcy by misusing their own power and draining that of their personnel through neglect of their legitimate concerns. People usually feel quite clearly when their personal power is being eroded in an abusive way, and this is one thing they do not easily forget. In fact, power has become such a controversial issue because we often see only the ugly side of it - people abusing power.

Following are a few concluding comments on the issue of power in the context of directing others:

1] We realize more and more that, when we are directing others, the only truly effective use of power consists of using it as a tool for the empowerment of those people whom we are directing. This holds true for any directing position that solicits power projections: manager, teacher, therapist, doctor, social worker, supervisor, and so on. It is most effective, in a self-management sense, for the person who directs, for those who are being directed, and for the interaction process that flows between them. It is most effective in terms of motivation, in terms of work satisfaction, and certainly in terms of work productivity, not to speak of the overall quality of life at work. When we take power away from somebody, not only will we not be able to build a constructive relationship with that person but we will compromise any form of organizational cooperation with him. This is self-destructive, as any organizational success is rooted in the ability of its members to work together constructively. By empowering the very people he directs, the leader liberates himself from the burden of their unproductive projections, encourages their motivation to learn, and promotes their vision of quality and competence.

2] When, in the direction of others, a leader gets unduly involved in the details of another's work to the extent of controlling it, and in so doing takes power away from the other, it is a sure sign that the leader is insufficiently in touch with her own power. In turn, in order to be able to empower others it is necessary to have access to one's own personal power. In more pragmatic terms, one cannot teach anything of real value to anybody unless one has already mastered what one is teaching. Similarly, the best manager is very likely to be the one who herself masters the operations she asks her employees to accomplish. And she will be even better at it if she masters not only the operations but also the learning process that leads to their accomplishment. One may be in a position of power in a group, but unless one has access to one's personal power in a particular area one will not be able to empower others in that area; it will remain a "token" power.

A complementary aspect is this: empowering others will be facilitated if the leader can be at ease with many different ways of being. Indeed, by empowering others, he supports the development of their own personal style of work. And by encouraging their self-management processes he deliberately risks losing them if they should eventually choose to work for another department or to change careers. Many leaders and supervisors are quite defensive about seeing the real, motivated person come forward after being an uncomplaining employee. Often they are afraid to listen to what the employee has to say – they take it for granted that the listening is only one way and want the employee to do the listening. When pointing this out to many people in a supervising position, it is somewhat surprising to observe their complete unawareness of this state of events. They are not really interested in what these people like or what moves them. Usually it is because they do not know how, or do not dare, to be in touch with what they themselves like, with what moves them, and so on. A leader will likely be more able to empower others to the extent that he can genuinely ask them questions such as, "What do you like to do?" "What moves you?" "What shakes you?" "What dreams do you have?" "Can I help you?"

He can then ask himself a question such as, "Is it realistic for me to help this person in what he wants?" The higher a degree of freedom he enjoys himself, the more he will be able to bestow freedom on others.

It is interesting to observe the fact that the more one is able to empower someone else, the more one empowers oneself at the same time. One example of this is the manager who lends power to an employee to negotiate contracts on her behalf, leaving the employee some freedom in negotiating the terms, or even sharing in the rewards that may come with the contract. The employee will surely be motivated, especially if the added responsibility awakens his sense of self-esteem. But by acting in this way, the manager herself reconnects with her own power also. She frees herself from one task in order to take on others that are now more interesting to her. Helping another person to tap into his own power can be a rewarding experience.

3] Empowering others does not mean condoning whatever they do. Empowering someone means to help him get in touch with what moves him, not blindly to accept what he does. In general, once a person is in touch with what moves him, he is happy, "in good spirits," and motivated. As he is in touch with these qualities and the resulting desire to be competent, he will generally be receptive toward constructive feedback as well. When someone is in a state in which he wants only approval of whatever he does, it definitely indicates he is out of touch with his personal power. An attitude of empowerment will require from the leader, not that he condone such a state, but that he demonstrate a certain trust in the process, a sense of integrity, and an uncompromised ability to relate to the employee in clear terms. At the same time, it requires the leader to be in touch with his own personal power and his own self-management processes.

4] We want to emphasize that physical force and violence are not expressions of power. On the contrary, they are symptoms of the inability to be in touch with personal power, and to communicate. In fact, the only way to end someone's tendency to use physical force is to help him restore the personal power that comes with "connection," not to return physical force. We could formulate a useful and paradoxical hypothesis here – the most effective way to end someone's physical violence is to empower the person. We would like to hazard the thought that the use of mental force and the use of violence belong to the same category. And we could formulate this more or less as follows. Whenever a person mentally forces his ideas and beliefs on someone else, this is in fact not an expression of power, but rather an admission of his inability to communicate creatively with realities different from his own, as well as an indication of his need to reconnect with his own self. We might add that with the awareness of one's own power comes a respect for the personal power of the people we interact with. To the extent that one uses one's power judiciously, one will also be able to help others to do the same.

The foregoing notes all have significant implications for the theory and practice of performance appraisals in organizations. This is the subject of our last section.

## A New Look at the Appraisal of Performance in Organizations

Organizations often have a constant preoccupation with the appraisal of performance and of work output. Typically, the appraisals are carried out at regular intervals, and they are based on predetermined criteria or standards that, ideally, cover all relevant dimensions of the work. We want to focus here on the fact that many times this is a procedure people submit to rather unwillingly, even in the best of cases, where they are allowed some participation in the process. From the viewpoint of the self-management approach, a number of observations can be made:

1] With the increasing importance of the relational components of work and of information systems, we observe a shift in the nature of the dimensions deemed essential in the conscientious accomplishment of an assignment. Indeed, the important dimensions of work are rapidly becoming more intangible and less measurable in objective terms. Instead of measuring the number of items produced in a given time period, we find ourselves wanting to measure communication and interpersonal skills, initiative, ethical sense, personality and character, the way an employee functions in a group context, and so on. With dimensions such as these, it becomes nearly impossible to avoid being subjective and unbiased in the expression of evaluative judgments. The standards against which the person is compared in each dimension simply lack an objective basis. For example, another's style tends to be judged as a function of one's own. But also, the way a particular individual "scores" on such a dimension cannot be isolated from the environment in which he works, or from the opportunities present in that environment. For example, an individual may receive a low score on "initiative" from a supervisor who insists on maintaining his own tight control on details of the work. In the same vein, the score an individual receives from his supervisor cannot be separated from the score that he would give his supervisor if he had a chance to do so.

2] The foregoing point highlights the need for two-way communication. Ordinarily when communication is smooth and a relationship reaches a fair degree of clarity and closeness, no performance appraisals are necessary. Feedback will be exchanged immediately and actions are adjusted in the process. In ordinary circumstances, there is a tendency to express evaluative comments when there is dissatisfaction on either side and when communication is seen as difficult or impossible. When communication is rich and creative, no need is felt for "evaluation" on either side. In turn, by formalizing this normal feedback function and by making it into an essentially one-way communication device, the personal power of the evaluator is being "recognized" and enhanced while that of the evaluee is being "ignored" or reduced, at least in the interpersonal context in which the appraisal takes place. As a result, the appraisal process tends to reduce and impoverish communication rather than enhance it. The employee may feel either flattered (if the appraisal was "good") or insulted (if the appraisal was "bad"). In both cases future communication is likely to be more difficult rather than easier, trust is likely to dwindle, and so on. In view of these facts, it would seem that communication will be furthered if instead of the supervisor appraising the employee, supervisor(s)and employee(s) are appraised together, based on how well they succeed in working together constructively toward the accomplishment of the job. Ideally we can imagine a process whereby the employee would express expectations that were not being met, and the supervisor would listen with an open mind, without interrupting. Then the supervisor would explain his expectations and the employee would listen, without feedback. After this exchange, each could give each other feedback on their respective statements. When an exercise such as this is done in an open-minded atmosphere, and preferably outside the work environment, it may become a realistic and enriching process for both parties. It would certainly go a long way toward expelling much of the unproductive information or misinformation that often piles up after days, months, and sometimes years of unexpressed feelings and unverified assumptions about each other.

3] The idea that performance appraisals function as a kind of feedback, and contribute to better communication between members of an organization is only rarely valid, unless our notion of communication is a very crude one. Instead we have found the function of performance appraisals to be closer to the concept of an organizational defense mechanism, in that their stated or non-stated purpose is to protect certain belief systems inherent in the organizational culture from types of communications that might threaten them. Performance appraisals also tend to be more prevalent in all situations where outlays of money have to be justified and where the perception is present that possible misuse of such money occurs. They are equally prevalent in situations where trust is low and where power struggles and conflicts float just beneath the surface of the explicit communications. Especially where tax money is concerned, performance appraisals can be conveniently used by managers to protect themselves in case dissatisfactions are expressed by clients, the organization, or sponsors. In other cases, the appraisal system is used as a tool to control recruitment, or to keep a tight control on who is and is not promoted. These practices are obviously a far cry from the avowed purpose of "enhancing communication"; instead, they become a tool for the exercise of interpersonal power in the organization. In fact, we can see that in many cases the appraisals are more conducive to power struggles and conflicts than to the enhancement of creative group power. This is understandable, as multiple-way communications tend to raise everyone's power, while one-way communications tend to negate the power of the person being "talked at."

4] It would seem that any set of criteria and standards of evaluation reflect a set of values, or what is important for the evaluator (or for the organization) in this work context. For example, the evaluator may think it is important that a large quantity of letters be typed by the secretary. However, for the secretary it may be more rewarding to deliver a quality job and to have a mature relationship with his or her employer. In comparing different secretaries on the basis of her own values, the evaluator may be comparing very different personalities. We may then ask, "What good does it do to evaluate three very different persons on the basis of one single set of values?" Another employer may value highly the number of initiatives taken by an employee. By neglecting the value the employee attaches to "gestation" and appropriation, he may judge this employee's work as unsatisfactory. It would seem that some form of mutual exploration of the best interests of both, and of where these interests or values can meet, would constitute a useful practice.

5] We have observed on many occasions that employee or executive appraisal procedures generate conflict and tension. People rarely submit to evaluations serenely. One of the possible reasons for this is that the objectives which the employee or the manager is expected to attain are extended by imagined or even hypothetical task additions. They are actually pseudo-objectives which are not always consistent with the fundamental mission of the organization. These pseudo-objectives take a toll on the behavior and the motivation of employees and often paralyze their sense of initiative. For example, in many government agencies delivering health and social services we may observe an almost obsessive preoccupation with the production of reports on activities performed, rather than a genuine concern with the quality of the service. The kind of confusion generated by such practices often goes together with considerable stress and a falsified perception of the organization's mission. An administrator who is required to fill out a specific number of forms per week can attain her "quota" and score well on her appraisal, but what does this have to do with the organization's ultimate aims?

The distance she feels between herself and the organization will sooner or later express itself in work-related stress. If the individual tries to change the existing system to reduce such dissonance, chances are she will only succeed in augmenting her frustration, for resistance against such efforts may be formidable. If she fails at this stage, it is very likely that her self-esteem will suffer and, consequently, her future efforts on behalf of the organization will be diminished.

An administrator who practices a self-management approach would, in these conditions, evaluate her own performance in relation to personally established objectives and thereby relieve the pressure associated with externally imposed criteria. It would make sense for her to differentiate clearly the goals of the organization from those of her immediate supervisors and from her own.

6] From the self-management viewpoint, it would seem that performance can hardly be appraised without taking into consideration the level of opportunities the organization opens up for processes of appropriation, relation, decision, and action. Further, a more productive approach would consist of leveling with the employee on the existence or non-existence of such opportunities and on the obstacles (organizational or other) that would prevent one from moving toward self management. As for the person who directs others, the most important performance-related question would more likely be: "What opportunities have you opened up with respect to the processes of appropriation, relation, decision, and action, both for yourself and your employees?" Our contention is that these general categories can very well be operationalized in specific organizational contexts.

7] Finally, we note that some organizations have set up training and development programs based on the results of executive evaluations. The concept of self management we have presented could provide a useful and inspiring framework for such management training programs. To focus on self management and on the lessons that come with the processes of appropriation, relation, decision, and action, may lead a training department to find a renewed interest in management and organizational development. In particular, programs tackling the effective learning and increased awareness of self management in organizations will constitute a useful strategy in the prevention, or at least the reduction, of work-related stress.

In summary, the observations made above make it clear that the self-management approach has implications for the appraisal of job performance in organizations. Of particular importance is the proposition that lessons associated with self management processes constitute a vital link between efficiency and the personal power of individuals who participate in the organizational dynamics.

"But it's morning. I have been given another day.
Another day to hear and read and smell and walk and love and glory.
I am alive for another day."

Hugh Prather

# CONCLUSIONS

All changes in our ways of being with each other in work settings entail changes in the cognitive maps we use to manage the immediate reality in which we find ourselves enmeshed. At some point, many people in organizations have experienced themselves as having little freedom of action and have gradually given up trying to be someone who counts in the work place. Others have overcompensated for their feelings by draining energy from their immediate environment. In both cases, their maps of the world in which they operate are basically impoverished. They do not perceive a very wide range of options for choosing their actions, and their actions are not the outcome of a deliberate process in which they are making free choices. Rather than risk making the wrong choice yet again, they have learned to live with a world they see as offering very few choices. We have become aware of the fact that many people experience similar difficulties and concerns. We might add that very often they do not find anyone who would consider these concerns legitimate enough to talk about them seriously.

Environments also change rapidly and drastically; many people find themselves caught in the middle, between the old and the new, between what has run its course and what is coming their way. The strain of these changes is assumed more and more by individuals themselves. The following are just a few scenarios illustrating changes individuals may go through with respect to work situations in organizations:

- A junior management employee or trainee in a relatively new company is moved up to a regular management job. He has to prepare himself to appropriate the new tasks. In doing so he needs to look beyond the official job description to what is really important in the job and what is of secondary importance. He has to find his new support system – for example, to find out how he has to act with whom, who he can rely on, etc. He needs to feel his way in the decision process, and to act. He may need first of all to establish a feeling of security. Once he feels comfortable in the position, and productive, he may then feel the necessity to grow and move to another type of work. He will need to prepare for his next challenge, know what he wants, etc.

- Someone rises a few layers in her organizational hierarchy and finds herself wanting to try a business of her own, perhaps with a partner. Consequently, she will need to work through a lot of appropriations, relations, decisions, and actions in a very short time. How will she manage all this? She will find herself in a very new frame of mind, dealing first-hand with management tasks, risks, uncertainties, personal conflicts, and doubts. For example: Will her family be able to live on what she makes?
- Someone wonders how he will manage himself while his organization is being merged with another. He does not know whether or not his job will still be there after the merger. He has been treasurer of his organization all his working life. Can he handle the new job as treasurer for both companies? Does he have the skills to merge the two accounting systems? Does he want that? Or does he really want to take a new job elsewhere, with the resultant need to appropriate that new organization, etc.?
- Some people change from one company to another within the same industry. Others change to a different industry, for example from insurance to banking. They then face the prospect not only of appropriating the new industry's culture, but also the new company's specific culture, with all its unknowns and uncertainties.
- Someone transfers from a business job to a government position. Public service is a different context from the private company. It tends to be more attuned and sensitive to public wants, while at the same time there are usually more controls. Such a transfer may require drastic changes in attitudes in order to be more aware of government procedures, some of which may be conflicting.
- When transferring from a government or business position to university teaching, for example, one encounters a whole new world and culture – the world of the conceptual and the abstract, where anything is possible (the "if" world). There, it is required to develop ideas and concepts, and communicate them. Relations are difficult – how does one touch base with colleagues, each of whom has a

specialized area of expertise, different from one's own? To overcome such barriers strains to the utmost one's ability to manage oneself.

- The transfer from a U.S.-based industry, government, or teaching position to work overseas in such places as Europe, China, and India. Each is a radically different culture with which one has to link up somehow (to appropriate, to relate, etc.). Without such links one will not get very far. One will need a high level of openness in order to function with another language, other customs, other clothing, other food, etc.

The above examples all have to do with changes in the work settings of individuals. But all kinds of other existential changes occur in people's environments and in their own lives, affecting them deeply – separation or divorce, sickness, death, the birth of a child, etc. The same problems present themselves. There are questions of relations, new situations have to be appropriated, decisions are made, and people act.

We have been concerned with elaborating the beginnings of a map that would help us organize our experiences in different areas of life and, in particular, that would help us better understand what has seemed unclear and at times bewildering in the organizations of which we have been members. We express the wish that such a map will also help the reader become more keenly aware of where he is in his organization, what does not work in his best interest, and what he wants for himself in this organizational context. We hope he will not merely pursue what he thinks he should want, but will become aware of options and whether he really wants to follow up on them, so that his choices in life become clearer.

Life reveals itself to be a flowing, changing process in which nothing is fixed forever. The flow of events and experiences carries us in directions and toward goals that we may be only dimly aware of at the outset. This can be the focus of much fascination and fright. We have come to believe that there is no fixed, closed system of behavior, action, or set of principles by which a person best develops. A person's development is preferably seen as a spiralling process guided by the continuously changing nature and understanding of experience.

In working together, as well as through our other relationships, we have also come to realize that, however tempting this may be at one point or other, we cannot simply follow in the footsteps of someone else. We can be open to what others have to say, we can learn from others, borrow techniques from them, form an interest group together, and so on. But we each find our own truths in our own experience, and these serve to guide us in our own choices. The challenge for individuals in the years ahead may very well be the ability to be with others and at the same time to be intensely themselves. Already the many changes and uncertainties inherent in organizational settings forewarn us of this.

The affirmation of personal power, then, leads to the cultivation of genuine self-esteem anchored in the experience and the expression of one's potentials as they manifest themselves. It is also the management of self-doubt, by intensively learning in those areas where one is not very sure of oneself. In the same context, we have realized that we can only grant someone the freedom to explore and understand his own experience to the extent that we can allow ourselves to be open to our own experiential process and the understanding of it. The reconnection to personal power through self management results not in competition whose aim is to destroy the other, but in a lively camaraderie in which one's own power can always be felt and where the experience of one's power is never destroyed simply to satisfy someone else. The destruction of someone else's power makes for the worst of all possible relationships.

The main thrust of the book is to clear the way toward a map for the individual's mental hygiene, as she finds herself in complex organizational environments. With the increasing number of informational messages she must process, with the number of diverse techniques and tools available that speak to personal preferences, and with ever more external sources claiming her attention, we hypothesize that the need for a person to be genuinely centered in herself is indeed crucial. Consequently, the need to manage, to the best of her ability, her appropriations, relations, decisions, and actions gains relevance. The concept of self management as defined here emerged from an attempt to find answers to the psychological bewilderment of a great number of managers, executives, and operative personnel alike, whose relationships with their organizations may have been experienced as ambivalent and sometimes disappointing. In doing so, we have steered away from established belief systems and from the multiple assumptions that dominate the culture of many contemporary businesses and other organizations. Instead, we have built on our own experiences in diverse organizational settings as well as those shared with us by friends, colleagues, and many others.

The model presented in this book may help reestablish for the reader, as it has for us, his connection with an often forgotten fundamentally human dimension in organizations.

# QUESTIONS FOR DEVELOPING INSIGHTS ON SELF MANAGEMENT

The following questions constitute a tool for developing further insights into the process of self management in particular for:

- enabling one to organize one's thoughts and identify important issues in one's self-management
- focusing on examples of obstructions pertaining to one's appropriation, relation, decision and action processes;
- finding ways to bring one's self-management more in line with what one wants.

We have found that management of oneself becomes more accessible to the extent that one can interact with persons with whom a significant and trustworthy relation can be established. After selecting and answering for oneself a series of questions from the list below, it may be beneficial to open up a discussion with a trusted support group. Much pertinent material may be generated by selecting even a limited sample of up to fifteen questions.

*Self Management Process: General Questions*

1] In what area do you perceive the most important obstruction with respect to self management in your organization. For example, what aspect of yourself do you find most difficult to express?

2] Find a few striking incidents from your experience in organizations that have contributed to shaping your own theory about how to manage yourself.

3] Suppose you find yourself in a management or supervisory position in your organization. Using your own experience as an employee, write a scenario of how you would act and how you would not act in that position.

*Appropriation Process*

1] Find an example of a situation in which you have experienced an obstruction in your appropriation process, in the organization of which you are currently a member.

2] Find an example of a situation in which you have experienced the opening up of your appropriation process.

3] Identify several factors that have contributed to the feeling that your appropriation process was blocked. Then identify several factors that at one point or another led your appropriation process to open up.

4] Give three examples of significant lessons you have gleaned from your work during the past six months.

5] What does it take to be able to continue learning for yourself in the context of this organization?

6] What do you wish to appropriate in the next six months in your work environment?

7] What personal needs are being filled by being a member of this organization? Which significant personal needs are not being filled?

8] What are your interests and preferences in your work? Ideally, what would you like to contribute to your organization?

9] Name a few opportunities present in your organization that correspond to those interests and preferences.

10] What conditions prevent you from tuning into opportunities?

11] What values are important for you to express in your work (equity, sense of community, friendship, competence)?

12] Give an example where you notice a reasonable fit between the values that are important to you and those you perceive as prevalent in your organization.

13] Give an example where your personal values clash with the values prevalent in the organizational culture.

14] What information channels do you use to decipher your organization's values, culture and myths, and, in general, to find out what goes on? Between verbal and nonverbal channels of information, which ones are easier for you?

15] What attitudes or beliefs do you find yourself "protecting" against influence from the organization?

16] Can you find an example of a situation in which you felt a danger to your personal identity? How does the organization influence your sense of identity, or by what mechanisms have you resisted such influences?
17] Are you satisfied with the ways in which information circulates in your organization? Explain.
18] Do you feel comfortable in your job? Explain.
19] Do your colleagues feel comfortable in their jobs? How do you know that they do or that they do not?
20] Identify at least one myth, or general assumption, that your colleagues and yourself would agree upon, which prevails in your organization.
21] Is there a slogan that would characterize some of the ideals shared in your work group? Explain.
22] Give an example of a major political or social change that has affected your organization in the past year.
23] What concrete steps or actions (initiated by yourself or by others) would facilitate your appropriating the many different facets of your organization and of your work?
24] What conditions could interfere with your appropriating different facets of your organization or your work?

*Relation Process*

1] Find an example of a situation in which you have experienced an obstruction in your relation process in your organization.
2] Find an example of a situation in which you have experienced the opening up of your relation process in your organization.
3] Identify several factors that have contributed to the feeling of obstruction and to the feeling of opening up in your relation process.
4] What do you desire in terms of contacts or exchanges with your work colleagues? What stands in the way of concretizing such exchanges?
5] What do your work colleagues desire in terms of contacts or exchanges with you? What stands in the way of your responding to such desires or expectations?
6] Recall a situation in which you needed help from others at work?

What kind of behaviors or attitudes did you find helpful or unhelpful?

7] Identify several colleagues whom you experience as generally supportive toward you. Then identify several colleagues whom you experience as generally unsupportive. Identify several people whom you experience as indifferent toward you. What feelings do you have toward each of them? Try to describe what support really means to you, and what it may mean to others.

8] In what ways are others supportive of you? In what ways are they not supportive?

9] Describe a conflict or misunderstanding that you resolved in your work group in the last 6 months. How did you feel about it?

10] Do your work colleagues often level with each other? If so, under what circumstances? Do you level with your colleagues? Give one example of such an incident in the past six months. How did you feel about this incident?

11] Name some of the obstacles that you have perceived between colleagues in communicating with each other. Give two examples in the last six months where positive or negative feelings were expressed by yourself or your colleagues.

12] Give an example of a relationship in your work environment that is genuinely nurturing to you. What is it in the relationship that makes it nurturing? Is it mutual?

13] How many of your work colleagues acknowledge you as a person? What actions on their part do you experience as acknowledgement or recognition of yourself?

14] How do you acknowledge or express recognition to your colleagues?

15] What fears or apprehensions do you have in being yourself with your colleagues? What aspects of yourself would not be accepted by your colleagues? What would happen if your worst fears materialized?

16] What fears or confusions do you imagine your colleagues have in "being themselves" at work?

17] Describe how you affirm yourself in your work group.

18] How often do you meet with colleagues after work? Under what circumstances do you enjoy meeting with them after work?

19] How many of your work colleagues are your friends? With how many of them do you feel at ease having lunch? What affinities do you discover in them?

20] In what ways do you express affection with some colleagues (for example, by exchanging intimate information on family, houses, aspirations, ideals, preferences, hobbies)?

21] In what ways have you disengaged affectively from some of your colleagues? Give one example.

22] What concrete steps or actions, initiated by yourself or by others, would facilitate the relation process in your work group?

23] What conditions could interfere with a more adequate relation process?

*Decision Process*

1] Find an example of a situation in which you have experienced an obstruction of your decision process in your organization.

2] Find an example of a situation in which you have experienced the opening up of your decision process in your organization.

3] Identify several factors that have contributed to the feeling of obstruction and to the feeling of opening up in your decision process.

4] How do you usually go about finding alternative options before making a decision? Do you usually analyze the advantages and disadvantages of both? Give an example.

5] When confronted with several options, how do you overcome the ambivalence and finally decide? Give an example of a situation.

6] In a decision you recently made, how did you go about clarifying personal values?

7] List some of your priorities in life. In what ways do they coincide or conflict with the priorities of your work group? What goals or priorities can you identify that drive your colleagues, your work group? Do differences between your own priorities and those of others sometimes prevent you from making a decision you feel would be right? Explain.

8] Are there sometimes conflicts between a decision you make on behalf of the organization and your personal values? If so, describe one such conflict.

9] Are your personal values getting clearer as you make more and more decisions? Give an example.

10] How did you evaluate the right time and place with respect to a recent decision? Give an example.

11] What prevents you from learning from your past decisions? Explain.

12] Name a few conditions that facilitate decision for yourself making in terms of support, environment, etc.?

13] What are some of the most unfavorable conditions for your decision making that you have encountered?

14] When you make decisions on behalf of the organization, how do colleagues or supervisors support you? In what ways are you not supported? Give an example. What consequences are there when your decisions are not supported?

15] How do you deal with the limiting effects of decisions made by others? Do you benefit sometimes from such decisions? Give an example.

16] What concrete steps or actions, by you or others, would facilitate the flow of your decision process in the organization?

17] What conditions could interfere with the implementation of concrete steps or actions to facilitate your decision flow?

*Action Process*

1] Find an example of a situation in which you have experienced an obstruction in your action process in your organization.

2] Find an example of a situation in which you opened up your action process in your organization.

3] Identify several factors that have contributed to the feeling of obstruction and to the feeling of opening up of your action process.

4] Are your actions in your organization congruent with your personal priorities? If so, in what ways? In what ways are they not? How does this affect you?

5] What kind of appropriations, relations, decisions tend to energize your action process? What kind of appropriations, relations, decisions tend to inhibit your action flow?

6] In what circumstances do you feel like being intensely active at work? Give an example.

7] Under what conditions do you feel like slowing down your actions at work? Give an example.

8] Give at least one example where you have witnessed the impact an action of yours had on other people. How did you feel?

9] Can you recall at least one incident where you felt pressured to act even though you did not feel it was appropriate for you to do so at the time?

10] Can you recall one incident where you pressured others in your work environment to act?

11] Give an example of a situation where you thought action was better than inaction? And the reverse?

12] What organizational or personal aspects can you identify from your experience that hampered your desire or your ability to implement decisions? Give an example of each.

13] What organizational or personal aspects can you identify that have facilitated the implementation of your decisions? Give an example of each.

14] In general, what would facilitate the flow of your actions in your organization?

15] What could interfere with the implementation of conditions that facilitate the flow of your actions in your organization?

# AFTERWORD

At the end of this volume, it seems appropriate to briefly outline the process by which we produced a collectively authored text.

The three authors agreed to meet regularly, and we respected the agreement. The authors have very different backgrounds in terms of work experience (in business organizations, government institutions, international agencies, small business enterprises, several universities on three different continents, and consulting assignments). We have very different emotional backgrounds and personalities. We have confronted our experiences and have retained the ideas and concepts we could consensually agree upon. Our views often clashed, but writing the book remained a pleasurable experience because of the synergy maintained during the creative process. No doubt our meetings have influenced our individual self-management processes. Our decisions and ways of solving various problems were affected by our exchange of ideas. A kind of support network gradually developed among the three of us.

While we remained anchored in our separate selves, a discrete and unstated bond has grown among us during the production of this work – the excitement of creating something together and sharing our perspectives and differences.

# REFERENCES USED IN THE TEXT


Argyris, Chris. *Reasoning, Learning and Action.* San Francisco: Jossey-Bass, 1983.

Aronson, Elliot. *The Social Animal.* New York: Freeman, 1972.

Asch, Solomon E. *Social Psychology.* Englewood Cliffs, N.J.: Prentice-Hall, 1952.

Bateson, Gregory. *Mind and Nature, Necessary Unity.* New York: Bantam, 1979.

Bateson, Gregory. *Steps to an Ecology of Mind.* New York: Ballantine, 1972.

Bettelheim, Bruno. *The Empty Fortress.* New York: Free Press, 1967.

Bion, W. R. *Experiences in Groups.* New York: Free Press, 1961.

Culbert Samuel A. *The Organization Trap.* New York: Basic Books, 1974.

Freud, Sigmund. *Psychopathology of Everyday Life.* Translated by A. A. Brill, New York: New American Library (Mentor 1257), undated.

Gibb, Jack. *Trust: A New View of Personal and Organizational Development.* Los Angeles: Guild of Tutors Press, 1978.

Goffman, Erving. *The Presentation of Self in Everyday Life.* New York: Doubleday, 1959.

Gruber, H. E. & Voneche, J. *The Essential Piaget.* New York: Basic Books, 1977.

Hall, E. T. *The Dance of Life.* New York: Doubleday, 1984.

Hawking, Stephen W. *A Brief History of Time.* New York: Basic Books, 1988.

Jacquard, Albert. *Endangered by Science.* New York: Columbia University Press, 1985.

Jacquard, Albert. *In Praise of Difference.* New York: Columbia University Press, 1964.

James, William. *The Principles of Psychology.* Boston: Harvard University Press, 1981.

Janis, I. L. & Mann, L. *Decision Making A Psychological Analysis of Conflict, Choice and Commitment.* New York: The Free Press, 1977.

Jaques, E. *The Changing Culture of a Factory.* London: Tavistock, 1951

Jung, Carl G. *Synchronicity, An Acausal Connecting Principle.* Princeton, N.J.: Princeton University Press, 1973.

Jung, Carl G. *The Practice of Psychotherapy. Essays on the Psychology of the Transference and Other Subjects.* Princeton, NJ: Princeton University Press, 1954.

Kant, Immanuel, *Critique of Pure Reason.* New York: St. Martin's Press, 1965.

Kets de Vries, Manfred, F. R. *The Irrational Executive.* New York: International University Press, 1984.

Kets de Vries, Manfred, F. R. & Miller, Danny. *The Neurotic Organization.* San Francisco: Jossey-Bass, 1984.

Kets de Vries, Manfred, F. R. & Miller, Danny. *Unstable at the Top: Inside the Troubled Organization.* New York: New American Library (Mentor), 1987.

Kopp, Sheldon. *If You Meet the Buddha on the Road, Kill Him!* New York: Bantam, 1976.

Laing, Ronald D. *Self and Others*. New York: Penguin, 1971.

Lao Tzu. *Tao Te Ching* (Translated with an introduction by D. C. Lau). New York: Penguin, 1963.

Milgram, Stanley. *The Individual in a Social World Essays and Experiments*. Reading, MA: Addison-Wesley, 1977.

Prather, Hugh. *Notes to Myself: My Struggle to Become a Person.* New York: Bantam Books, 1970.

Sartre, Jean-Paul. *No Exit*. New York: Knopf, 1947.

Schein, Edgar H. *Organizational Culture and Leadership*. San Francisco: Jossey-Bass, 1986.

Siu, Ralph G. H. "Management and the Art of Chinese Baseball." *Sloan Management Review*, 19(3), 1978, pp. 83–89

Von Bertalanffy, L. *General Systems Theory; Foundations, Development, Applications*. New York: Braziller, 1968.

Weyl, Herman. *Philosophy of Mathematics and Natural Science*. Princeton, NJ: Princeton University Press, 1949.

Wheeler, Daniel D. & Janis, Irving L. *A Practical Guide for Making Decisions*. New York: Free Press, 1980.

# FURTHER READINGS

**The readings below constitute a list of works that have stimulated our thinking in connection with this volume. In different degrees and on different levels, they combine to weave the background of the realities that we have perceived and selected.**


Adams, John D. *Transforming Work A Collection of Organizational Transformation Readings*. Alexandria, VA: Miles River Press, 1684.

Beer, Stafford. *Designing Freedom*. Toronto: CBC Publications, 1974.

Blanchard, Kenneth & Peale, Norman Vincent. *The Power of Ethical Management.* New York: William Morrow, 1988

Bloom, A. *The Closing of the American Mind.* New York: Simon & Schuster, 1987.

Bolman, Lee G. & Deal, Terrence E. *Modern Approaches to Understanding and Managing Organizations*. San Francisco: Jossey-Bass, 1984.

Bourdieu, P. *Le sens pratique*. Paris: Editions de Minuit, 1980.

Bradford, David L. & Cohen, Allan R. *Managing for Excellence.* New York: Wiley, 1984.

Branden, Nathaniel. *The Disowned Self.* Los Angeles: Nash, 1971.

Campbell, Joseph (with B. Moyers). *The Power of Myth*. New York: Doubleday, 1988.

Culbert, Samuel A. & McDonough, John J. *Radical Management: Power Politics and the Pursuit of Trust*. New York: Free Press, 1985.

Deal, Terrence E. & Kennedy, Allen A. *Corporate Cultures: The Rites and Rituals of Corporate Life*. Reading, MA: Addison-Wesley, 1982.

Drucker, Peter. *Innovation and Entrepreneurship: Practice and Principles*. New York: Harper & Row, 1985.

Freud, Sigmund. *Civilization and its Discontents*. New York: W.W. Norton 1961.

Fromm, Erich. *The Sane Society*. Greenwich, CT: Fawcett, 1955.

Geertz, Clifford. *The Interpretation of Cultures*. New York: Basic Books, 1973.

Gendlin, Eugene T. *Focusing*. New York: Bantam, 1978.

Gleick James. *Chaos: Making a New Science*. New York: Viking, 1987.

Goffman, Erving. *Stigma: Notes on the Management of Spoiled Identity*. Englewood Cliffs, N.J.: Prentice-Hall, 1963.

Goodman, Paul S. & Associates. *Change in Organizations: New Perspectives on Theory, Research and Practice*. San Francisco: Jossey-Bass 1982.

Hackman, J. Richard & Suttle, J. Lloyd. *Improving Life at Work : Behavioral Science Approaches to Organizational Change*. Santa Monica, CA: Goodyear, 1977.

Harrington, Alan. *Life in the Crystal Palace*. New York: Avon, 1959.

Hickman, Graig R. & Silva, Michael A. *Creating Excellence: Managing Corporate Culture, Strategy, and Change in the New Age*. New York: N.A. L., 1984

Jacquard, Albert. *Inventer l'homme*. Brussels: Editions Complexe, 1984.

Jones, Michael Owen; Moore, Michael D. & Snyder, Richard C. (eds.). *Inside Organizations : Understanding the Human Dimension*. Newbury Park, CA: Sage, 1988.

Jung, Carl G. *Man and His Symbols*. New York: Bell, 1964.

Kopp, Sheldon. *An End to Innocence: Facing Life Without Illusions*. New York, Bantam, 1978.

Kopp, Sheldon, *Mirror, Mask and Shadow: The Risks and Rewards of Self-Acceptance*. New York: Bantam, 1980.

Laing, Ronald D. *The Divided Self*. New York: Penguin, 1960.

Levering, Robert; Moskowitz, Milson & Katz, Michael. *The 100 Best Companies to Work for in America*. Reading, MA: Addison-Wesley, 1984.

Likert, Rensis & Likert, Jane Gibson. *New Ways of Managing Conflict*. New York: McGraw Hill, 1976.

Maslow, Abraham H. *Eupsychian Management*. Homewood, Ill., Richard D. Irwin: 1965.

Maslow, Abraham H. *The Farther Reaches of Human Nature*. New York: Viking, 1971.

May, Rollo. *The Meaning of Anxiety*. New York: Pocket, 1950.

McClelland, David C. *Power: The Inner Experience*. New York: Irvington, 1975.

McCoy, Charles S. *Management of Values: The Ethical Difference in Corporate Policy and Performance*. Boston: Pitman, 1985.

Morgan, Gareth. *Images of Organization*. New York: Sage, 1986.

Naisbitt John. *Megatrends: Ten New Directions Transforming Our Lives*. New York: Warner, 1982.

Nuttin, Joseph. *Motivation, Planning and Action; A Relational Theory of Behavior Dynamics*. Hillsdale, NJ: Lawrence Erlbaum Associates, 1984.

Pagès, Max et.al. *L'emprise de I'organisation*. Paris: Presses Universitaires de France, 1979

Perls, Frederick; Hefferline, Ralph F.; Goodman, Paul. *Gestalt Therapy*. New York: Dell, 1951.

Peters, Tom. *Thriving on Chaos: Handbook for a Management Revolution*. New York: Knopf, 1987

Peters, Tom & Austin, Nancy. *A Passion for Excellence: The Leadership Difference*. New York: Random House, 1985.

Porter, Michael E. *Competitive Advantage: Creating and Sustaining Superior Performance*. New York: Free Press, 1985

Rogers, Carl R. *A Way of Being*. Boston: Houghton Mifflin, 1980.

Rogers, Carl R. *On Personal Power*. New York: Dell, 1977.

Rubin, Theodore I. *Compassion and Self-Hate*. New York: Ballantine, 1975.

Sainsaulieu, Renaud.*L'identité au travail: les effets culturels de l'organisation*. Paris: Presses de la Fondation Nationale des Sciences Politiques, 1977.

Shostrom, Everett L. *Actualizing Therapy: Foundations for a Scientific Ethic.* San Diego, CA: Edits, 1976.

Tichy, Noël M. *Managing Strategic Change: Technical Political and Cultural Dynamics.* New York: Wiley, 1983.

Toffler, Alvin. *The Third Wave.* New York: William Morrow, 1980.

Vickers, Geoffrey. *Freedom in a Rocking Boat: Changing Values in an Unstable Society.* New York: Basic Books, 1971.

Watzlawick, Paul. *How Real is Real?: Communication, Disinformation, Confusion.* New York: Random House, 1976.

# Index


**A**

action 8, 32, 36, 38, 45, 98, 115, 128
  adaptive 156
  flow of 156
  ill-timed 152
  integration of 152
  meaningful 118, 173
  paralyzed 39
  process 37, 144, 155
  pseudo- 154
  repetitive 150
actualization 47
affection 122, 131, 164, 186
alienation 107
alternation 108, 111, 115, 140, 145, 153
ambiguity 73, 76, 81f., 83, 117, 137ff., 176
ambivalence 117f., 120
anger 102, 120, 129, 135, 166, 181, 183, 186
anxiety 37, 131f., 145
appropriation 8, 32, 36, 45, 52, 115
  multidimensional nature of 53
  overburdened 39, 62
  process 24, 30, 43, 44, 51, 53, 56ff., 64, 69, 72, 77, 79ff., 83, 124
  withdrawal from 42
Argyris 15
Aronson, E. 130
Asch, S. 130
association
  professional 63
attachment 86, 91
attitude 120, 178
  defensive 109
  inflexible 136
  non-discriminating 176f.
  self-destructive 132
attribution 185, 186
authenticity 96, 97
authority 99, 125
authority figure 128, 129
autonomy 92, 162
awareness 15, 45, 52, 55, 58, 68, 71, 75, 81, 90, 94, 101, 111, 124, 125, 126, 127, 129, 130, 131, 162, 164, 165, 180, 184, 192, 196

**B**

barrier
  environmental 165
  individual 163
  overcome 201
  self-imposed 42
Bateson, G. 75, 170
behavior 48, 79, 115
  antisocial 40
  authoritarian 40, 43, 131
  automatic 159
  clinging 103
  compulsive 131
  defensive 39ff.
  ill-adapted 37, 60, 64
  mechanical 35
  outcomes of 89
  patterns of 51
  repetitive 39
  robotic 35
  standards of 47, 74
Bettelheim, B. 78
blame 59
blind spots 62, 63
boredom 104, 122
breakdown 152
burnout 74, 158, 181

**C**

change 33, 45f., 80, 82, 153, 156f., 174f., 199, 201f.
  management 48
  resistance to 49
charisma 185

choice 120ff., 133ff., 136, 140, 144, 173, 177, 199, 201f.
  conscious 126
  compulsive 120
climate
  defensive 111
  organizational 113
closeness 102f., 112, 162, 186, 193
commitment 107, 122, 139, 161, 163
communication 54f., 76, 86ff., 94, 98, 103, 112, 136f., 162, 168, 170, 178f., 180, 186, 193f.
  obstacles 86
competence 33, 82, 91f., 109, 150, 158, 180, 186, 190
  professional 137
competition 84, 106, 163
competitiveness 38
complexity 62, 66, 96, 145
compulsion 163
conditioning 155
conflict 47, 55, 67, 72, 75, 87, 90f., 109f., 113, 149, 176, 194, 195, 200
  internal 42, 121
conformance 43, 47, 61
confrontation 179f.
confusion 76
congruence 116, 122
conscientiousness
  professional 107
conscious 31
constraint 177
contact 97f., 135
control 47f., 78f., 99, 106, 116, 146, 151, 160f., 188, 193f.
  conscious 31
  dogmatic 154
  external 154
  manipulative 154
  position of 180
  sense of 180
cooperation 38, 84, 189
coping 44, 47, 161
criteria 145, 166, 179, 192, 195f.
  external 144
  for evaluation 151
  for healthy management 164
  internal 144
Culbert, S. A. 50
culture
  organizational 57, 63f., 81f., 107, 113, 123, 126, 135, 176, 194
curiosity 35, 56, 61, 78, 80, 83f., 159

D

decision 8, 32, 36f., 38, 45, 98, 115, 123, 134, 146, 173
  flow 123
decision process 30, 35f., 115, 135
defense mechanism 43, 70, 125, 127ff., 141, 142, 194
denial 127
dependency 93ff., 100, 102, 105f., 109, 119, 180, 184
depression 36, 43, 76, 122, 126, 131, 165, 179
desire 123f., 128, 130, 133, 148, 172
detachment 122
  emotional 117
development 73
  constructive 72
  needs for 72
  organizational 196
  personal growth 42
  professional 14
  unbalanced 39
direction 123, 127, 129, 133, 134, 138, 140, 171ff., 182
  sense of 36
discernment 119, 167
disengagement 83, 102f., 108, 110, 112
dissipation 179, 181
dissonance 69f., 121, 155, 196
domination 183
double bind 60, 136
double-talk 64, 73, 75ff.

E

effectiveness 148, 180
efficiency 76, 77, 100, 147ff., 197
  notion of 146
effort
  creative 29
empathy 78, 101, 158, 172, 181
empowerment 189, 191
emptiness 29, 89

energy 113
environment 31, 45, 48, 51f., 55f., 59, 61f., 64f., 69, 70, 78, 80, 82, 155, 165, 173, 193f., 199, 201f.
    control of 43
    opportunities 26
    organizational 63, 65, 68, 73, 79, 146, 149
    rejection of 43
    theories about 44
    work 86
equilibrium 27, 147f., 151, 175, 176
    dynamic 47
    emotional 149
ethical sense 193
evaluation 148
    mutual 147


VAKAT


exchange 35, 80, 86ff., 92, 111, 113, 122, 146, 180, 194
expectation 92, 94, 97ff., 102, 113, 126, 133, 148, 150, 173, 175, 179, 181, 187, 194

**F**

fear 41f., 44, 58ff., 70, 89f., 92, 97. 99, 122, 131f., 139, 150f., 155ff., 162, 166, 182, 186
feedback 55, 67, 80, 83, 104, 111, 120, 144, 147, 155, 160ff., 191, 193, 194
    punitive 53
flexibility 34, 118, 119, 120, 162
focusing 58, 72, 104, 138, 140, 157
    capacity 139
freedom 125, 130, 133, 138, 144, 191, 199
    degrees of 102
    experienced 125, 130
    level of 162
    sense of 129f.
Freud, S. 31, 52, 69, 141
frustration 37f., 129, 157, 196
fulfillment 168

**G**

Gibb, J. 30
group 32, 67, 89f., 92, 104, 133, 137, 154, 182, 185ff., 190, 193
    conformity 140
    dynamics 87, 174
    facilitator 142
    process 130
    session 142
    work 89
Gruber, H.E. 25
guilt 37, 41, 76, 78, 99, 131, 140, 155, 165f., 184

**H**

Hall, E. T. 85
harmony 28, 38, 45, 130
    creation of 55
    level of 120
    maintenance 112
    restoration of 23, 48, 49, 81, 106, 128
Hawking, S. W. 18
helplessness 126, 129
hostility 99
humor 31, 99
hyperactivity 129

**I**

identification
    with the role 102, 105
identity 57, 75, 112
    crisis 37
ignorance 58ff.
image 97, 100ff., 104, 107, 167, 187
    company 106
    conforming to 101
imagination 167
implementation 144, 147ff., 167
impulsiveness 156
inaction 37
incongruity 76, 90, 119, 121
inflexibility 33
information 55, 58f., 61ff., 79ff., 83f., 88ff., 95, 120, 126, 128, 130, 137ff., 141f., 150, 154, 172, 175, 181, 187f., 192, 194
    access to 79, 139
    confirming or disconfirming 54f.
    discovery of new 140
    exchange of 88
    flow 88

input 60
output 60
overload 41, 44
processing 42
search 117
seeking of 124
withholding 108
inhibition 35, 39, 161
initiative 136, 145, 161f., 193, 195
inquiry 55f.
integration 32, 35, 54, 58f., 61, 84, 158, 173, 181
integrity 155
intention 144ff., 152f., 157, 159, 165f., 175
clarification of 157
realization of 147
interaction 24, 101, 111, 181
action 25
appropriation 25
decision 25
organizational 96
relation 25
intimacy 26, 29, 86, 88f., 93, 96ff., 100, 102, 107, 111, 122, 132
introjection 131f.
intuition 56, 140ff.

J

Janis, I. L. 42, 130
Jaques, E. 87
jealousy 166
job description 162, 199
Jung, C. G. 114

K

Kant, I. 66
Kets de Vries 10, 87
knowledge 99, 110, 127, 165f., 168, 186
integration of 150
Kopp, S. 72

L

Laing, R. D.
Lao Tzu 182
leadership 73, 106ff., 111, 171, 173, 181f., 190
learning 105, 157, 162, 174, 177, 178, 184, 189, 196, 202
ability 95
circumstances of 139
commitment to 105
concept of 52
desire to 150
from one's action 150
inability 94
personal 152
refusal 94
limitation 32, 47f., 51, 62, 105
self-imposed 31
loss 129

M

management
generic processes 31
manager 31f.
manipulation 78, 130
Mann, L. 42
meaning 48f., 77f., 81f.
mental block 80
mental map 51, 53ff., 61ff., 70f., 79ff.
messages 77
ambigiuous 57, 73, 75, 76, 78
organizational 73
Milgram, S. 130
models 59, 64, 80, 141, 159, 172ff., 203
motivation 78, 118, 121, 124f., 133f., 137, 176, 189, 190, 195
demotivation 133, 158
myths 52, 57

N

needs 39, 51, 81, 88, 101, 105, 109, 110ff., 117, 122ff., 128ff., 133, 145, 148, 153f., 176
deficiency-motivated 134
social 36
support 36
norms 79, 125, 132, 184
culture-induced 90

O

objective 148f., 160, 165, 180, 188, 195f.
pseudo- 195

obstruction 34ff., 44ff., 62, 79, 81, 103, 105, 106, 110, 111, 118f., 122, 126, 156f., 184
  diffusive character 34
  first type 33
  second type 33, 38
  symptoms of 58, 60f., 102, 152
  third type 33, 39
openness 35, 61, 79, 94f., 108, 119f., 123f., 128, 201
opportunity 32, 37, 39f., 45, 58, 81, 109, 119, 147, 153, 158, 159f., 163ff., 175ff., 182, 193, 196
option 139
organization 31, 33, 61, 63
  adaptive 14
  effectiveness 15
  healthy 14
  mental image 36
  power and influence 14
  process 21

**P**

perception 69, 175
perception
  distortion 71
performance 67, 71, 74, 98, 100, 140, 145, 180f., 196
  appraisal of 57, 171, 192, 193f., 197
  evaluation 16, 74
  optimal 149
  rewards 161
  task 108
Perls, F. 69, 131
perspective 52, 54f., 81, 103, 179
  sense of 31, 101
Piaget, J. 25
potential 39, 46, 86, 92, 96, 108, 150f., 167, 173, 176f., 179, 181, 184, 202
  creative 48
  personal 27
power 59, 73, 77, 98, 104, 108, 127, 154, 160, 162, 171, 173, 183ff., 190, 191f., 194
  abuse of 188
  centre 137
  failures 184
  illusions 183
  in groups 185, 188, 195
  issue of 182
  personal 153f., 158, 182, 183, 185f., 188ff., 193, 197, 202
  powerlessness 126, 129
  projection 189
  struggles 194
  symbolic 187
  token 190
Prather, H. 198
prejudice 42, 125, 158
priorities 29, 36, 72, 88, 115ff., 121f., 127, 135, 138, 145, 147, 151, 172
  organizational 119
  priorities 27
priority 88, 145, 147, 151, 172
processes 22, 113, 118
  obstruction 28
  action 24, 27, 29, 37, 39, 144, 155
  alienation 33
  alternation 30, 32, 86, 87
  appropriation 26, 43, 51, 53, 56ff., 64, 69, 72, 77, 79ff., 124
  attributes 19
  coexistence 30
  contamination 33f.
  creative 21, 23
  cycles 29f.
  decision 24, 27, 36, 115, 135
  dynamic aspects 20
  flow of 23
  global perspective 20
  group 31, 130
  healthy 28ff., 40, 47, 62
  impoverished 33
  managing of 19, 21, 23, 159, 160
  organizational 21, 23
  output measures 20
  phases 19, 29f., 39, 46
  polarities 19, 30, 39, 46
  regularities 20, 49
  relation 24, 26, 29, 35, 47, 77, 86, 87, 92, 105, 112
  rhythms 19, 29f., 32, 39, 46, 103, 104, 108
  self-organizing 21, 23
  subconscious 138
  synchronization 32f., 38, 46

procrastination 152, 157
productivity 139, 157, 189
programming 126
  cultural 124f., 127, 130f., 183
project 144f., 151, 157
  life 150, 174
projection 45, 64ff., 72, 73, 97, 99f., 102, 105, 127, 142, 173, 185f., 188, 190
  characteristics of 68
  creative aspects of 71
  creative role 65
  defensive aspects of 65, 69
  dissolving 72
  negative 71
  positive 71
projects 159

**R**

rationalization 42, 70
reaction
  defensive 127
reflex
  of the mind 128
  physical 128
reinforcement 181
relation 8, 32, 35ff., 45, 99f., 115
  flow of 86
  harmonious 106, 110
  intimate 141
  meaningful 107
  network of 86
  network of supportive people 26
  process 29, 30, 35ff., 39, 47, 77, 86f., 92, 105, 112
  supportive individuals 86
relationships 87, 91, 93, 102f., 107, 109, 111, 113, 119, 132, 146, 157, 162, 173, 180, 186, 189, 195, 202
  authentic 58
  organizational 129
  supportive 58
resentment 181, 183, 186
resistance 196
  passive 148, 149
resources 32, 95, 119, 139, 141, 145, 153, 157, 164, 176, 181
  capacity to mobilize 167
  creative 30
  development of 150
responsibility 161ff., 167, 174, 176f., 181
  professional 35
risk 90, 97, 149, 159
role 87, 96, 97, 99ff., 105, 112, 130, 141, 172, 173
  helping 121
  identification with 102, 105
  organizational 93
  professional 47, 84, 120
  punitive 100
Rorschach test 64
rule 131, 144
rumor 57, 80

**S**

Sartre, J. P. 30
scapegoat 71
Schein, H. 53
security
  basic 142
  emotional 116
  feeling of 200
  sense of 150
self management 6ff.
  values inherent 10
  abilities 9, 14
  assumptions 9
  attitudes and behaviors 6
  autonomy 8, 12
  belief in people's potential and ability 10
  challenge 9
  criteria of success or failure 8
  difficulty 9, 13
  directing others 9
  effective 16
  egoism 6
  ethical 8
  faith in life 10
  learning opportunities 6
  learning process 6
  narcissism 6
  open-mindedness and curiosity 11f.
  opportunism 8
  optimal 44, 45

organizational culture 12f.
personal competence 9, 14
personal development 7
personal power 9
practical philosophy 5f.
process 19, 22f.
relevance 14
sense of confidence 10
supportive 7
trust 7
value system 7, 9
self-confidence 142, 150
self-esteem 41, 59, 62, 88, 97, 99, 104, 108, 116, 120, 148f., 157, 161, 180f., 202
self-fulfilling prophecies 44
self-protection 36
sensitivity 132, 138, 148, 157
shame 41, 76
Siu, R. G. H. 143
skill 32, 82, 104, 105, 120, 134, 171, 177f., 200
feedback 104
listening 104
observational 104
in direction others 177
interpersonal 193
self-management 175
team-building 174
stereotype 97, 109
stress 74, 104, 117, 158, 164, 174, 195, 197
subconscious 31f., 87, 131, 138ff., 142, 150
supervision 171, 176ff., 190, 193f., 196
support 80, 91ff., 100, 102, 105, 107, 135, 139, 162, 199
lack of 161
network 91f., 96, 97, 102
synergy 32

T

team
creative 107
teamwork 15, 97, 98
tension 99, 107, 111, 195
timing 146f., 151
training 173f., 196
trust 30, 88, 92, 95, 107f., 163, 189, 191, 193f.

U

unblocking 105
uncertainty 126, 200, 202

V

values 57, 87, 91, 107ff., 115, 117, 121ff., 126, 131, 135, 138, 168, 180, 195
violence 191f.
vision 33, 190
Voneche, J. 25
vulnerability 132, 154, 188

W

Weyl, H. 4
Wheeler, D. D. 130
wholeness 101, 142
wishful thinking 42
work design 149